Katherine Mansfield and F

KATHERINE MANSFIELD STUDIES

Katherine Mansfield Studies is the peer-reviewed, annual publication of the Katherine Mansfield Society. It offers opportunities for collaborations among the significant numbers of researchers with interests in modernism in literature and the arts, as well as those in postcolonial studies. Because Mansfield is a writer who has inspired successors from Elizabeth Bowen to Ali Smith, as well as numerous artists in other media, Katherine Mansfield Studies encourages interdisciplinary scholarship and also allows for a proportion of creative submissions.

Katherine Mansfield Studies

Volume 8

Katherine Mansfield and Psychology

Editors
Clare Hanson, Gerri Kimber and Todd Martin

Editorial Assistant
Louise Edensor

EDINBURGH
University Press

Edinburgh University Press is one of the leading university presses in the UK.
We publish academic books and journals in our selected subject areas across the
humanities and social sciences, combining cutting-edge scholarship with high editorial
and production values to produce academic works of lasting importance. For more
information visit our website: edinburghuniversitypress.com

Edinburgh University Press Ltd
The Tun – Holyrood Road, 12(2f) Jackson's Entry, Edinburgh EH8 8PJ

Typeset in 10.5/12.5 New Baskerville by
Servis Filmsetting Ltd, Stockport, Cheshire,
and printed and bound in Great Britain by
CPI Group (UK) Ltd, Croydon CR0 4YY

A CIP record for this book is available from the British Library

ISBN 978 1 4744 1753 2 (hardback)
ISBN 978 1 4744 1755 6 (webready PDF)
ISBN 978 1 4744 1754 9 (paperback)
ISBN 978 1 4744 1756 3 (epub)

Contents

Contents

REVIEW ESSAY

List of Illustrations

Acknowledgements

The editors would like to thank the judging panel for this year's Katherine Mansfield Society essay prize, Professor Laura Marcus and Dr Isobel Maddison, for reading and commenting on the submissions. The winning essay by Polly Dickson is featured in this volume.

The editors would also like to thank the Richard Green Gallery, London, and in particular Rachel Boyd Hall for her assistance, together with the Fergusson Gallery, Perth and Kinross Council, Scotland, and especially Amy Waugh, for permission to reproduce the front cover painting, 'Poise', by J. D. Fergusson. They would also like to thank the Harry Ransom Center at the University of Texas at Austin for permission to use the image of the postcard of the Chalet des Sapins, Switzerland, and the Alexander Turnbull Library in Wellington, New Zealand, for permission to use the photo of Katherine Mansfield and John Middleton Murry. Further appreciation is extended to Christopher Browning, Daphne du Maurier's literary executor, for permission to print excerpts from du Maurier's unpublished letters, courtesy of Special Collections, University of Exeter Archives.

Also available in the series:

Frontispiece. Postcard of the Chalet des Sapins, Switzerland (with Mansfield's handwriting, bottom left), where Katherine Mansfield first read *Cosmic Anatomy*, January 1922. Katherine Mansfield Collection, Harry Ransom Center, The University of Texas at Austin, with kind permission.

Introduction

Clare Hanson

Psychology emerged as a discipline in the second half of the nineteenth century, predating and forming the intellectual context for
psychoanalysis and continuing to develop in tandem with it, although
its cultural impact has arguably been less strong.[1] The dominance of
psychoanalysis in twentieth- and twenty-first-century culture has been
such that, as Perry Meisel argues, 'Freud's work has itself become an
example of those unconscious determinations that influence us when
we least suspect it.'[2] As he also suggests, Freud's work can be seen as
a set of imaginative texts in which the concept of the unconscious
is itself a trope, a literary rather than a scientific device, grounded
in an approach to language which seals the thematic and 'technical'
affinities between literature and psychoanalysis.[3] More pertinently for
Katherine Mansfield, many critics have argued for the mutual imbrica-
tion of psychoanalysis and modernist literature, with Stephen Frosh
contending that 'psychoanalysis, at least in its pre-World War II form,
is an emblematic modernist discipline; conversely, modernist perceptions of subjectivity, individuality, memory and sociality are all deeply
entwined with a psychoanalytic sensitivity.'[4] Yet it is also the case that
modernist writers are creatures of the nineteenth as much as the twentieth century, given that their formative influences usually date back
to the earlier century. In Mansfield's case, as Sydney Janet Kaplan has
shown, the writing of Walter Pater and Oscar Wilde had a major impact
on her understanding of gender, genre and the dynamics of consciousness.[5] There are several allusions to Pater and Wilde in Mansfield's early
notebooks and no comparable references to specific works of psychology; none the less, in 1908 we find her thinking about a projected story
in terms which meld Pater's Lockean impressionism with the language
of psychology when she writes, 'I should like to write a life very much

1

in the style of Walter Pater's 'Child in the House' [...] A story, no it would be a sketch, hardly that, more a psychological study of the most erudite character.'[6] The term 'psychological' almost certainly refers not to Freud but to the wider network of psychological theories that pre-dated and enabled his work, which included evolutionary psychology, Wilhelm Wundt's experimental psychology and the dynamic psychology of William James.[7] Despite wide differences between them, what these early psychologists shared was a materialist perspective which empha-sised the intricate interrelation of the mind and body. This focus on the permeable boundary between consciousness and sensation converged with the interests of modernist writers, including Mansfield, who were exploring the affective dimensions of perception and emotion.

This volume focuses on aspects of early psychology in the belief that, as Judith Ryan has argued, its impact on twentieth-century literature was greater than is often recognised and that it formed a significant part of Mansfield's intellectual history.[8] In addition, it reads Mansfield's work in the light of psychoanalytic theory from Freud onwards, taking in Melanie Klein, Jacques Lacan, Mladen Dolar and Maud Ellmann, demonstrating the openness of her fiction to multiple psychoanalytic perspectives. Mansfield's familiarity with the main tenets of psychoa-nalysis has been explored in a recent article by Patricia Moran, where she points out that Mansfield moved in circles where Freud's work was widely discussed, as it was, for example, at Ottoline Morrell's gather-ings at Garsington Manor.[9] In addition, Mansfield's letters attest to her knowledge of – and exasperation with – D. H. Lawrence's intimate engagement with Freud's work, as, for example, when she writes,

> I shall *never* see sex in trees, sex in the running brooks, sex in stones & sex in everything [...] But I shall have my revenge one of these days – I sug-gested to Lawrence that he should call his cottage The Phallus and Frieda thought it was a very good idea.[10]

Yet it can be argued that what Mansfield was reacting to here was a par-ticular use of Freud's work, as Lawrence appropriated and distorted it to shape his idiosyncratic sexual philosophy[11]; similarly, when she attacks what Virginia Woolf called 'Freudian Fiction', her target is the cultural uses made of Freud's work rather than Freudian theory *per se*.[12] When she writes to Murry to complain about the '"mushroom growth" of cheap psycho analysis', then, her point is that popular versions of psychoanalysis (such as the articles on the subject published in the *Athenaeum* which Murry was then editing) are in danger of distract-ing writers from a purpose which can, paradoxically, be understood in Freudian terms. As she writes:

I do believe one ought to be able to – not ought – ones novel if it is a good one will be capable of being *proved* scientifically to be correct. Here – the thing that's happening now is *the impulse to write is a different impulse*. With an artist – one has to allow – oh tremendously for the subconscious element in his work. He writes he knows not what – hes *possessed*. I dont mean of course, always, but when he's *inspired* – as a sort of divine flower to all his terrific hard gardening there comes this subconscious . . . wisdom. Now these people who are nuts on analysis seem to me to have *no* subconscious at all.[13]

Mansfield is here arguing, in effect, for the inter-implication of literature and psychoanalysis: just as Freud illustrates his 'case studies' with reference to literary texts, so the process of writing is conceptualised as a flowering of subconscious knowledge. In this sense, she anticipates Shoshana Felman's influential argument that literature and psychoanalysis are distinct and yet folded within one another so that the border between them is undecidable.[14]

Felman's essay is the starting point for the first essay in this volume, Polly Dickson's prize-winning exploration of hunger and desire in Mansfield's fiction. Taking 'Bliss' as emblematic of Mansfield's concern with these themes, Dickson traces the way in which the narrative stages a desire which it simultaneously precludes. She argues that in 'Bliss' a desire for the emergence of an authentic self is articulated through a rhetoric ambivalently poised between the expression and frustration of appetite. Drawing on Maud Ellmann's work, she reads the luscious fruit in Bertha's dining room as a signature of the bodily pleasures from which Bertha is (self-)exiled, thus unable to make herself 'matter' in the world. Developing this point, she draws on Sara Ahmed's queer phenomenology to highlight the way in which domestic space, like the interior of the body, is unsettled and disorientated in this text, as when Bertha's dining room table melts away and a blue bowl floats in the air, becoming insubstantial. Yet such moments of disturbance, of a potential queering of the relationship between self and world, are no sooner articulated than they are disavowed, a pattern Dickson also finds in the late story, 'A Cup of Tea'. Although it is ostensibly about nourishment, Dickson suggests that this text too depends on hunger and regression, as an identification with another woman which promises to bridge the gap between desire and its expression is inhibited by the imperatives of the heterosexual order.

The next three contributions read Mansfield through the lens of early twentieth-century psychology and psychoanalysis. My own essay argues that the vitalist psychology of William James and particularly Henri Bergson (whose work she knew) shaped Mansfield's understanding of the mutability and multiplicity of the self. It suggests that Bergson's emphasis on the heterogeneity of consciousness finds an echo in the distinctiveness of Mansfield's characterisation, as she tracks the fluid interplay between different levels and intensities of consciousness. Drawing on the vitalist understanding of personality, it argues that Mansfield tracks the expression and transmission of emotion between characters in terms of affect and involuntary action, disclosing the porosity of the self and its openness to the unpredictability of human interactions. Delving further into Bergson's account of consciousness, it suggests that Mansfield shares his understanding of the self as caught between a virtual past and a virtual future, transformed moment by moment under the pressure of a past which breaks through into the present and a future which is constitutively unknowable. Accordingly, for Mansfield as for a number of modernist writers, character is framed in terms of a situational self which is responsive to the changing environments in which it finds itself, and consciousness is rendered as endlessly productive of novelty, of that which cannot be predicted from the familiar and already known. As Vincent O'Sullivan has suggested, Bergson's speculative thought may also have set the scene for Mansfield's controversial engagement with M. B. Oxon's *Cosmic Anatomy*, which is the subject of Maurizio Ascari's essay. Challenging the disdain or embarrassment which has marked previous critical commentary on this book, Ascari explores the intricate network of connections which framed Mansfield's response to it. In particular, he points out that it was an early mentor of Mansfield, A. R. Orage, who introduced the author of *Cosmic Anatomy* to a wider public. Publishing his work in the *New Age*, Orage placed it in dialogue with articles on psychoanalysis by A. R. Randall and David Eder, generating a debate which turned on contrasting views of the human: on the one hand was the positivist view associated with mainstream psychoanalysis and on the other a more holistic view of matter as rooted in a spiritual dimension. Ascari argues that it was this syncretic, holistic understanding that appealed to Mansfield as she confronted chronic illness and her fear of inner division, formulating in response a philosophy of 'entering into' the external world and becoming one with it. In addition, Ascari connects Oxon's holistic perspective with Mansfield's interest in 'plurisignification' and her use of symbolism to create for the reader a sense of the simultaneous unfolding of multiple meanings. In the final essay in this section, Meghan Marie Hammond explores points of contact between Mansfield's fiction and the psychology of William James, Carl Lange and Théodule Ribot, who together challenged the scientific orthodoxy that assimilated emotional to intellectual states, suggesting instead that emotion first arises in the body,

4

so that it precedes, although it does not determine, thought. For writers like Mansfield, who were fascinated by the 'depths' of consciousness and who became adults in the era of early psychology, these ideas were important. However, as Hammond points out, Mansfield offers an implicit challenge to the view of childhood that marked early psychology. Where James and Lange saw children as rudimentary or 'primitive' beings, Mansfield endorses the worth of the distinctive emotional life of the child, particularly during the transition from the affective world of infancy to the demands of adult life. In this respect, Hammond reads 'The Child-Who-Was-Tired' as a story which is acutely aware of the link between the body and the emotions, arguing that the eponymous child is suffering from emotional and cognitive instability because of her bodily exhaustion. Stress leads to the outburst in which she kills the baby, driven by the need to return to a state of pure feeling denied to her as an adolescent with adult responsibilities.

The essays that follow use a range of psychoanalytic perspectives to open up new readings of Mansfield's fiction. Rebecca Thorndike-Breeze employs Lacanian theory to prise open the psychological complexities of cross-class engagement in 'The Garden Party'. She suggests that in this story, Mansfield depicts the relationship between the working class and the middle class as one of simultaneous alienation and intimacy, which, for the middle-class Sheridans, entails the abjection of the working class as uncanny other. Developing this argument, she reads Laura's growing apprehension of the otherness of working-class life in terms of Mladen Dolar's concept of 'extimacy': that is, the uncanniness inherent in the 'internalised otherness' which is, for him, the condition of possibility of the subject. Tracing Laura's journey from the garden party to Mrs Scott's dark and smoky kitchen, Thorndike-Breeze suggests that, in confronting the widow's swollen, grief-stricken face, Laura experiences herself as *unheimlich*, momentarily apprehending the presence of the abject within. She argues that, despite the apparently peaceful resolution of the story as Laura gazes at the body of the dead carter, its enigmatic final lines suggest that such resolution cannot be sustained. Turning to Mansfield's early writings, Louise Edensor argues that Mansfield's understanding of the self resonates both with aspects of William James's work and with Freud's topographical model of the self. Concentrating on 'Vignette: Summer in Winter' and 'The Education of Audrey', Edensor adapts Claire Drewery's work on liminality to draw out Mansfield's interest in the transitional spaces of adolescence, which are figured in these texts through the motifs of the window and the mirror. Such threshold spaces are sites where the relationship between inner and outer selves is revealed as fractured and uncertain, as the protagonists struggle to break free of an enclosed, unstable subjectivity. Citing Kate Fullbrook's discussion of Mansfield's pessimism and the 'sudden shifts of tone' which signal her 'discontinuity of vision', Edensor concludes by noting Mansfield's radical uncertainty about the possibility of realising an integrated and harmonious self. Taking a different path, Allan Pero reads 'Bliss' through a set of oppositions drawn from Lacanian psychoanalysis. Alluding to Mansfield's description of her 'two kick-offs' in the writing game, he proposes that this passage suggests an awareness of the split between ego and subject which, for Lacan, underwrites two distinct forms of knowledge. On the one hand is the ego-led misrecognition of the self as unified and coherent which Lacan terms *méconnaissance*, and on the other is the knowledge which emerges from the subject's relation to the symbolic order (*savoir*) which represents the truth of unconscious desire. He then invokes the Lacanian distinction between masculine enjoyment (which is tied to sexuality), and feminine or Other *jouissance* (which entails the experience of feminine infinitude), to argue that Bertha Young's 'bliss' can be construed in terms of both *savoir* and a *jouissance* that eludes interpretation. None the less, Bertha's over-identification with the phallic economy drives her to seek a form of enjoyment which remains within its terms, deferring and displacing a *jouissance* that has no place in the domestic sphere. Finally, Avishek Parui explores the intersection of post-war mourning and masculinity crisis in 'The Fly', arguing that the boss's inability to weep over the loss of his son corresponds to his failure to assert his masculinity through a strategic and self-preserving ritual of recall. For Parui, such strategic remembering is linked with the phallogocentric principles of control which informed the war and which are the object of Mansfield's critique. The boss is depicted in terms which recall Pierre Janet's analysis of the hysterical subject, with the difference that the boss hystericises himself in a ritual of remembrance that progressively erases traumatic memory. The subsequent 'inset drama' of the fly stages a sadomasochistic drama in which the distinction between subject and object is undone and the fly's death is an end point signalling the boss's inability to survive the loss of his son. Mapping the intricate entanglement of private remembrance and a public discourse of denial, 'The Fly' encodes a paradigm shift in memory, dramatising the post-war struggle of memory against forgetting.

The first creative piece in this volume is a short story by Paula Morris, a reworking of 'The Garden Party' which reflects on class divisions in contemporary New Zealand. This is followed by three poems by Nina Powles which invoke key moments in Mansfield's biography and reflect on her multiple afterlives. Creative non-fiction is represented by

Introduction

Eve Lacey's reflections on working in a Mansfield archive, an experience which prompts her to reflect on the effect of Mansfield's publication history on the reception of her work. Lacey suggests that the publication of so much of her unfinished work enhances the reader's sense that her writing has the 'ruminative and reminiscent' quality that Mansfield associated with 'talks in the afterlife'. The first two pieces in the Critical Miscellany reflect on the recent recovery of *Poise*, a painting by the Scottish Colourist J. D. Fergusson, which, it has been suggested, may be a portrait of Mansfield. Angela Smith dissents from this view on the grounds that the 'vigorous blue-eyed' figure in the portrait is more like Kathleen Dillon, one of the dancers who worked with Fergusson's partner, Margaret Morris, and who was the model for his painting *Rose Rhythm* (1916). In addition, Smith argues that Mansfield's comments on *Poise* in a letter to Murry lack the self-consciousness that would be in evidence if this were indeed a portrait of Mansfield. Making the opposite case, Rachel Boyd Hall reads Mansfield's response to the painting as 'passionate' and invokes the closeness of the friendship between Mansfield and Fergusson in support of the argument that Mansfield had sat for Fergusson and that *Poise* was the painting that came out of these sessions. Meanwhile, in 'Patriarchal Pink', Bronwen Fetters offers a reading of colour-coding in 'The Little Governess', arguing that Mansfield invokes stereotypical gender codes in this story only to subvert them. In a comparative study, Setara Pracha considers symbolism in Daphne du Maurier's 'The Apple Tree' and in Mansfield's 'Bliss'. Rounding up the volume, Todd Martin's review essay returns us to the theme of psychology as he examines the models of the self that underpin Meghan Marie Hammond's *Empathy and the Psychology of Literary Modernism* and Gerri Kimber's *Katherine Mansfield and the Art of the Short Story*. He then considers Sarah Ailwood and Melinda Harvey's collection of essays, *Katherine Mansfield and Literary Influence* alongside Janka Kaščáková and Gerri Kimber's *Katherine Mansfield and Continental Europe*, before turning to Anna Plumridge's new edition of *The Urewera Notebook*. All these studies, he suggests, demonstrate how Mansfield's work enriches our understanding of the self and our relationship with others: in a word, of psychology.

Notes
1. For a detailed account of the emergence of psychology see Rick Rylance, *Victorian Psychology and British Culture, 1850–1880* (Oxford: Oxford University Press, 2000).
2. Perry Meisel, *The Literary Freud* (London and New York: Routledge, 2006), p. 1.
3. Meisel, p. 3.
4. Stephen Frosh, 'Psychoanalysis in Britain: "the rituals of destruction"', in

David Bradshaw, ed., *A Concise Companion to Modernism* (Oxford: Blackwell, 2002), pp. 116–37 (p. 116).

5. See Sydney Janet Kaplan, *Katherine Mansfield and the Origins of Modernist Fiction* (Ithaca, NY: Cornell University Press, 1991).

6. Margaret Scott, ed., *The Katherine Mansfield Notebooks*, 2 vols (Minneapolis: University of Minnesota Press, 2002), Vol. 1, pp. 111–12.

7. Freud did not become well known in Britain until the years immediately before the First World War. The *New Age* began to pay attention to his work in 1912 and *The Interpretations of Dreams* was published in English in 1913, followed by *The Psychopathology of Everyday Life* in 1914 (both translations were by A. A. Brill).

8. See Judith Ryan, *The Vanishing Subject: Early Psychology and Literary Modernism* (Chicago: University of Chicago Press, 1991), for a discussion of the influence of psychology on modernist literature.

9. Patricia Moran, '"the sudden 'mushroom growth' of cheap psychoanalysis": Mansfield and Woolf Respond to Psychoanalysis', *Virginia Woolf Miscellany*, 86 (Fall 2014/Winter 2015), pp. 11–14 (p. 11).

10. Vincent O'Sullivan and Margaret Scott, eds, *The Collected Letters of Katherine Mansfield*, 5 vols (Oxford: Clarendon Press, 1984), Vol. 2, pp. 261–2. Hereafter referred to as *Letters*, followed by volume and page number.

11. Lawrence was both intrigued by and hostile to Freud's emphasis on sexual repression and developed an alternative version of psychoanalysis in *Psychoanalysis and the Unconscious* (1921) and *Fantasia of the Unconscious* (1922).

12. See Virginia Woolf, 'Freudian Fiction', *Times Literary Supplement* (25 March 1920), reprinted in Andrew McNeillie, ed., *The Essays of Virginia Woolf, Vol. 3: 1919–1924* (London: Hogarth Press, 1988), pp. 195–8.

13. *Letters*, 4, p. 69.

14. Shoshana Felman, 'To Open the Question', *Yale French Studies*, 55/6 (1977), pp. 5–10.

CRITICISM

CHAPTER 1

Interior Matters: Secrecy and Hunger in Katherine Mansfield's 'Bliss'

Polly Dickson

'Hungry people are easily led.'

'A Cup of Tea' (1922), Katherine Mansfield

In *Literature and Psychoanalysis. The Question of Reading, Otherwise,* Shoshana Felman calls for a disambiguation of the relationship between literature and psychoanalytical thought, hoping to 'disrupt altogether the position of mastery' which psychoanalysis has traditionally been given over literature, and privileging instead a 'relation of *interiority*', where each may be seen to inhabit the other.[1] It is in reading alongside this notion of mutual interiorities that psychoanalytic thought might be most productively and generously engaged in readings of texts such as those of Katherine Mansfield: not in its being applied to her work, that is, but rather 'implied' within it, touching on some of its darker, hungrier moments.

This article, in addressing the experience of hunger, understands the identity of a subject to be formed as much by what it allows to enter itself as by what it refuses to ingest. Mansfield's short story 'Bliss' (1918), a tale which, as I shall show, stages the preclusion of a hidden desire, pays keen attention to the interiority at once of the text, of the body, and of the home, as sites of secrecy. Mansfield's characteristically disembowelling irony emerges through the articulation of a desire within a narrative which renders that desire impossible. The potential emergence of an authentic self – what we might, here, call 'bliss' – is twinned with its contingent and simultaneous prohibition. The subject Bertha, craving authentic integration into the world, is stifled by the very matter through which she attempts to define herself. I will suggest, in moving from Sara Ahmed's writing on the domestic interior to Maud Ellmann's on hunger and starvation, that hunger anchors the human subject in domestic space and that our relationship to food is prototypical for our relationships to others. Ingestion shapes the way in which the subject learns to recognise itself as an embodied being, distinguishing outside from inside. Hunger thus concerns the will to be integrated into materiality, making a subject 'matter'.

There are compelling ethical difficulties in writing about hunger. There is no approach to hunger that does not trouble the place of the body and the way we are to inhabit it. Hunger, like pain, as Ellmann points out, is the kind of pressingly interior bodily phenomenon that cannot be known or shared from without. '[B]oth sensations', she writes, 'demonstrate the savage loneliness of bodily experience.'[2] That is why, in this piece about interiors, I shall draw so much attention to shapes, lines and surfaces. I want not to be probing or incisive in my readings, but rather to be tactful, holding on to the sense of *tact* as touch. I want to pay attention to an interior without attempting to master it; I want always to be aware of the matter, the surfaces and skins that come before it. The task, then, is not to voice somebody else's hunger but rather to acknowledge its existence, to say what it sounds or looks – and seems to feel – like. Again, it is to be tactful, and in being tactful to be sensitive to the self-reflexive nature of touch. In coming so close to another's body, I come up against the limits of mine. This is the old knot of psychoanalysis: that to speak of another's desire is so often also – by transference and counter-transference, whether acknowledged or not – to enunciate one's own. And 'Bliss' is, as I shall show, a text in which an experience of hunger emerges as a story of watching others eat.

In 'Bliss', Bertha Young and her husband Harry host a dinner party. Bertha, who has never felt physical desire for her husband ('she'd been in love with him, of course, in every other way, but just not in that way [. . .] after a time it had not seemed to matter'), and whose baby seems to have a closer relationship to its nanny than to her, yearns to pursue a feeling of 'bliss' that seems to gesture momentarily at a life beyond the constraints of domesticity.[3] The feeling gains strength and contour as Bertha gazes at the cool figure of Pearl Fulton, one of her dinner-party guests, with whom she feels a rich, silent affinity: '"I believe this does happen very, very rarely between women. Never between men," thought Bertha' (149). But just before Pearl leaves, Bertha catches sight, or seems to catch sight, of Harry and Pearl clutching at one another in mutual greedy desire.

The rigid constraints of the dinner party, the posturing of the guests' pretentious, avant-gardist conversation – '"Well, Warren, how's the play?" said Norman Knight, dropping his monocle' (146) – and Bertha's feeling of bodily incarceration, of being 'shut up in a case like a rare, rare fiddle' (142), mark the space of the interior as a formative mould for the body and as an encroachment on its horizons. Normative regimes of domestic space threaten to plunge the body into inertia. In *Queer Phenomenology*, Sara Ahmed puts queer studies in dialogue with phenomenology to explore how our bodies are shaped through how we inhabit space – through repeated orientations. Compulsory heterosexuality, for Ahmed, is the result of a collective and inherited directionality: 'Space and bodies become straight as an effect of repetition.' She emphasises those objects of the home – such as dinner tables and family photographs – which act as 'points of pressure' of this inscriptive heterosexuality, pushing us along the straight and narrow of domestic alignments.[4] Bodies are mired in a straightness enforced by the turns and tendencies they have learned to repeat. Space for Mansfield, as for Ahmed, collaborates in the articulation of the body. Both writers take an ironic swipe at the kind of Romantic vision of the home articulated by Gaston Bachelard in *The Poetics of Space*. Here, the home is the shelter of the imagination, an osmotic site of memory, identity and dream:

> [The] house we are born in is physically inscribed in us. It is a group of organic habits [. . .] We are the diagram of the functions of inhabiting that particular house, and all the other houses are but variations on a fundamental theme. The word habit is too worn a word to express this passionate liaison of our bodies, which do not forget, with an unforgettable house.[5]

In 'Bliss', too, the home touches and presses down on the dreaming mind and body – but its touch is hard and unforgiving. In a story ostensibly about collective nourishment in the form of a dinner party, food loses all qualities of sustenance and becomes a spectacle of alienation. Eating is ornamental, an act of display – 'she loved having them there, at her table [. . .] what a decorative group they made' (148) – cast not as an act of collective nourishment but as a precipitator of the hungry lack present in the lines of the domestic sphere, a marker not of the body's incorporation of and being incorporated into its surroundings but of its emptiness. In my reading of the text, Bertha's 'bliss' speaks of the lure of a liberating disembodiment, ecstasy's sense of having been put outside oneself. In this sense, 'bliss' shares something with the psychoanalytic approach to hunger articulated by Maud Ellmann in *The Hunger Artists*. For Ahmed in *Queer Phenomenology*, our identity is formed through our alignment with, and integration into, the external matter of the domestic frame. For Ellmann, eating enunciates the very origin of identity: '[f] or it is by ingesting the external world that the subject establishes his body as his own'.[6] In turn, for Mansfield, the sense of material fullness and satiety associated with domestic life – 'Really – really – she had everything [...] and their new cook made the most superb omelettes' (145) – is haunted by the spectre of a form it shut out at its genesis and constitution: a spectre which returns as lack, which longs insatiably 'to run instead of walk, to take dancing steps on and off the pavement, to bowl a hoop' (141) – which longs, that is, for an uninhibited, a pre-socialised (perhaps, we might suggest, a pre-Oedipal) body.

In preparation for her guests, Bertha arranges fruit in her dining room, piling evocatively fleshy tangerines and pears, 'bright round objects' – 'stained with strawberry pink', 'smooth as silk' – into 'two pyramids', luridly suggestive of the female body. The white iridescence of the ornamental dish (its 'strange sheen [...] as though it had been dipped in milk') is both maternal and pearly; the display briefly eluci-dates the promise that Pearl seems to represent and the ample forms of a 'bliss' which it all too promptly slips beyond – for, as Bertha piles the pieces on top of one another in strata of dark colours, the table appears to 'melt into the dusky light', to turn from matter into formlessness (142–3). This seems to enact one of those 'giddy' or 'queer' moments described by Ahmed, for '[t]he sameness of the table', as she writes of Husserl's phenomenological table, 'is spectral: the table is only the same given that we have conjured its missing sides'.[7] One way of queer-ing the received world with its delineated exteriors, she suggests, is to let this spectrality surge forth. By foregrounding the 'bracketed out', the excluded parts of the material world, by letting her table embody its own disintegration, perhaps Bertha experiences a moment of re- or disorientation; perhaps the household, and by extension the body, is to begin a newly invigorated, 'slantwise' existence. If a queer inhabit-ance of the world involves such 'moments of disorientation', then this, and indeed the whole giddy experience of the story ('she felt quite dizzy, quite drunk' [145]), might seem to present Bertha with a new and enlivened form of domestic embodiment. But the matter of food as display seems more an experience of reification than of liberation: for in this moment, a body crystallises in the forms within which cen-sorship of bodies takes place. The ornamental world with all its pretty objects seems to embody the pearly material secret at the centre of the story, that 'something' that Bertha hungers to know – 'the way she has of sitting with her head a little on one side, and smiling, has something behind it, Harry' (144) – a 'something' which ultimately reveals itself crushingly *not* to be (lesbian) desire itself, but rather the return of that desire's expulsion. Pearl proves herself to be Harry's, and not Bertha's, beautiful, dreamed-of woman (and if the possessive here jars, note Bertha's own misjudged 'little air of proprietorship' [147]). The fruit represents a brief monument to a female body whose hidden capacity for pleasure is killed in its being articulated, a desire outed and stifled in the outing. Disavowal is foregrounded as ornament. Ahmed's objects, as long as they remain anchored in their native domestic setting, might exist only as such ornaments of disavowal, traumatically re-evocative of, and in unhappy dialogue with, the order they attempt to queer.

'Bliss', as disallowed desire, is articulated within the matter and the structures which preclude its fulfilment. A table surfaces again as an inhibiting structure at the story's climax – this time in written form, the book of poetry 'Table D'Hôte'. The camp, posturing Eddie points Bertha towards the book, and to a line within it, 'Why Must it Always be Tomato Soup?', at the very moment of her vision of Harry and Pearl in the hallway:

> His lips said: 'I adore you,' and Miss Fulton laid her moonbeam fingers on his cheeks and smiled her sleepy smile. Harry's nostrils quivered; his lips curled back in a hideous grin while he whispered: 'Tomorrow,' and with her eyelids Miss Fulton said: 'Yes.'
>
> 'Here it is,' said Eddie. 'Why Must it Always be Tomato Soup?' It's so *deeply* true, don't you feel? Tomato soup is so *dreadfully* eternal.' (151–2)

Such dismal lines, like the repeated lines of banal, pretentious conversation, are found to be written deep in the matter – the bookshelves, tables – of the house itself. The relentless sameness of un-nourishing food, tomato soup (Bertha has just served her guests a 'beautiful red soup' [148]), coincides with the compulsive return of the heterosexual dyad (for the adulterous pair will see each other again – 'Tomorrow' – when again Bertha will face the same '*dreadfully* eternal' repetition of her displacement). Bertha's attraction to Pearl climaxes in a sickening recall of the heterosexual order when Pearl reveals herself to be one half of the binary that excludes and displaces her: right from the outset, in marriage's failure to satiate her; and then again in the 'hideous grin' of the story's toothy climax, in mocking mirrored double.

Maud Ellmann argues that 'eating is the origin of subjectivity', as the infant subject establishes, through ingestion and expulsion, the boundaries of its body in relation to the other.[8] Disturbances involving food are common stock of psychic fixations on the oral stage: the stage of development during which, according to Freud,

> sexual activity has not yet been separated from the ingestion of food [. . .] the sexual aim consists in the incorporation of the object – the prototype of a process which, in the form of identification, is later to play such an important psychological part.[9]

Pre-Oedipal memories invariably register themselves in the mouth and the throat. This is the logic to which the 'hysterical' labelling of aphonia and other pathologies of the throat subscribe. Critics such as Patricia Moran have noted that Bertha is pictured as a hysteric, with her feelings of discomfort figured as a kind of choking – having 'swallowed a bright piece of that late afternoon sun' (142).[10] And her linguistic prowess is correspondingly wan. Over and over she fails to express the things she aches to – 'What had she to say?' to Harry on the telephone (144); 'She wanted to cry' about the moon (147); 'she longed to tell [the guests] how delightful they were' (148). Her attitude towards married life seems to consist of paltry and unconvincing aphorisms borrowed from elsewhere – 'Really – really – she had everything,' where the repeated 'really' gestures at a stifled pretence at satisfaction (145). And Bertha feels the pain of words inside herself – 'ardently! Ardently! The word ached in her ardent body!' (151). That the word 'ardently', a word of passion, is part of her own material composition, longing to be enunciated, suggests that the language of desire that she has interiorised hurts from the inner space of her body in a renewed kind of hunger. Mansfield provides a clue to the link between language and satiety in a letter to Murry dated 16 November 1919, writing about a novel by Virginia Woolf that she considers pretentious and unsatisfying: 'the more I read the more I feel all these novels will not do. After them Im a swollen sheep looking up who is not fed [*sic*].'[11] We might get fatter on words – on lines, even – but this does not lessen our hunger for the ones that will properly feed us. Sometimes, 'famished by an excess', the more of them we choke down, the hungrier we become.[12]

If, moreover, as Ellmann argues, the subject's very constitution depends on ingestion, then 'his [*sic*] identity is constantly in jeopardy, because his need to incorporate the outside world exposes his fundamental incompleteness'; indeed, 'the very need to eat reveals the "nothing" at the core of subjectivity.'[13] The suggestion both that eating manages our identities, and that eating might produce or exacerbate, rather than fill, a lack, is one that Mansfield also attends to – and with more acerbic wit. In the stilted conversation at the dinner table, masculine creativity stages itself under the names of food and body parts: the guests speak of 'Michael Oat', the playwright, who wrote '*Love in False Teeth*', who might call his new play 'Stomach Trouble', whose lover has apparently 'taken a dreadfully good snip off her legs and arms' (148). Masculine orality, here, is strangely twinned with feminine diminution. The gendered cannibalistic subtext is mirrored in the figure of Mrs Knight, dressed garishly in items of food – with a 'dress out of scraped banana skins' and earrings 'like little dangling nuts' – and who laughingly recalls how during her journey the train 'rose to a man and simply ate me with its eyes' (146). The appetite of the gaze, here, returns. Ellmann points out the relationship between the verbs 'to stare' and 'to starve' – which used to mean 'to freeze or turn to stone' – such that both words retain the suggestion of 'reifying bodies into spectacles'.[14] Hungry eyes have oral potency. In the decorative fruit episode, food on display turns into the emptiest kind of matter, making a spectacle of the perforations in domestic show. Bertha watches the nanny feed her baby 'like the poor little girl in front of the rich girl with the doll' (143). And finally, in that last scene of Harry and Pearl in the hallway – 'And she saw . . . ' – what Bertha witnesses is a vision of the heterosexual matter which displaces her (151); the ellipsis suggests a dwindling of language in a vision of her own emptied space. Matter, in ungenerous proliferation before the hungry eye, is stripped of its sense. Elsewhere, Bertha's own language wanes into silence and incompletion as Harry's discourse on bodies expands. The link between the 'big' paternal male's corporeality and his loquacity is a frequent one in Mansfield's stories – 'Sexuality and power are [. . .] inscribed in the father's orality,' as Burgan puts it in the context of Mansfield's early depictions of her father, Harold Beauchamp.[15] Bertha's attitude to her husband, ostensibly loving and reverent, is marked by linguistic sparseness and omission, figured in the ironic ellipsis of parenthetic remarks such as 'a little ridiculous perhaps. . . . ' (147), whilst the narrative voice's claim (referring to Harry's recurrent body-talk) that 'Bertha liked this, and almost admired it in him very much,' – note the awkward 'almost' – is symptomatic of disavowal (145). The emaciation of language, again, speaks volumes. Where alienation, in the stifling privacy of the interior, can claim to look like marital satisfaction, assent can be a mark of fear; and 'bliss' can be another face of hunger.

If both ingestion and starvation have the power to 'undo the self in the very process of confirming its identity' by bringing to light the body's hungry dependence on matter, then speaking about food has, I think, the same effect – as the fruit decoration, which disintegrates as it is made, is confirmed and undone simultaneously. By forming us, by giving us a form, the other (and the world) has also stolen something from us: every other future horizon, every other form our body might have been or taken. Relinquishing oneself to hunger is a form of safeguarding the body from its material circumscription to the outside: for Ellmann, 'the only means of *saving* subjectivity from the invasion of the other in the form of food'.[16] It is a desire of lack which propels everything forward, which constantly needs a response, which looks to the ghosts of those futures which have been denied it. Subject to the demands made of her body by marriage and maternity, and caught constantly by Harry's tendency 'to talk about food' (148), Bertha seems to retreat *into* her hunger. In an earlier story by Mansfield, 'Germans at Meat' (1910), the smothering expansiveness of the nourishing maternal instance is more cuttingly presented as a site of threat as the bewildered young narrator is derided for her vegetarianism, linked in the conversation of her German companions with her childlessness: 'Who ever heard of having children upon vegetables?' – which is linked in turn with their scorn at female independence – 'you never have large families in England now; I suppose you are too busy with your suffragetting.' Gluttony and fertility are the key features of a raucous conversation about food and women, away from which the shy narrator is quick to rush, leaving behind her the resounding cry of 'Mahlzeit' ('meal-time').[17]

Bertha's is not the narrative of an anorexic, nor of a hunger artist – not quite – but she certainly seems to be caught by the seduction of that out-of-kilter state of being which threatens to shatter her material existence, a move towards flight from the knowable and the nameable, towards what Ellmann terms 'the supremacy of lack'.[18] In looking to the opening of the piece for a description of 'bliss', we find it coded as a longing to remaster her body, 'to run instead of walk' and to re-inhabit the world like a child, 'to throw something up in the air and catch it again' (141–2) – linked to the desire for a pre-Oedipal body, for a childlike inhabitance of the world, for the 'ecstasy of disembodiment'.[19] This 'bliss', then, is characterised as a need, as a propulsion towards something else, giving her mirror image the appearance of 'waiting for something . . . divine to happen . . . that she knew must happen . . . infallibly' (142). In a way that is characteristic for Mansfield, the ellipses here speak mute volumes, as though what Bertha wants to say cannot be expressed in the words or materials she has to hand. It is the dissatisfaction with her current state of being which makes itself heard through these gaps – following the logic of wilful hunger as 'what it means for the body to reject itself'.[20] Such wilful hunger is a bodily self-enunciation at the same time as it is a desire for self-annihilation.

Psychoanalytic thought holds that our internal conception of our body – the imaginary anatomy – is derived from a psychical cartography based on a sensory 'record of past impressions'.[21] Such bodily schemas work through metabolic exchange between the self and the external world. Didier Anzieu writes in *Le Moi-Peau (The Skin Ego)* of the skin as more-than-organ, emphasising its intermediary nature and its incorporation of space, through touch and the metabolic function, into the constitution of the soma: as 'the interface which marks the border with the outside and keeps that outside out'.[22] We have no native conception of our body, but one pieced together through the memory of external stimulation. Our bodily orifices, in particular, bear the sensory mementoes of maternal touch; our very digestive tract remembers the body of the mother. This is why, for Ellmann, Klein and others, eating 'confounds the limits between self and other' as it looks back to our primal and greediest relationship.[23] For these thinkers, the body is more than matter: it is indeed precisely the making *more* of matter, a dynamic function of drawing space and exteriority into the ego. The articulation of the subject's body is dependent on this metabolic act of incorporation and rejection of the outside: introjecting aspects of the other whilst recognising its distinction, autonomy and separation. Post-Freudian psychoanalytic accounts of motherhood see the maternal instance as the paradigmatic formative space for the infantile ego: Nancy Chodorow writes that '[t]he beginning perception of [the infant's] mother as separate [. . .] forms the basis for its experience of a self.'[24]

As Bertha remodels herself on the (m)other, her desire for Pearl seems to set itself out in visual terms. Bertha, dressed in a 'white dress, a string of jade beads, green shoes and stockings', seems to model herself subliminally on a bridal image, on the vision of the ghostly tree illuminated against 'the jade-green sky' (145), on Pearl 'all in silver, with a silver fillet binding her pale blond hair' (147), and on the alimentary colour scheme that Harry greedily describes – 'his "shameless passion for the white flesh of the lobster" and "the green of pistachio ices"' (148). Bertha seems to use the fantasy of Pearl as a method by which to accede to her role in her marriage, finding within the construct of the other – of the woman of Harry's fantasy – a stimulus for her own desire. Pearl, shining silvery and frequently described as 'cool' and 'sleepy' (149), re-evokes Bertha's 'cold mirror' at the beginning of the story and the dark face it gives back to her (142). And the link between the 'cold' mirror and Bertha's lack of desire for her husband, which she describes, again, as her being 'so cold', further entrenches the biting boundary-line of material difference re-marked in each encounter with the other (150). As Burgan puts it, Mansfield uses the mirror to 'portray the ordeal of the self as it confronts a reflection that presents neither ontological reassurance nor psychological integration'.[25] The mirror – the Lacanian site of the radically split self – is an intermediary structure situating an attempt to model the self by or through the other. Bertha's coy mimicry reminds us why a reading of the story by Moran and others as 'the sexual abandonment of woman by woman' does not ring true.[26] The body of the other, on the contrary, provides a reflective scheme for self-recognition. When she imagines articulating the fantasy to Harry – 'I shall try to tell you when we are in bed tonight what has been happening. What she and I have shared' – Pearl is not to be allowed *into* the marital bed but becomes, rather, a tool, a matter of Bertha's own self-articulation (150). In the terms of Ahmed's queer phenomenology, Bertha seeks a 'queer', in the sense of a more curious and a non-perfunctory inhabitance of her world, a re-articulation of her own appetite and a twisting of the 'lines' we might repeat in moments of intimacy. She hungers after Pearl as matter to be incorporated into the embodied self. The final reflection, though, in the snarling, grotesque vision of heterosexuality, slips beyond Bertha's will to reconfiguration – with Pearl's 'moonbeam fingers' re-inscribing the vision of the pear tree and Harry's 'hideous grin' recalling the orality of the devouring male (151). Bertha is left staring – starving – before a reflection of her sense-less marital existence; she watches others eat.

'A Cup of Tea' (1922) is comparable to 'Bliss' in its patterns of self-constitution through reflection and in its troubling of need within sus-tenance. The 'extremely modern, exquisitely well dressed' Rosemary takes a hungry street girl home and gives her tea and sandwiches (461), a move motivated by an uncomfortable kind of pity and the feeling 'that women *were* sisters', but more so by the desire to stage the self in a new way: 'she heard herself saying afterwards to the amazement of her friends: "I simply took her home with me."' This imagined projection of Rosemary's own voice inhabits the renewed projection of the self, through the thin, childlike other, as maternal 'fairy godmother': 'she pushed the thin figure into its deep cradle' (463–4). The satisfaction that both figures might obtain through this instance of nurture is pre-cluded by Rosemary's husband, Philip, when he articulates his recogni-tion of the beggar girl as a sexual being: 'she's so astonishingly pretty' (466). Seeing the scrawny girl for the first time as a rival, Rosemary rushes back to displace her. Her own infantile behaviour at the end of the piece, sitting on Philip's knee, begging him for treats and desper-ate for the assurance that he desires her too – 'Philip [. . .] am I *pretty?*' (467) – keeps the marital relationship mired in a state suggestive of the Oedipal father and daughter. 'A Cup of Tea' is thus a story ostensibly about nourishment and motherhood, which reveals and depends on a subtext of hunger and regression. It shares with 'Bliss' a sense of the self's foiled attempt to take up an authentic relationship to the world. In both texts, the subliminal over-identification with another woman, as a route to remodelling the self and articulating desire, fails. Again, the discovery of female desire coincides with the discovery of the inhibitions on that desire. The hunger for identification is the hunger for matter, to make the self 'matter' as an embodied subject, relevant within the material economy of the world. Hunger intensifies the material, as

Ellmann suggests, by exacerbating the dependency of the inner being on its external surroundings. What desire – hunger – seems to produce is exactly that which will continue to initiate it. This is the logic by which hunger is self-propelling in Mansfield's work, and real nourishment impossible, even in narratives ostensibly about food.

Hunger, in 'Bliss', is described in the very terms by which its satisfaction is denied: Bertha's desire is 'revealed only in the structures that hide it' – and inscribe it as part of the domestic landscape.[27] Hunger, as such, keeps the subject inert. 'Hungry people are easily led,' as Rosemary discovers of the beggar girl (463). As readers, we may be as hungry to interpret the text as the text seems to hunger after interpretation – but eating, for Mansfield, does not necessarily lead to satiety. We might hunger to get inside the text to know what is hidden there – but here the interior element will voice itself only through the material lines holding it in place. Eating is also the prototype of the secret, for there is no better hiding place than the stomach: as Bachelard puts it, 'Digestion corresponds, indeed, to the taking possession of a fact that is more obvious than any other and whose certainty cannot be questioned [. . .] Its entire coenaesthesia lies at the origins of the myth of inwardness.'[28] The best way for a text to hide a secret is to incorporate it completely within the very logic of its own words. What is inside will voice itself only through the material structures or lines which keep it there. To be sensitive readers of hunger we must inhabit the story in its own terms, following Felman's model of co-inhabiting interiorities, not master it from the outside or put it out of place. The hunger we find, dependent on external forces to be voiced in any way at all, is a hunger which does not abate, does not relinquish its grip on the body, always demands an answer, or a further struggle: 'Oh, what is going to happen now?' (152).

Notes

1. Shoshana Felman, 'To Open the Question', in *Literature and Psychoanalysis. The Question of Reading: Otherwise* (Baltimore and London: Johns Hopkins University Press, 1982), pp. 5–10 (pp. 7, 9).
2. Maud Ellmann, *The Hunger Artists: Starving, Writing and Imprisonment* (London: Virago, 1993), p. 6.
3. Gerri Kimber and Vincent O'Sullivan, eds, *The Collected Fiction of Katherine Mansfield*, 2 vols (Edinburgh: Edinburgh University Press, 2012), Vol. 2, p. 150. Hereafter references to this volume are placed parenthetically in the text.
4. Sara Ahmed, *Queer Phenomenology: Orientations, Objects, Others* (Durham, NC, and London: Duke University Press, 2006), pp. 90–2.
5. Gaston Bachelard, *The Poetics of Space*, trans. by Mari Jolas (Boston: Orion Press, 1964), pp. 14–15.
6. Ellmann, p. 30.

7. Ahmed, p. 36.

8. Ellmann, p. 30.

9. Sigmund Freud, *Three Essays on the Theory of Sexuality*, trans. by James Strachey (New York: Basic Books, 1975), p. 64.

10. See Patricia Moran, *Word of Mouth: Body Language in Katherine Mansfield and Virginia Woolf* (Charlottesville: University Press of Virginia, 1996), p. 44.

11. Vincent O'Sullivan and Margaret Scott, eds, *The Collected Letters of Katherine Mansfield*, 5 vols (Oxford: Clarendon Press, 1984–2008), Vol. 3, p. 97.

12. Ellmann, p. 29.

13. Ellmann, p. 2.

14. Ellmann, p. 102.

15. Mary Burgan, *Illness, Gender, and Writing: The Case of Katherine Mansfield* (London: Johns Hopkins University Press, 1994), p. 29.

16. Ellmann, pp. 30–1.

17. Kimber and O'Sullivan, *The Collected Fiction of Katherine Mansfield*, Vol. 1, pp. 166–7.

18. Ellmann, p. 27.

19. Ellmann, p. 2.

20. Ellmann, p. 15.

21. Elizabeth Grosz, *Volatile Bodies: Towards a Corporeal Feminism* (Bloomington: Indiana University Press, 1994), p. 66.

22. Didier Anzieu, *Le Moi-Peau* (Paris: Dunod, 1995), p. 61. My translation.

23. Ellmann, p. 51. See also Melanie Klein on the formative implications of infantile feeding in Juliet Mitchell, ed., *The Selected Melanie Klein* (London: Penguin, 1986), pp. 211–29.

24. Nancy Chodorow, *The Reproduction of Mothering: Psychoanalysis and the Sociology of Gender* (London: University of California Press, 1999), p. 67.

25. Burgan, p. 38.

26. Moran, p. 61.

27. Armine Kotin Mortimer, 'Fortifications of Desire: Reading the Second Story in Katherine Mansfield's "Bliss"', *Narrative*, 2 (1994), pp. 41–52 (p. 50).

28. Gaston Bachelard, *La Formation de l'esprit scientifique: Contribution à une psychanalyse de la connaissance objective* (Paris: Vrin, 1972), p. 69. My translation.

Katherine Mansfield and Vitalist Psychology

Clare Hanson

In Katherine Mansfield's short story 'Psychology' (1920), the protagonists reflect ruefully on the fact that psychology is invading the territory of literature and speculate that 'the young writers of today – are
trying simply to jump the psycho-analyst's claim.'[1] For the (unnamed)
female speaker this is a dismal prospect, as it was for Mansfield, who
complained to John Middleton Murry that 'cheap psycho analysis' was
no substitute for the artist's vision, although she went on to observe in
the next breath that 'with an artist – one has to allow – oh tremendously
for the subconscious element in his work.'[2] These contradictory comments reflect the ambivalence of Mansfield's engagement with psychology. While deploring fiction that turns 'Life into a *case*',[3] she uses the
language of psychology to explain her self-understanding as an artist,
and there is no doubt that the central concerns of her fiction resonate
powerfully with the landscape opened up by psychology and psychoanalysis. In consequence, an extensive body of criticism has grown up
which draws on insights from these disciplines to discuss Mansfield's
fiction. Psychoanalytic theory predominates, as we would expect, given
the pervasiveness of Freudian theory in modernist culture, and with the
exception of Meghan Hammond's illuminating discussion of Mansfield
and empathy, there has been relatively little examination of the connections between her writing and other branches of twentieth-century
psychology.[4] This article aims to redress the balance by assessing the
relationship between Mansfield and vitalist psychology as represented
by William James and Henri Bergson.[5] It suggests that this is a connection which is ripe for reconsideration in light of the resurgence of interest in vitalism: for example, in Elizabeth Grosz's recent re-evaluation of
Bergson's work.[6]

James and Bergson were the most significant vitalist thinkers of the late nineteenth and early twentieth centuries, and their ideas were widely disseminated in intellectual culture. James's *Principles of Psychology* was an unexpected bestseller and the famous phrase, 'the stream of consciousness', had entered literary criticism by 1918.[7] Mansfield's knowledge of his work is evidenced by the fact that she quotes from his *The Will to Believe* (1897) in a 1920 review of Hugh Walpole's *The Captives* and her familiarity with Bergson's work is also a matter of record.[8] She is likely to have read T. E. Hulme's pioneering essays on Bergson, which were published in the *New Age* at around the same time as her *German Pension* stories, but the main point of contact was Murry, who had read *L'Evolution créatrice* in the original in 1907 and, like T. S. Eliot, had attended Bergson's lectures in Paris.[9] Energised by Murry's enthusiasm, Mansfield nailed her colours to the mast of 'Bergsonism' in 'The Meaning of Rhythm', which she co-wrote with Murry when she became Assistant Editor of *Rhythm* in 1912. This essay–manifesto explores the aesthetic implications of Bergson's thought in the context of an emphasis on rhythmic energies, and presents the artist as one who is able to find 'some newness of life' in every passing moment.[10] This concern with the generativity of life – what Mansfield calls 'the *life* of life' – was central to her aesthetic and was nourished by this early encounter with vitalist psychology.[11]

Hundreds of Selves

As Omri Moses has shown, vitalism had a significant impact on the way in which many modernist writers understood 'character'.[12] Rather than understanding the self in terms of a transcendent ego, vitalists posited a self that was both multiple and mutable. As William James put it in *Principles of Psychology*, identity consists in '*resemblance among the parts of a continuum of feelings*', a continuum he likens to a herd of cattle united only by the 'judging thought' which oversees them.[13] Bergson extends this insight, distinguishing between the superficial multiplicity of personality and the qualitative multiplicity that characterises the deeper reality of consciousness. In *An Introduction to Metaphysics* he memorably describes the self as a sphere with a surface crust that consists of 'all the perceptions which come to it from the material world'. Memories adhere to these perceptions and cluster around them, accompanied by 'a stir of tendencies and motor habits [. . .] a crowd of virtual actions'. However, beneath these 'sharply cut crystals and this frozen surface' there exists a continuous flux which, Bergson writes, 'is not comparable to any flux I have ever seen. There is a succession of states, each of which announces that which follows and contains that which precedes it . . . In reality no one of them begins or ends, but all extend into each other.'[14] For Bergson, consciousness is heterogeneous precisely because it exists in duration, his term for subjective as opposed to objective time. Whereas objective time is quantitative and homogeneous, in the flux of duration even the 'simplest sensation [. . .] cannot remain identical with itself for two successive moments, because the second moment always contains, over and above the first, the memory that the first has bequeathed to it.'[15]

Mansfield conceptualises the self in similar terms in her account of 'the flowering of the self'. A surface and depth model is deployed in this famous passage, where the varied components of Bergson's 'surface crust' of identity are presented as wilful guests in 'a hotel without a proprietor', whose comings and goings are barely kept in order by the 'small clerk' who tries to register their movements. In conjunction with this, Mansfield invokes a deeper dimension, opaque to everyday consciousness (and akin to the centre of Bergson's sphere) where a self persists which is simultaneously 'continuous and permanent', a paradoxical phrase which captures the way in which identity is perpetually renewing and reforming itself.[16] In this respect, Mansfield articulates an understanding of identity that runs counter to the assumptions that underpinned most early twentieth-century psychology. Jung's 'personality psychology', for example, with its outlining of distinct personality types, was predicated on the belief that individuals possess a stable set of characteristics that pre-exist and determine their actions, while Freud's exploration of unconscious processes privileged the power of childhood experience to sculpt enduring dispositions.

It could be argued that the vitalist understanding of psychic life was particularly important in shaping Mansfield's approach to characterisation. In a recent article, Patricia Moran has offered an illuminating analysis of Mansfield's rejection of the developmental model of the self which underpinned both psychoanalysis and the modernist novel, as practised by her friend and rival, Virginia Woolf. She goes on to ascribe Mansfield's rejection of plot and narrative development to her 'sense of the self as multiple and performative' and writes that in her work 'personality is a fleeting and ephemeral construction.'[17] I would like to extend Moran's point about ephemerality to argue that Mansfield's protagonists are realised in terms of a Bergsonian heterogeneity that encompasses both the 'sharp crystals' of perception and the 'continuous flux' of the deeper self. Moreover, I would suggest that it is in the fluid interplay between multiple levels and intensities of consciousness that the distinctiveness of Mansfield's characterisation lies. For example, if we trace the contours of the 'character' of Beryl Fairfax, as revealed in the last section of 'At the Bay', we find a superficial emphasis (in line with Moran's account) on the constructed and the performative, as Beryl projects images of herself which are narcissistically focused on her self-conception as a 'lovely, fascinating girl' (243). These fantasies are interrupted by an awareness of the dumb and 'sorrowful bush', which segues abruptly into a sense of the unrepeatable, moment-by-moment nature of being: 'All that excitement and so on has a way of suddenly leaving you, and it's as though, in the silence, somebody called your name, and you heard your name for the first time' (242). From this point on, the narrative evokes the qualitative multiplicity which, according to Bergson, is constitutive of the 'depth of being'.[18] Beryl's heart beats when she first sees a shape in the darkness then 'leaps' in the moment before she consciously recognises Harry Kember. When he asks her to step outside, something 'stirs' in her and 'rears' its head. In the face of his mockery the desire grows 'tremendously strong' but once she is outside the garden gate, images of 'glittering' moonlight and shadows 'like bars of iron' convey her sense of being exposed and trapped. As she registers Harry's 'bright, blind, terrifying smile', horror morphs into resistance and she wrenches herself free of his grip (244). In this scene, the emotions of anticipation, trepidation, recklessness and fear modulate into and interpenetrate each other. We can distinguish them retrospectively, but as we read we are caught up in the subtle interplay between the 'sharply cut crystals' of Beryl's external perceptions and the flux of her deeper consciousness.

The immersive quality of this scene also derives from Mansfield's attention to the affective dimension of Beryl's emotions. Affect, defined in terms of pre-cognitive and pre-linguistic physiological responses, was central to the vitalist understanding of personality and James's account of emotion is exemplary in this respect, as he challenges the 'common sense' view that emotion precedes its bodily expression. Instead, he argues famously, that 'we feel sorry because we cry, angry because we strike, afraid because we tremble' and suggests that *the bodily changes follow directly the perception of the exciting fact and that our feeling of the same changes as they occur IS the emotion.*'[19] James does not privilege affect over emotion but stresses the way in which it inheres in both emotion and perception. Developing this point, Bergson argues in *Matter and Memory* that affect is 'that part or aspect of the inside of our body which we mix with the image of external bodies' and that, as it is produced by perception, 'there is no perception without affection.'[20] As Lisa Blackman has argued, the vitalist emphasis on the continuity of perception, affect and emotion leads to an understanding of consciousness as not only mutable but also open to the possibility of 'cleavages, accidents and ruptures' that reveal 'the more porous and permeable aspects of the self'.[21]

Such ruptures are at the heart of 'Psychology', breaking in on the consciousness of the protagonists, a woman playwright and a male novelist who meet to discuss the literary issues of the day. They pride themselves on the fact that their friendship is grounded in complete openness, persuading themselves that 'like two open cities in the midst of some vast plain their two minds lay open to each other' (112). On this occasion, their talk is disrupted by moments of unexpected self-consciousness, as when the woman offers cake and implores her friend to eat it with all his senses ('"Roll your eyes if you can and taste it on the breath"'). This prompts him to realise that while he usually sees food simply as '"something that's there [. . .] to be devoured"' (113), he not only is intensely aware of what he eats in these visits but also registers every detail of his surroundings:

'Often when I am away from here I revisit it in spirit – wander about among your red chairs, stare at the bowl of fruit on the black table – and just touch, very lightly, that marvel of a sleeping boy's head.'

He looked at it as he spoke. It stood on the corner of the mantelpiece; the head to one side down-drooping, the lips parted, as though in his sleep the little boy listened to some sweet sound. . .

'I love that little boy,' he murmured. And then they both were silent. (114)

The silence marks his realisation that what is 'precious' to him in these meetings is not the bright conversation but the *mise en scène* created in his friend's studio through the disposition of objects, colour and warmth, each of which appeals to the senses. The theme of sensuous apprehension is deepened by the reference to the head of the sleeping boy, sculpture representing a form of non-discursive apprehension. In this narrative pause, the characters experience a shared awareness of what Bergson calls 'the uninterrupted humming of life's depths',[22] a wordless knowledge which is expressed through the metaphor of the ripples that surround the boy's head as it metaphorically 'drops' into the pool of silence: they 'flowed away, away – boundlessly far – into deep glittering darkness' (114).

At this point and elsewhere, emotion is transmitted between the protagonists through the 'bodily changes' which (to echo James) *are* the emotion and communicate emotion. Their 'ordinary maddening chatter' (116) is derailed by the affective expression of feeling and the ensuing intimacy is experienced as profoundly discomfiting, almost as a form of infection. The implication is that when the boundaries of the self are breached, the self becomes strange to itself, opening up, in Blackman's words, 'the possibility of different kinds of action, conscious and non-conscious'.[23] In this case, the male novelist finds himself 'to his horror' making an excuse to leave, an involuntary move that cuts across his 'longing' to communicate with his friend differently. After his departure the woman behaves 'strangely', running up and down, lifting her arms then flinging herself down on the sofa. However, when she opens the door to another guest, an old friend who 'idolises' her, this second encounter opens up new channels of feeling. She is usually quick to dismiss her 'good friend' but on this occasion, aware once more of 'the silence that was like a question', she embraces her: 'This time she did not hesitate. She moved forward. Very softly and gently, as though fearful of making a ripple in that boundless pool of quiet, she put her arms round her friend.' The tumult of emotions released by the encounter with the novelist coalesces into a novel assemblage of feeling which is expressed in a gesture that makes her feel 'so light, so rested [. . .] even the act of breathing was a joy. . . .' (118). Nothing decisive happens in this story, but in registering a subtle re-alignment of the female protagonist's attachments and affections it conveys the mutability and permeability of consciousness with extraordinary immediacy.

Absorbing the Past

Bergson's account of memory is especially pertinent to Mansfield's work because it construes memory as a synthesis of past and present which is also oriented towards the future. For Bergson, the past exists outside us and it endures in perpetuity; it is 'preserved by itself, automatically' but its existence is entirely virtual except when it is accessed through memory.[24] Following James's discussion in *The Principles of Psychology*, Bergson distinguishes between two main types of memory, the first being habit memory, which is oriented towards future action and is 'lived and acted, rather than represented', as, for example, when we draw on prior knowledge of how to drive a car without being consciously aware of doing so. Accessing pure memory, however, entails a leap into the past, in 'an act *sui generis* by which we detach ourselves from the present in order to replace ourselves, first, in the past in general, then in a certain region of the past – a work of adjustment, something like focusing a camera'.[25] Yet pure memory also manifests itself continuously in the form of memory-images which are inseparable from our perceptions. As Bergson explains:

if there be memory, that is, the survival of past images, these images must constantly mingle with our perception of the present, and may even take its place. For if they have survived it is with a view to utility; at every moment they complete our present experience, enriching it with experience already acquired.[26]

That the interplay between perception and memory is the pre-condition of reflective consciousness is a point stressed by Mansfield in her comments in a letter to Murry on Margot Asquith's *Autobiography*:

> Perhaps I feel more than anything that shes one of those people who have no past and no future. She's capable of her girlish pranks and follies today – in fact she's at the mercy of herself now & forever just as she was then. *And thats bad.* We only live by somehow absorbing the past – changing it – I mean really examining it & dividing what is important from what is not (for there IS waste) & transforming it so that it becomes part of the life of the spirit and we are *free of it* [. . .] With Mrs A this process (by which the artist and the 'living being' lives) never takes place.[27]

Mansfield here expresses a Bergsonian sense of the continuity of past, present and future and underscores the agency of memory, which draws the past into the present and thereby changes both. Her characterisation of Asquith as having no future because she has no past resonates too with Bergson's understanding of the influence of the past on the future. As Grosz explains, when the past is drawn into perception it can shed a novel light on the present that modifies future action. For this reason, the past is a resource which can be

> more or less endlessly revived, dynamized, revivified precisely because the present is unable to actualize all that is virtual in it. The past is not only the past of *this* present, but the past of every present, including that which the future will deliver.[28]

Bergson's rhetorical question, 'What are we, in fact, what is our *character*, if not the condensation of the history that we have lived from our birth?'[29] reverberates throughout Mansfield's retrospectively framed 'A Married Man's Story'. Indeed, its unnamed narrator is explicit about this story's Bergsonian affiliations as he affirms the continuing freshness of the past and its centrality to his own identity:

> The Past – what is the Past? I might say the star-shaped flake of soot on a leaf of the poor-looking plant, and the bird lying on the quilted lining of my cap, and my father's pestle and my mother's cushion belong to it. But that is not to say they are any less mine than they were when I looked upon them with my very eyes and touched them with these fingers. No, they are more, they are a living part of me. Who am I, in fact, as I sit here at this table, but my own past? (433–4)

As the narrator orients himself towards the virtual dimension of the past, his memories unspool to reveal a dialectic that has structured his childhood, between a home environment associated with artifice, even corruption, and an inner sense of vitality and potential. His mother spends hours looking at circus posters outside her window, gazing at 'the slim lady in a red dress hitting a dark gentleman over the head with her parasol [. . .] or at a little golden-haired girl sitting on the knee of an old black man in a cotton hat' (430). Her preoccupation with these disturbing, quasi-erotic images is matched by the activities of the narrator's father, a chemist who peddles drugs to sex workers:

> In the evening his customers were, chiefly, young women; some of them came in every day for his famous fivepenny pick-me-up. Their gaudy looks, their voices, their free ways fascinated me. I longed to be my father, handing them across the counter the little glass of bluish stuff they tossed off so greedily. God knows what it was made of. Years after I drank some, just to see what it tasted like, and I felt as though someone had given me a terrific blow on the head; I felt stunned. (431)

His memories resemble a phantasmagoria which barely contains the violence latent in his parents' constrained lives. The narrator presents himself, however, as a plant alternately shut in a cupboard and thrust into the sun according to his parents' whim. The image irresistibly recalls Mansfield's notebook entry on 'the flowering of the self' and is here tied to a moment of intuition in which, according to the narrator, the plant in the cupboard comes into flower. This is a moment in which Mansfield re-inscribes the iconic Paterian image of the 'thick wall of personality' that isolates us from others as the narrator plays with a candle, with a lake of liquid wax surrounded by a white, smooth wall.[30] Repeatedly he pierces the wall then seals it up, as though playing with the possibility of opening himself up to the world, before experiencing a revolution of feeling in which he claims to see everything with new eyes: 'I saw it all, but not as I had seen before. . . . Everything lived, everything. But that was not all. I was equally alive and – it's the only way I can express it – the barriers were down between us – I had come into my own world!' (437). This transformation could be interpreted in terms of what Bergson would call an intuition of the vital, in which we become conscious of the sympathies that connect us with others. However, such a reading is vitiated by the narrator's revelation that, from this point on, he has turned away from the world of human beings 'towards my silent brothers' (437; the feral wolves invoked earlier in the story). This strange shift in feeling is unmotivated from the point of view of conventional psychology but is explicable in terms of Bergson's suggestion that we think with only a small part of our past, but it is with our entire past, including the original bent of our soul, that we desire, will and act. Our past, then, as a whole, is made manifest to us in its impulse; it is felt in the form of a tendency.[31]

The narrator presents his behaviour (which we know has included cruelty towards his wife) in terms of 'impulses' that derive not from specific events or experiences but from the weight of the entirety of the past, which Bergson suggests we 'drag behind us unawares'.[32] The memories disclosed in this story fail to conform to the explanatory logic of mainstream psychology (or psychoanalysis), the text insisting that there is no such overarching logic, that the past imposes itself on the present in necessarily unforeseeable – and in this case, unnerving – ways.

While 'A Married Man's Story' revolves around a chaotic unfurling of memories, in 'The Daughters of the Late Colonel' Mansfield explores the inhibition of memory in characters who are unable to access the potential of the past or the future. The middle-aged sisters, Constantia and Josephine, have been victims of their father's bullying for decades and have been permanently damaged by it, as is indicated by the way in which he haunts them after his death. For example, Josephine has a moment of terror when she realizes that she has buried her father without his permission, so ingrained is her habit of submission to his will. In death his vitality is far greater than that of his daughters, so that when they enter his old room Josephine feels that he is lurking in there, ready to spring out at them at any moment. As Constantia recalls her previous life, 'running out, bringing things home in bags, getting things on approval, discussing them with Jug, and taking them back to get more things on approval', there is an implicit parallel between the 'goods' and the sisters, whose lives have also had a provisional quality as they have sought paternal approval which has perpetually been withheld (284). Their father's death opens up the prospect of another life, but just as they begin to explore this possibility their conversation is interrupted by the sound of a barrel-organ outside. Stunned by the realisation that they will never again be ordered to stop the music, the sisters allow themselves to enter a space of reflection.

Josephine's attention is caught by their mother's photograph, its faded quality invoking the motif of time passing, and she speculates about the difference it would have made if their mother had lived. She remembers the 'mysterious man at the boarding-house' who once left a note for one of the sisters, opening up the possibility of flirtation, even marriage (283). However, the fact that the message was obliterated by steam means that they never knew which of them it was for, signalling their loss of individual identity under the regime of their father. Meanwhile Constantia gazes at a statue of the Buddha and remembers creeping out of bed in the moonlight and stretching herself on the floor as though she was crucified, together with occasions when she has wandered by the sea singing, memories that point to a mysticism which has found no external support. Perception and memory are mingled in these reflections, which are directed towards the future as well as the past, as is suggested by Constantia's subsequent desire to 'say something to Josephine, something frightfully important, about, – about the future and what. . . .' (284). However, in the conversation which follows, neither sister is able to take the lead and they descend into bickering about who should go first, re-enacting the kind of petty dispute that has marked their life together. After a while Constantia confesses, '"I can't say what I was going to say, Jug, because I've forgotten what it was"' (285). This forgetting and loosening of memory is reminiscent of Bergson's account of the amnesia of hysterics, in which 'the recollections which appear to be abolished are really present' but cannot be retrieved because the subjects have lost 'intellectual vitality'.[33] Years of victimisation have created a condition akin to hysteria, in which the sisters' ability to access the creative interplay between the past, the present and the future has been stunted. This loss of vitality (Bergson's *élan vital*) is perfectly captured in Mansfield's comment on the story:

> All was meant, of course, to lead up to that last paragraph, when my two flowerless ones turned with that timid gesture, to the sun. "Perhaps *now*." And after that, it seemed to me, they died as truly as Father was dead.[34]

Virtual and Actual Futures

Mansfield's fiction is imbued with a particular sense of the future which can also be illuminated with reference to Bergson's thought. As we have seen, Bergson conceptualises the past, present and future as seamlessly interlinked but stresses that the existence of the past is virtual except when it is linked to the present, when it can inform and shape action. According to Bergson, the future is also virtual, but it has a different relationship to the present moment, from which it must necessarily differentiate itself. He explains this in his critique of the possible: that is, the common assumption that the possible pre-exists the real. He argues that the possible in this sense is a retrospective construction and that it is only when the real comes to exist that we persuade ourselves that it must 'have been always possible'.[35] In place of an opposition between the possible and the real, he suggests that we should understand the future in terms of the relationship between the virtual and the actual. The virtual is an immanent force which in no way resembles the actual; rather, the actual is produced in a movement of creative divergence from it. The 'break' between the virtual and the actual produces a future which is constitutively unpredictable and unforeseeable.

Such a sense of the indeterminacy of the future is the pre-condition of Mansfield's articulation of character in terms of what Moses terms the 'situational self'.[36] As he points out, the dominant model of the self in Western culture is a substantialist one which assumes that people have a psychological consistency deriving from a set of enduring traits and that they make decisions in the light of these enduring dispositions. In contrast, he argues that the situational self that features in the work of several modernist writers is contingent and relational, responsive to the successive environments in which it finds itself, endlessly capable of devising unpredictable ways of thinking, behaving and performing. Mansfield's protagonists are similarly framed as 'situational selves', closely embedded in and responding to their psycho-social environments, adjusting their behaviour and self-understanding in the light of ongoing interactions. In 'Bliss', for example, the narrative tracks the way in which Bertha Young's sense of self is reconfigured through her interactions with a dinner guest, Pearl Fulton, and her husband Harry. The story opens with Bertha's sudden, intense feeling of pleasure in her own vitality, rendered in powerfully visceral terms:

> What can you do if you are thirty and, turning the corner of your own street, you are overcome, suddenly, by a feeling of bliss – absolute bliss! – as though you'd suddenly swallowed a bright piece of that late afternoon sun and it burned in your bosom, sending out a little shower of sparks into every particle, into every finger and toe? . . . (91–2)

The image of swallowing the sun points to the interconnectedness of the cosmos and closely echoes a passage in *Creative Evolution* where Bergson writes that:

> The thread attaching [the sun] to the rest of the universe is doubtless very tenuous. Nonetheless it is along this thread that is transmitted down to the smallest particle of the world in which we live the duration immanent to the whole of the universe.[37]

Like Bergson, Mansfield is alert to the fine web of connections between living beings and the wider universe, a web that supports but does not finally explain Bertha's 'bliss'. There are suggestions that this feeling is prompted by anticipation over seeing Pearl Fulton, especially as it resurfaces as Bertha stands looking out of the window with Pearl. She thinks of the two of them as 'understanding each other perfectly [. . .] wondering what they were to do in this [world] with all this blissful treasure that burned in their bosoms and dropped, in silver flowers, from their hair and hands?' (102).

The allusions to bosoms, hair and hands suggest an intense sexual awareness of the other woman, but Bertha's sexuality is not easily categorised as lesbian or indeed as heteronormative. There is an especially queer moment when she thinks of what she and Pearl 'have shared' then leaps to the image of herself and Harry in bed together. This passage has been read in terms of displaced lesbian desire and could also be read in terms of an apprehension, at a level below conscious thought, of the sexual relationship between Harry and Pearl (Harry being what she and Pearl have 'shared').[38] However, there is something undecidable in Bertha's sexuality, just as there is something provisional in her self-understanding. She recreates herself from moment to moment to such a degree that she is opaque to those around her, and the reader also struggles to read her in terms of conventional characterisation. Her responses often seem slightly off-key but are the product of an alert, fluid consciousness which is oriented to an open future, as is suggested by her final line in the story: '"Oh, what is going to happen now?" she cried' (105).

In 'At the Bay', the narrative focuses on points of contact between characters whose interactions, as Meghan Hammond suggests, entail a considerable degree of 'feeling with' each other.[39] Linda Burnell, for example, knows her brother-in-law Jonathan well and demonstrates a sympathetic understanding of his inability to break out of the 'prison' of his job. However, her most significant encounter is with her baby son, who is not, of course, a fully formed 'person'. He responds to the world only in terms of somatic and sensory impressions but is able to engage Linda through a form of proto-affect. He peeps, dimples, smiles, waves his arms, squeezes his eyes and rolls his head, gestures which Linda interprets in terms of interpersonal address, as the third-person narrative reveals ('"I'm here!" that happy smile seemed to say. "Why don't you like me?"'; 'He didn't believe a word she said' [223]). These interactions lead to a moment of emergence when something unprecedented emerges from a matrix of feelings and perceptions:

> Linda was so astonished at the confidence of this little creature. . . . Ah no, be sincere. That was not what she felt; it was something far different; it was something so new, so. . . . The tears danced in her eyes; she breathed in a small whisper to the boy, 'Hallo, my funny!' (223)

As often in Mansfield's work, the ellipses signal a movement of feeling which is singular and unquantifiable. For Linda, this access of feeling is entirely novel and confounds her self-understanding, as she regards herself as being traumatised by her pregnancies and having no warmth left to give her children. As the narrative perspective switches immediately to the baby (who has forgotten his mother), Linda's experience is framed as singular, fleeting and mutable, in line with Mansfield's understanding of consciousness as endlessly productive of novelty, of experience that cannot be predicted from what is already known.

A Blow for Freedom

In 1922 Mansfield wrote to her old friend, S. S. Koteliansky, of D. H. Lawrence's *Aaron's Rod*:

> There are certain things in this new book of L's that I do not like. But they are not important or really part of it. They are trivial, encrusted, they cling to it as snails cling to the underside of a leaf. But apart from them there is the leaf, is the tree, firmly planted, deep thrusting, outspread, growing grandly, alive in every twig. It is a living book; it is warm, it breathes.[40]

What she values in Lawrence is his commitment to the irreducible energy of living things, a commitment that pervades his work and grounds it in a holistic ontology which she shares. In this respect, Mansfield's engagement with vitalist thought can be seen as part of a wider tendency within modernism which is currently being reconsidered in studies such as Kirsty Martin's *Modernism and the Rhythms of Sympathy: Vernon Lee, Virginia Woolf, D. H. Lawrence*. As Martin argues, the vitalist strand in modernism can be understood in part as a response to the slaughter of the First World War and to a climate in which it seemed that the intricacies of human life and feeling were neither respected nor valued. To this extent, vitalism posed an ethical challenge to prevailing ideologies, as it did in its emphasis on a distinctive conception of freedom. This is most fully articulated by Bergson, who rejected both free will and determinism on the grounds that both assume the existence of a stable subject distinct from the choices available to them. For Bergson, the subject is always in process and is continuous with the options she participates in making, so that he (re)defines freedom in terms of being able to act in the moment with the entirety of one's being. In *Time and Free Will* he writes that 'We are free when our acts spring from our whole personality, when they express it, when they have that indefinable resemblance to it which one sometimes finds between an artist and his work.'[41] This is close to Mansfield's position in the letter quoted above when she writes:

Why do we not gather our strength together and LIVE [...] In youth most of us are, for various reasons, slaves. And then, when we are able to throw off our chains, we prefer to keep them. Freedom is dangerous, is frightening.

If only I can be a good enough writer to strike a blow for freedom! It is the one axe I want to grind. Be free – and you can afford to give yourself to life! Even to believe in life.[42]

Mansfield is expressing a belief that is grounded in a complex, long-standing engagement with contemporary psychology and philosophy. The freedom she advocates finds expression in embodied action and constitutes a kind of autopoiesis. As Bergson argues in *Creative Evolution*, we are the 'artisans' of the moments of our life, each one of which is 'a kind of creation'.[43] And as both he and Mansfield suggest, the work of art is an analogous expression of freedom, affirming the transformative energies diffused in living beings.

Notes

1. Katherine Mansfield, *The Collected Stories*, Introduction by Ali Smith (London: Penguin Classics, 2007), p. 115. Hereafter, page numbers are placed parenthetically in the text.
2. Vincent O'Sullivan and Margaret Scott, eds, *The Collected Letters of Katherine Mansfield*, 5 vols (Oxford: Clarendon Press, 1984–2008), Vol. 4, p. 69. Hereafter referred to as *Letters*, followed by volume and page number.
3. *Letters*, 4, p. 69.
4. See Meghan Marie Hammond, *Empathy and the Psychology of Literary Modernism* (Edinburgh: Edinburgh University Press, 2014), pp. 90–117.
5. For a previous discussion of Bergson's influence on Mansfield, see Eiko Nakano, 'Katherine Mansfield and French Philosophy: A Bergsonian Reading of *Maata*', *Katherine Mansfield Studies*, 1 (2009), pp. 68–82.
6. See Elizabeth Grosz, *In the Nick of Time: Politics, Evolution and the Uncanny* (Durham, NC, and London: Duke University Press, 2004) and *Becoming Undone: Darwinian Reflections on Life, Politics, and Art* (Durham, NC, and London: Duke University Press, 2011).
7. May Sinclair was the first to use the phrase in a literary context in her review of Dorothy Richardson's *Pointed Roofs*. See May Sinclair, 'The Novels of Dorothy Richardson', *Egoist* (April 1918), pp. 57–9 (p. 58).
8. See Clare Hanson, ed., *The Critical Writings of Katherine Mansfield* (Basingstoke: Macmillan, 1987), p. 106.
9. See Mary Ann Gillies, *Henri Bergson and British Modernism* (Montreal: McGill–Queen's University Press, 1996), pp. 60–1, for a discussion of Murry's encounter with Bergson's thought.
10. J. Middleton Murry and Katherine Mansfield, 'The Meaning of Rhythm', *Rhythm*, 2: 5 (June 1912), pp. 18–20 (p. 19).
11. Mansfield writes of her commitment to 'the detail of life – the life of life' in a notebook entry dated by Murry to May 1915. See Margaret Scott, ed., *The Katherine Mansfield Notebooks*, 2 vols (Minneapolis: University of Minnesota Press, 2002), Vol. 2, p. 57. Hereafter referred to as *Notebooks*, followed by volume and page number.

12. Omri Moses, *Out of Character: Modernism, Vitalism, Psychic Life* (Stanford: Stanford University Press, 2014).

13. William James, *The Principles of Psychology*, 2 vols (New York: Henry Holt & Company, 1896), Vol. 1, pp. 336–8, James's italics.

14. Henri Bergson, *An Introduction to Metaphysics*, trans. by T. E. Hulme (London: Macmillan, 1913), p. 9.

15. Bergson, pp. 10–11.

16. *Notebooks*, 2, p. 204.

17. Patricia Moran, '"the sudden 'mushroom growth" of cheap psychoanalysis: Mansfield and Woolf Respond to Psychoanalysis', *Virginia Woolf Miscellany*, 86 (Fall 2014/ Winter 2015), pp. 11–14 (p. 13).

18. Bergson, p. 9.

19. James, 2, p. 449, James's italics.

20. Henri Bergson, *Matter and Memory* (1896), trans. by Nancy Margaret Paul and W. Scott Palmer (Mansfield Centre, CT: Martino, 2011), p. 60.

21. Lisa Blackman, 'Affect, Relationality and the "Problem of Personality"', *Theory, Culture and Society* 25: 1 (2008), pp. 23–47 (p. 30).

22. Henri Bergson, *The Creative Mind* (New York: Citadel Press, 1974), pp. 149–50.

23. Blackman, p. 30.

24. Henri Bergson, *Creative Evolution* (1911), trans. by Arthur Mitchell (London: Macmillan, 1960), p. 5.

25. Bergson, *Matter and Memory*, p. 171.

26. Bergson, *Matter and Memory*, p. 70.

27. *Letters*, 4, pp. 89–90.

28. Grosz, *In the Nick of Time*, p. 178.

29. Bergson, *Creative Evolution*, p. 5.

30. Walter Pater, *Studies in the Renaissance* (London: Macmillan & Co, 1873), p. 209.

31. Bergson, *Creative Evolution*, pp. 5–6.

32. Bergson, *Creative Evolution*, p. 5.

33. Bergson, *Matter and Memory*, p. 170.

34. *Letters*, 4, p. 249.

35. Bergson, *The Creative Mind*, p. 101.

36. For a discussion of the situational self, see Moses, pp. 74–6.

37. Bergson, *Creative Evolution*, p. 11.

38. Pamela Dunbar argues for a lesbian reading of 'Bliss' in *Radical Mansfield: Double Discourse in Katherine Mansfield's Short Stories* (Basingstoke: Macmillan, 1997), pp. 104–13.

39. See Hammond, p. 114. The point is made in relation to *Prelude* but applies equally to the other Burnell stories.

40. *Letters*, 5, p. 225.

41. Henri Bergson, quoted in Grosz, *Becoming Undone*, p. 65.

42. *Letters*, 5, p. 225.

43. Bergson, *Creative Evolution*, p. 7.

A Raft in the Sea of Loneliness:
Katherine Mansfield's Discovery of
Cosmic Anatomy

Maurizio Ascari

21.V.18. I positively feel, in my hideous modern way, that I cant get into touch with my mind. I am standing gasping in one of those disgusting telephone boxes and I cant 'get through'. 'Sorry. There's no reply' tinkles out the little voice. 'Will you ring them again, exchange? A good long ring. There must be somebody there.' 'I cant get any answer'.[1]

Katherine Mansfield had a recurrent fear of loneliness: not only external loneliness, being cut off from other human beings and nature at large, but also inner loneliness, being cut off from herself, from that innermost dimension that she strove to reach with all her strength. The opposite of loneliness is relatedness, which is what her discovery of M. B. Oxon's *Cosmic Anatomy and the Structure of the Ego* (1921) helped her achieve, according to the vibrant words she wrote on 4 January 1922:

> I have read a good deal of Cosmic Anatomy – understood it far better. Yes, such a book does fascinate me. Why does Jack hate it so? To get even a glimpse of the relation of things, to follow that relation & find it remains true through the ages enlarges my little mind as nothing else does. Its only a greater view of psychology. (N2 313)

This cryptic passage is an apt description for a book that remains no less cryptic despite almost a century of Mansfield criticism. Although *Cosmic Anatomy* is at the core of the Mansfield myth, few scholars have attempted either to contextualize it within the cultural scenario that saw the development of modernism or to scrutinize it more closely.

In order to understand Mansfield's response to this book we need to take into account a complex network of interpersonal exchanges that spans the divide between the intellectual and the emotional, science and pseudoscience, rationality and its 'others'. It was Mansfield's old friend and mentor, A. R. Orage – a socialist thinker who had developed an interest in theosophy, and who edited the *New Age* between 1907 and 1922 – who sent the recently published *Cosmic Anatomy* to J. M. Murry, hoping to have it reviewed, but Murry 'intensely disliked this "book of occult doctrines"'[2] and it was Mansfield who started reading it.

The respectful trust Mansfield put in Orage is proved by a letter dated 9 February 1921, where she thanks him for his 'wonderful unfailing kindness in the "old days"' – suffice it to think of the number of stories she published in the *New Age* starting from 1910 – and expands on her many debts to him:

> you taught me to write, you taught me to think; you showed me what there was to be done and what not to do.
>
> My dear Orage, I cannot tell you how often I call to mind your conversation or how often, in *writing*, I remember my master.[3]

Mansfield's letter ends with this sentence: 'I'd like to send my love, too, if I wasn't so frightened. K.M.'[4] While testifying to the warmth of her feelings towards Orage, these words imply that she perceived her relation with him as asymmetrical, perhaps because he was fifteen years her senior or simply because his profile was larger than life, as proved by his exchanges with G. K. Chesterton, Ezra Pound and T. S. Eliot. Orage was the pivot around which a cultural circle revolved, whose nature cannot be fully grasped unless we take into account the role alternative – or, if you wish, 'occult' – approaches to knowledge played in this period.[5]

What's In a Book?

Cosmic Anatomy was a prominent feature of the Mansfield myth right from its inception, in the years following her death, when Murry orchestrated the publication of her uncollected writings. When Mansfield's *Journal* appeared in 1927 it introduced to the public a little-known volume that had changed the life of the author one year before her death. While the snow oppressively prevailed all around the Chalet des Sapins in Montana sur Sierre in January 1922, *Cosmic Anatomy* filled Mansfield's days, together with Shakespeare and the Bible. The book became further rooted in the collective imagination, thanks to the publication of the *Scrapbook*, which includes several long quotations from it.[6]

Ida Constance Baker's *The Memories of LM* also contributed to the legend, for Mansfield's reading of *Cosmic Anatomy* is presented here as marking 'the first step towards what she later found in Ouspensky'.[7] Baker deemed this as the real turning-point in Mansfield's life, while her decision to join Gurdjieff's community at Avon was simply 'the culmination of a gradual process'.[8] What is more, Baker considered the book to be at the root of Mansfield's estrangement from Murry.[9]

The writer's 'surrender' to irrationalism provoked a perplexed reaction in many a critic. Suffice it to think of Jeffrey Meyers, whose *Katherine Mansfield: A Darker View* describes her 'submission to the powerful charisma of Gurdjieff' as

> a culmination of almost all the ideas and events that had dominated her final year: her passion for all things Russian, her absorption in *Cosmic Anatomy*, her impatience with her illness, her disillusionment with doctors and desire to cure her soul, her inability to face reality and acquiescence in self-deception [. . .] .[10]

While the real man behind the pen name of M. B. Oxon was Lewis Alexander Richard Wallace, Meyers mistakenly identifies him as 'A. R. Wallace', the author of *Scientific Aspects of the Supernatural* and *Miracles and Modern Spiritualism*, a scientist and spiritualist writer who had actually died in 1913.[11] What follows is this biased cameo portrait: '[Wallace] wrote many abstruse articles, under his Oxonian pseudonym, to mystify its readers. Like Orage, he was enthusiastic about crankish projects.'[12]

To achieve a more balanced and reliable perspective, we need to turn to Vincent O'Sullivan, who expands on *Cosmic Anatomy* in his introduction to the fifth volume of Mansfield's *Letters*:

> there is a direct line from [Mansfield's] telling Violet Schiff early in the year that 'what saved me finally was reading a book called "Cosmic Anatomy" and reflecting on it' (8 January), to her final months in George Gurdjieff's Institute [. . .] It is a line and a conclusion that her biographers and commentators often feel uneasy with, yet it has an inevitable logic, and brought Mansfield undisputable satisfaction.[13]

In 2011 O'Sullivan re-assessed Mansfield's last year, wondering how she might develop such an interest for *Cosmic Anatomy*, which 'one is provoked on almost every page to describe [. . .] as either cranky or confused.'[14] Despite these understandable qualms, O'Sullivan engages intellectually with *Cosmic Anatomy*, trying to unravel meaning from its pages. He argues that Wallace's insistence on 'the unity underlying casual phenomena' must have been appealing for a woman who was haunted by a sense of impending death and inner division.[15] He also mentions Bergson as an influence, who possibly set the ground for Mansfield's reception of the book, which rescues 'time from mere mechanical process'.[16] While O'Sullivan ends his enlightening article with an analysis of late stories such as 'The Fly' and 'The Canary', I will now take a different direction and investigate Wallace's contribution to the *New Age*, the alternative thinking laboratory in which *Cosmic Anatomy* is rooted.

M. B. Oxon, Orage and the New Age

It was thanks to the financial help of George Bernard Shaw and Lewis Wallace – who both advanced £500 – that Orage was able to buy the *New Age* in 1907, together with his co-editor, Holbrook Jackson, who left shortly afterwards in 1908, while Orage remained at the helm until 1922. Wallace was a banker who had made money thanks to sheep-farming in New Zealand. He and Orage had met in theosophical circles and his material support continued in the following years, but Wallace also contributed a large number of articles and letters, notably concerning psychoanalysis.

What marks out the *New Age* is its dialectical nature. As Martin Wallace comments, under Orage's editorship, the *New Age* 'was a product not of journalism as traditionally conceived, but of men and ideas interacting in a period of cultural change'.[17] In particular, the journal played a seminal role in introducing psychoanalysis to the British public.[18] Already, on 15 February 1912, A. E. Randall published 'The Heart of Hamlet's Mystery',[19] summarising Ernest Jones's discussion of Shakespeare's play and Freud's view of the Oedipus complex. Two years later, the publication of *On Dreams* – David Eder's translation of Sigmund Freud's abridged edition of *Die Traumdeutung* – prompted Randall to publish 'Freud on Dreams'.[20]

The article criticises both those who oppose psychoanalysis on account of Freud's insistence on the sex instinct, and psychoanalysis itself for studying solely the 'egoistic' dimension of dreams, thus failing to take into account the possibility of prophetic and telepathic/coincidental dreams. While Freud advanced a 'materialistic' explanation of dreams as rooted in individual experiences and drives, spiritualists and psychical researchers related dreams to a wider sphere, studying their connections with hypnotism, thought transference and even possession. As Frederick W. H. Myers claims in *Human Personality and Its Survival of Bodily Death*:

> we are living a life in two worlds at once; a planetary life in the material world, to which the organism is intended to react; and also a cosmic life in that spiritual or metetherial world, which is the native environment of the soul.
> The waking personality is adapted to the needs of the earthly life; the personality of sleep maintains the fundamental connection between the organism and the spiritual world [. . .][21]

Given the existence of such radically different interpretations of dreams, it comes as no surprise that Randall's opinions triggered the heated reaction of Wallace, whose sympathies transpire from his pen name, evoking a kinship with M. A. Oxon, the pseudonym of spiritualist medium W. Stainton Moses.

In 'Dreams I' (23 July 1914) Wallace criticises Freud's theory of dreams as stemming from a pathological view of the human. What Wallace advocates is an alternative theory, which puts 'sex dirtiness into the background', leading 'into the great world of the old myths and the personal gods'.[22] In the following weeks, Oxon expanded on this theory ('Dreams II', 30 July; 'Dreams III', 6 August), which read as impressionistic rather than scientific or otherwise inspired. No wonder that on 13 August Randall counterattacked, while Oxon replied on 20 August. This intellectual boxing match went on[23] until Eder himself – Freud's translator and a contributor to the *New Age* – intervened with a letter in which he commented that Freud's theory of dreams had been subjected 'to the tests of experiment and experience' while Oxon had 'spun his view of dreams sitting in his armchair'.[24] Predictably, Wallace replied within a week, reasserting his dissatisfaction with Freud's pathological conception of dreams, which 'starts from the wrong end, and postulates as the cause of dreams a "quasi-material" mechanism'.[25]

The debate periodically re-ignited, as shown by an article Orage himself published on 31 January 1918 in the column 'Readers and Writers', which he signed as R. H. C.[26] The text opens with Orage's appreciation of a recent study by G. R. S. Mead for 'showing that Psycho-analysis has not yet distinguished in the subconscious the "higher" from the "lower," the rudimentary from the vestigial, the past from the future in a word, the psyche from the soul'.[27] The full import of this praise becomes apparent if we remember that Mead was an important member of the Theosophical Society, which he abandoned to create the Quest Society in 1909, with the aim of fostering the comparative study of religion, philosophy and science. Orage goes on to discuss his recent polemics with Randall on the subject of *Hamlet*, and only at the end does he launch into a passionate apology for psychoanalysis, which he describes as 'the most inviting' of all the new sciences, adding that 'Its immediate practical applications in the hands of competent psycho-analysts are already considerable; but the field both of theory and of practice has scarcely begun as yet to be cultivated.'[28]

These comments are revealing of the strategies Orage pursued while orchestrating the *New Age* debate on psychoanalysis in the attempt both to bring readers into contact with the new theories of the mind and to widen the researchers' field of inquiry. This syncretic tendency is exemplified by the articles Wallace published in the summer of 1919, when 'The Ancient View of Reincarnation' (3 July) was followed by 'Some Remarks on Psycho-Analysis' (14 August). These critical positions predictably invited a response, this time on the part of J. A. M. Alcock, a doctor whose 'Psycho-Analysis' appeared in the 'Letters to the Editor' on 21 August. This marked the beginning of an exchange of letters – embracing also Jung's theories – that lasted until 23 October.[29]

Far from being isolated, Wallace interacted dialectically with the group of intellectuals who gathered around Orage. According to James Webb, this 'psycho-synthesis group' included Havelock Ellis, David Eder, James Young and Maurice Nicoll – the latter two had studied with Jung at Zurich – while Rowland Kenney and J. A. M. Alcock were also involved.[30] Webb's use of the term psycho-synthesis alerts us to the connections between this collective quest and other attempts to go beyond Freud's method, such as those of Italian psychiatrist Roberto Assagioli, whose holistic approach to the psyche is akin to Jung's and resulted – as early as 1909 – in a doctoral dissertation entitled *La Psicosintesi*.

As Webb claims, 'The sort of psychoanalysis which the *New Age* favored was never far from the occult.'[31] Orage and his friends were trying to mediate between two contrasting views of the human: on the one hand a materialist, positivistic, scientific view, of whose reductionism they were critical, and on the other a holistic view which today we might label as 'new age', curiously echoing the title of Orage's journal.[32]

This attempt to foster transgressive approaches to the psyche is exemplified by James Young's 'The Psychology of Dreams' (30 October 1919). After describing Freud's theory as a great advance, Young analyses the relation between dreams and the unconscious in relation to the endo-psychic repression of forbidden tendencies, mainly of a sexual nature, and their re-emergence through dreams in a disguised form, as symbols. Considering Freud's insistence on the sexual nature of dreams as reductive, Young draws this parallel:

> If you say that a Beethoven symphony is 'nothing but' a collection of notes in a certain sequence, you allow rationalism to destroy wonder. You, as it were, kill the God in you. You destroy the value, and by no means explain the phenomenon.[33]

After mentioning Bergson to describe this reductive attitude as a misapplication of the law of cause and effect, Young proceeds to enunciate the 'synthetic or prospective view of dreams',[34] in which symbolism is no longer regarded simply as a disguise. What follows is a theory of archetypes that shifts the emphasis from the single individual to the species, from ontogenesis to phylogenesis, underlining the centrality of symbols in the primitive perception of reality. Unsurprisingly, 'Jung of Zurich'[35] is presented as the initiator of the synthetic or prospective view of dreams, which reconnects psychoanalysis to anthropology, mythology and comparative religions.

As we shall see, both dreams and symbolism were central to Mansfield's creative imagination, but this is not the only reason why I have dwelt on this article. Young was the doctor who visited Mansfield at the Select Hotel in Paris on her last birthday, on 14 October 1922, before discussing with Gurdjieff her admission to the Institute. While Young already lived at Le Prieuré, Orage himself arrived in Paris later that day to join Gurdjieff, and it is as a fellow member of the community that Mansfield affectionately described Young on 23 October 1922: 'Doctor Young, a real friend of mine, comes up and makes me up a good fire. In "return" I am patching the knee of his trousers today.'[36] As a doctor, Young was also present in Mansfield's room – unlike Murry – when she died.

Much has been written concerning the few months Mansfield spent at Le Prieuré together with Orage, Ouspensky, Young and the other disciples of Gurdjieff.[37] Although this article is concerned with Mansfield's first contact with *Cosmic Anatomy*, rather than with her final days, the two ends of this itinerary of self-discovery appear as inextricably connected. Webb even questions the accepted authorship of *Cosmic Anatomy*, advancing the hypothesis that the volume may have been 'cobbled together by Orage and the psychosynthesists'[38] to serve as an introduction to the lectures Ouspensky had started giving after his arrival in London in August 1921.

Although it cannot be excluded that *Cosmic Anatomy* was written or revised by various persons, Wallace still actively contributed to the *New Age* between 1919 and 1920, as shown by 'The "Libido"' (6 November 1919); 'The Self and Not Self' (13 November 1919); 'Practical Religion' (4 December 1919); 'Psycho-Egyptology' (19 February 1920); and 'Psycho-Egyptology-II' (26 February 1920). The fact that some of his concerns echo in the pages of *Cosmic Anatomy* does not rule out any joint form of authorship, but it does point to a continuity.

Inside Cosmic Anatomy

Far from offering a summary of this convoluted book, I will focus on just a few sections, starting from the introduction, whose title – 'Our present sorrows and a possible cure' – possibly in itself attracted the attention of Mansfield.

Addressing a widespread discontent that he regards as caused both by the war and by the scientific deconstruction of religious beliefs, the author attempts to contrast this loss of certainties by developing an alternative approach to the spiritual: 'Mankind is now moving from Reason and Intellect towards Feeling and Emotion, and needs instruction therein; but Religion has little to say on the subject, and Psychology is still too intent on pathology. Both of them should be working together . . .'[39] What Wallace perceives as a danger is the undisputed primacy of science as conducive to technology and economic growth. After complaining that 'We are all utilitarians now,' he invites his readers to explore their relationship with their inner dimension and their environment along different lines.[40] While physics and astronomy contribute to unveiling the material nature of the universe, individuals lack a 'scheme of life' (CA 6). As a result, 'man is now left a solitary mariner, shipwrecked on an uncharted ocean' (CA 7). Perhaps it is an echo of this line that we find in the words Mansfield noted on 3 February 1922, after reaching Paris and beginning Dr Manoukhin's X-ray treatment:

> This going to Paris has been so much more important than it seemed. Now I begin to see it as the result, the ending to all that reading. I mean that even Cosmic Anatomy is involved. Something has been built – a raft, frail and not very seaworthy, but it will serve. Before, I was cast into the water where I was 'alone'. (N2 323–4)

Given Mansfield's condition of illness and solitude, it is hardly surprising that she responded to Wallace's insistence on the correlation between individuals and the universe at large, as well as between soul and body, and on the ensuing possibility of curing the body through the soul.

Back to *Cosmic Anatomy*: its convoluted character results from a precise argumentative strategy, which Wallace articulates in contrast with what he labels as 'the modern craze for unification':

> If we can take millions of photographs of a common table, each of which will show it of a different shape, some with four legs, some with none – but all of them true pictures – it is, surely, probable that the same applies to that wonderful world in which we live. (CA 2)

This cubist emphasis on the plurality of perspectives is meant to explain the 'self-contradictory' (CA 8) nature of the book, which is presented as provisional and conducive to a reconciliation on a different plane.

Already in Chapter 2, on 'The Ancient View of Things in General', we are confronted with an interesting reflection concerning the human consciousness, behind the volatility of which Wallace recognizes 'that indefinable silent onlooker who seems to do nothing, the unchanging link between our changing moods which is the essence of our "I-ness"'

(CA 25). While modernist culture placed the emphasis on the stream of consciousness, Wallace aimed to reach a deeper level, which he defines as our 'foundation-stone', calling it 'Essence or Energy or Vishnu. This is what we call Eternal Life, as contrasted with earthly life' (CA 25).

This unorthodox view of the human is at the core of Chapter 9, 'On Psycho-Analysis', which tackles the problem of tracing a line between the self and the not-self. After lamenting the fact that physiologists and even psychoanalysts seem to see no difference between humans and animals, Wallace stigmatises Freud's and Jung's theories as 'childishly crude' (CA 119), describing dreams as 'the only recollections which most men have of the worlds other than the visible one' (CA 137).

Opposing the materialist attitude of scientists, Wallace advocates a reversed view of the world that posits matter as rooted in the spiritual dimension. In so doing, he is of course indebted to ancient and oriental philosophies and religions, but also to Plato, whose view of the androgynous is echoed in this passage:

> Man is not only anatomically but also mystically of double sex. Sex means in fact the division of the Twins. [. . .] when they have reunited, when a man has redeveloped his female half and the woman her male half, they will, so to speak, reproduce themselves in psyche. (CA 134)

This passage – which one may associate with Jung's dichotomy between animus and anima – probably resonated with Mansfield's own sexual concerns, with her complex perception of her identity. However, what attracted Mansfield even more was arguably the book's emphasis on wholeness, especially at a time when she felt so painfully severed from life.

What *Cosmic Anatomy* offers is an inclusive and dynamic view of the self, as comprising the masculine and the feminine, body and soul, but also overflowing the boundaries of a single life in terms of time, due to its insistence on reincarnation. The book may have proved liberating to Mansfield in other ways also, since Wallace redesigned the relation between the individual and the cosmos by underlining both their astrological connections and the paradigm of mutual mirroring that was at the core of the microcosm/macrocosm dualism according to Neo-Platonism and Renaissance magic. Wallace's assertion that 'we contain the whole world in us' (CA 132) brings us back to his polemics against psychoanalysis, notably in relation to the conception of the unconscious:

> What is the 'unconscious' and whence is it derived? It was first conceived to be a personal possession of each man; it is now looked on, by some, as the collective treasury of human experiences; it will, I think, turn out to be hardly distinguishable from the Universe. (CA 174–5)

Rejecting both the Freudian ontogenetic view of an individual unconscious and Jung's phylogenetic view of a collective unconscious that
developed in the course of evolution, Wallace embraces an esoteric
view of the unconscious as an inner infinite in which the outer infinite
is mirrored.

The Ordeal of the Self

Wallace's holistic theories undoubtedly appealed to Mansfield, whose
painful awareness of inner disconnectedness is rendered ironically in
this undated passage:

> True to oneself! Which self? [. . .] For what with complexes and suppres-
> sions, and reactions and vibrations and reflections – there are moments
> when I feel I am nothing but the small clerk of some hotel without a pro-
> prietor who has all his work cut out to enter the names and hand the keys
> to the wilful guests. (N2 203–4)

In order to overcome this energy-consuming and paralysing condition
of transience, Mansfield professes her

> belief in a self which is continuous and permanent, which, untouched
> by all we acquire and all we shed, pushes a green spear through the
> leaves and through the mould, thrusts a sealed bud through years of
> darkness until, one day, the light discovers it and shakes the flower free
> and – we are alive – we are flowering for our moment upon the earth.
> (N2 204)

Mansfield's emphasis on human 'flowering' reminds us of a technique
she experimented with in many of her stories, the *blazing moment* – a
climax of heightened consciousness, of *eudaimonia*, of reconnection
with reality and truth, an epiphany that she often depicts as taking
place in a garden. What the flowering of this underlying permanent
self brings about is the achievement of a paradoxical condition, in
which – as Mansfield explains – 'we are most ourselves and least personal' (N2 204). This is nothing else than the overcoming of the ego,
which Eastern traditions compare to a monkey endlessly jumping from
one branch to another, due to the mind's unceasing response to external stimuli under the aegis of fears and desires.

Mansfield's fear of inner multiplicity – of inhabiting only the change-
able surface of her being without attaining the unruffled transparency
of her inner depths – significantly combined with the 'religion' of work
she was pursuing in this period, an ethical attitude that likewise entailed
an escape from the ego. Already in 1921 she jotted down a few lines in

47

which she complained about her pride, about catching herself 'preen-ing' her feathers, and then concluded that

> anything that I write in this mood will be no good; it will be full of *sediment*. [. . .] One must learn, one must practice to *forget* oneself. I can't tell the truth about Aunt Anne unless I am free to enter into her life with-out selfconsciousness. Oh God! I am divided still. (N2 296)

The same message transpires from an entry Mansfield wrote on 2 February 1922, immediately after reading Wallace: 'To do anything, to be anything, one must gather oneself together and one's faith make stronger. Nothing of any worth can come from a disunited being' (N2 322–3). Unity is presented here as the key to both literary creativ-ity and personal development, two dimensions that Mansfield increas-ingly regarded as coinciding. Mansfield fully articulated this nexus on 14 October 1922, her thirty-fourth birthday and the day when Young went to see her in Paris. On this climactic day, when Mansfield acknowledged that her relationship with Murry was dying and sud-denly felt ready to plunge into the unknown by joining Gurdjieff, she also felt the need to remind herself of her priorities – that is, health and work:

> By health I mean the power to live a full, adult, living breathing life in close contact [with] what I love – the earth and the wonders thereof, the sea, the sun. All that we mean when we speak of the external world. I want to enter into it, to be part of it, to live in it, to learn from it, to lose all that is superficial and acquired in me and to become a conscious, direct human being. (N2 287)

Reconnecting with the external world and with her permanent self are presented here as two sides of the same coin, and unsurprisingly health is seen as conducive to writing:

> Then I want to *work*. At what? I want so to live that I work with my hands and my feeling and my brain. I want a garden, a small house, grass, ani-mals, books, pictures, music. And out of this – the expression of this – I want to be writing. (Though I may write about cabmen. That's no matter.) (N2 287)

While these lines betray a knowledge of Gurdjieff's theory of the three centres – intellectual, emotional and moving – on which the human pivots, they also testify to the dilemma Mansfield was experiencing in this period. While her final aim was to write, in order to achieve this goal she needed 'to be rooted in life' (N2 287), but her invalid condi-tion was severing her precisely from this source of nourishment.

In a life that was progressively deprived of sensory contacts with the external world, writing understandably acquired a compensatory value. While Mansfield's talent for observation was probably innate, the need to cross the border between self and not self – which transpires from her oft-quoted 1917 manifesto of boundless empathy, 'When I write about ducks I swear that I am a white duck'[41] – arguably strengthened in the last period of her life due to her condition of chronic illness. Overcoming individuation to identify with other forms of life enabled her to escape from her aching body, which she described in February 1922 as an 'almost unendurable' prison, 'like being a beetle shut in a book' (N2 326).

Writing was, for Mansfield, a way to renew her ties with *external life*, although we can easily shift our perspective and comment that she needed to be in contact with external life in order to write. The act of writing, moreover, was a way to explore her *inner life*, and was correspondingly rooted in it. A letter dated 13 October 1920 gives vent to Mansfield's criticism of 'the sudden "mushroom growth" of cheap psycho analysis everywhere', notably in novels, then renders her view of inspiration as follows:

> With an artist – one has to allow – oh tremendously for the subconscious element in his work. He writes he knows not what – hes *possessed*. I don't mean of course, always, but when he's *inspired* – as a sort of divine flower to all his terrific hard gardening there comes this subconscious [. . .] wisdom. Now these people who are nuts on analysis seem to me to have *no* subconscious at all.[42]

While distancing herself from those authors whose writing springs from a rational view of the psyche, Mansfield locates her source of inspiration precisely in the 'subconscious', although the 'possession' she experiences combines with her passion for technique – a highly controlled and demanding activity that she labels here as 'terrific hard gardening'.

Dreams and Symbolism

At a time when Mansfield felt painfully disconnected from her body, her psyche and her inspiration, reading *Cosmic Anatomy* gave her new hope in a form of personal rebirth, but it also resonated with her aesthetic concerns, for these two dimensions were inextricably interlaced, as we have just seen. Several of the daily entries Mansfield wrote in her notebooks in January 1922 revealingly open with an account of her dreams, which is often followed by reflections on Wallace's study.

> A long typical boat dream. I was, as usual, going to N.Z. But for the first time my stepmother was very friendly – so nice. I loved her. A tragic dream

as regards Ida. She disappeared & it was too late to find her or tell her to come back at last.

Read Cosmic Anatomy. (N2 313)

I cannot help seeing a parallel between Mansfield's 'typical boat dream' and stories such as 'Six Years After', which she wrote in November 1921. Far from being conducive simply to an exploration of her psyche, dreams were at the origin of Mansfield's stories, as she had earlier commented with regard to 'Sun and Moon' (1920): 'I *dreamed* a short story last night even down to its name, which was *Sun & Moon.* [. . .] I didn't dream that I read it. No I was in it part of it and it played round invisible me.'[43] This story, pivoting on the sun and the moon intended as archetypes of the masculine and the feminine, brings us to the issue of symbolism.

While David Daiches described Mansfield's symbolism as the polar opposite of her quest for truth, in so far as it depends 'entirely on the mind of the observer',[44] I believe that Mansfield's exploration of symbolism was actually an attempt to get at the root of the human, repositioning it – with an anti-modernist move – within the wider realm of nature. While explaining her enthusiastic response to *Cosmic Anatomy*, Mansfield underlines the importance Wallace's archetypal reading has for her writing:

> It helps me with my writing for instance to know that hot + bun may mean Taurus, Pradhana, substance. No, that's not really what absorbs me, its that reactions to certain causes & effects always have been the same. It wasn't for nothing Constantia chose the moon & water – for instance!' (N2 313)

Here Mansfield is referring to the final section of 'The Daughters of the Late Colonel' (1922). A week after the death of their tyrannical father, the two title characters – Josephine and Constantia – hear an organ playing. Their first reaction is to give money to the organ grinder, telling him to go away so as not to disturb their father, but they soon realise that this precaution is no longer necessary. The music sets Constantia's mind working, thinking of all the opportunities that failed to materialise, until her monotonous and constrained material existence begins to look unreal and the few moments of solitude when she was in touch with natural forces – and thus authentically alive – come to the fore:

> She remembered the times she had come in here, crept out of bed in her nightgown when the moon was full, and lain on the floor with her arms outstretched, as though she was crucified. Why? The big, pale moon had made her do it. [. . .] She remembered too how, whenever they were at the

seaside, she had gone off by herself and got as close to the sea as she could, and sung something, something she had made up, while she gazed all over that restless water. There had been this other life, running out, bringing things home in bags, getting things on approval, discussing them with Jug, and taking them back to get more things on approval, and arranging father's trays and trying not to annoy father. But it all seemed to have happened in a kind of tunnel. It wasn't real. It was only when she came out of the tunnel into the moonlight or by the sea or into a thunderstorm that she really felt herself.[45]

In this passage Constantia is portrayed as communing with natural elements that have been archetypically codified as female, and that even *force* her to acknowledge – once again symbolically, through the sign of the cross, which becomes here a form of body language – her inner truth: that is, her victimisation at the hands of her father.

As Gerri Kimber comments, in Mansfield's later stories symbolism acquired an 'esoteric undertone', as if she was 'assuming a subconscious understanding of the workings of the universe through her use of recurring symbols'.[46] Significantly, *Notebook 20* – which is characterised by Mansfield's sketches of her dreams and by her comments on *Cosmic Anatomy* – opens with these words: 'What is the universal mind?' (N2 311). Relatedness here acquires a much wider meaning, which goes beyond the human and yet contains it.

This emphasis on a holistic perception of things can help us understand Mansfield's interest for *plurisignification*: that is to say, the possibility of communicating simultaneously at various levels. After relating Mansfield's 'polyphonic treatment of narrative matter' to her familiarity with music, Andrée-Marie Harmat discusses her use of symbols to create 'in the reader an impression of the simultaneous and parallel unfolding of several – and often contrary – meanings and of the manifold strands that constitute the human psyche'.[47] 'The Daughters of the Late Colonel' aptly illustrates this polyphonic technique, since it is the music of the barrel organ that triggers Constantia's reflections, which carry readers into her subconscious, until this train of associations results in a protective act of removal: 'A pause. Then Constantia said faintly, "I can't say what I was going to say, Jug, because I've forgotten what it was [. . .] that I was going to say."'[48]

While Mansfield's interest in symbolism antedates her reading of *Cosmic Anatomy*, Wallace's diagrams and interpretations of ancient texts resonated with her tendency to codify various layers of meaning in a polyphonic narrative, and of course also with a corresponding vision of the human psyche as multilayered. Harmat is well aware of this latter connection, since her reflections on Mansfield's symbolism culminate in her analysis of the mirror as a means of psychological investigation which allows 'the contrapuntal treatment of separate levels of consciousness in human beings'.[49]

Beyond Psychoanalysis

While approaching my conclusion, I cannot help thinking of the possible relations between Mansfield's and Lawrence's use of symbolism and conception of the human. In his autobiography, Murry recounts how, after the publication of *Sons and Lovers* (1913), Dr Eder 'called more than once on Lawrence to discuss the doctrine [of psychoanalysis], when I happened to be there'.[50] Was Mansfield also present? Did she discuss this and other related subjects with Lawrence? Despite their estrangement, Mansfield and Lawrence pursued, in some respects, similar paths. As Susan Reid remarks, there is much in what Mansfield wrote during her last year 'that resonates with Lawrence's writing'.[51] In July 1922, after reading *Aaron's Rod*, Mansfield even wrote: 'I feel nearer L. than everyone else. All these last months I have thought as he does about many things.'[52]

In the early 1920s Lawrence gave vent to his criticism of psychoanalysis while propounding an esoteric approach to knowledge, the psyche and the cosmos. In *Psychoanalysis and the Unconscious* (1921), Lawrence rejects Freud's view of the unconscious and the Oedipal theory to offer – in Bruce Steele's words – 'an alternative account based [. . .] on his own intuition, experience and insights'.[53] After discarding a loaded term such as 'soul', due to its pre-conceived religious connotations, Lawrence defines the unconscious as 'that essential unique nature of every individual creature, which is, by its very nature, unanalysable', envisaging an alternative form of self-knowledge, since the unconscious 'can only be experienced'.[54] Refusing a subjugation of the unconscious to the intellectual principle that dominates Western culture, Lawrence advocates the advent of a 'science of the creative unconscious',[55] the pre-requisite of which is a new epistemological attitude. Lawrence soon developed his project in *Fantasia of the Unconscious* (1922), which is explicitly presented as an esoteric book that is addressed to initiates ('The generality of readers had better just leave it alone'), and moreover as resting on an anti-positivist premise: 'I am not a scientist [. . .] I proceed by intuition.'[56]

These concise references are meant to underline that Lawrence was dissatisfied both with the Freudian model of the psyche[57] and with positivism, intended as an attempt to expand the domination of the mind over life – from the human body to nature at large – to the detriment of life itself: 'Our science is a science of the dead world. Even biology never considers life, but only mechanistic functioning and apparatus of life.'[58] Yet, Lawrence's distrust of mind and mechanism does not imply that he was sympathetic to Gurdjieff and his milieu. While in November 1922 – writing from Le Prieuré – Mansfield described Lawrence and E. M. Forster as 'the two men who *could* understand this place, if they would',[59] Lawrence later resisted Mabel Luhan's attempt to convert him to Gurdjieff's worldview, as Meyers reminds us.[60]

Back to Mansfield: her reading of *Cosmic Anatomy* is but a chapter in a quest that was fuelled by a condition of physical deprivation, and that proved as undaunted as her juvenile quest for physical plenitude, her experiences with lovers of both sexes, her desire to *know* both with her mind and with her body. I can see a continuity between the flashes of intuition Mansfield noted already in her youth – such as 'Although there were no God, God would remain the greatest notion man has had. Evolution is eventually God – nicht?' (N1 122) – and the holistic tendencies she fully manifested later on. No wonder that, on 19 October 1922, she wrote to Koteliansky: 'I have gone through a kind of private revolution. It has been in the air for years with me.'[61] As these words indicate, Mansfield's quest for truth and wholeness spanned a much longer time than the last year of her life.

Having said this, her response to *Cosmic Anatomy* marked an important step in this itinerary of self-searching. Despite its mystifying density, Wallace's book enabled Mansfield to articulate more clearly her tension towards unity and meaning, providing her with a sense of direction, inviting her to translate words into action, as she confided to *Notebook 20*: 'To act and not to dream' (N2 311). Even before getting in touch with Ouspensky and Gurdjieff, Mansfield was aware of the hypnotic and mechanical character of everyday life, as shown also by 'The Daughters of the Late Colonel'. Somehow, *Cosmic Anatomy* worked as a mirror, and – like one of her characters, when facing reflection – she recognised her true self in its pages.

Notes

1. Margaret Scott, ed., *The Katherine Mansfield Notebooks*, 2 vols (Minneapolis: University of Minnesota Press, 2002), Vol. 2, p. 134. Hereafter, all page references to volumes 1 and 2 are placed parenthetically within the text thus: for example, '(N2 134)'.
2. Antony Alpers, *The Life of Katherine Mansfield* (New York: Viking Press, 1980), p. 353.
3. Vincent O'Sullivan and Margaret Scott, eds, *The Collected Letters of Katherine Mansfield*, 5 vols (Oxford: Clarendon, 1984–2008), Vol. 4, p. 177. To A. R. Orage, 9 February 1921. Hereafter referred to as *Letters*, followed by volume and page number.
4. *Letters*, 4, p. 177. To A. R. Orage, 9 February 1921.
5. See Leon Surette, *The Birth of Modernism: Ezra Pound, T. S. Eliot, W. B. Yeats, and the Occult* (Quebec City: McGill–Queen's University Press, 1993); and Leigh Wilson's *Modernism and Magic: Experiments with Spiritualism, Theosophy and the Occult* (Edinburgh: Edinburgh University Press, 2013).

6. John Middleton Murry, ed., *The Scrapbook of Katherine Mansfield* (New York: Alfred A. Knopf, 1940), pp. 234–7, 242–4, 248–50, 253, 273–4.

7. Ida Baker, *Katherine Mansfield: The Memories of LM* (London: Michael Joseph, 1971), pp. 173–4.

8. Baker, p. 213.

9. See Baker, p. 204.

10. Jeffrey Meyers, *Katherine Mansfield: A Darker View* (first published as *Katherine Mansfield: A Biography* in 1978; New York: Cooper Square Press, 2002), p. 238.

11. See Michael Shermer, *In Darwin's Shadow: The Life and Science of Alfred Russel Wallace* (Oxford and New York: Oxford University Press, 2002).

12. Meyers, p. 238.

13. O'Sullivan, in *Letters*, 5, p. viii.

14. Vincent O'Sullivan, 'Signing Off: Katherine Mansfield's Last Year', in Gerri Kimber and Janet Wilson, eds, *Celebrating Katherine Mansfield: A Centenary Volume of Essays* (Basingstoke: Palgrave Macmillan, 2011), pp. 13–27 (p. 16).

15. See O'Sullivan, 'Signing Off', p. 19.

16. O'Sullivan, 'Signing Off', p. 19.

17. Martin Wallace, *The New Age under Orage* (Manchester: Manchester University Press; 1967), p. 16.

18. See Natalya Lusty and Helen Groth, *Dreams and Modernity: A Cultural History* (Abingdon: Routledge, 2013), pp. 88–120.

19. See A. E. Randall, 'The Heart of Hamlet's Mystery', *New Age*, 10: 16 (15 February 1912), pp. 377–8.

20. See A. E. R. [Randall], 'Freud on Dreams', *New Age*, 15: 2 (14 May 1914), p. 40. The article appeared under the heading 'Views and Reviews', which was the title of Randall's weekly column.

21. Frederick W. H. Myers, *Human Personality and Its Survival of Bodily Death* (Tasburgh, Norwich: Pelegrin Trust in association with Pilgrim Books, 1992), pp. 90–1.

22. M. B. Oxon (Lewis Wallace), 'Dreams', *New Age*, 15: 12 (23 July 1914), p. 275.

23. Randall contributed a letter on 27 August while Oxon replied on 3 September; Randall wrote again on 10 September and Oxon had the last word on 17 September.

24. M. D. Eder, 'Dreams', *New Age*, 15: 21 (24 September 1914), p. 511.

25. M. B. Oxon, 'Dreams', *New Age*, 15: 22 (1 October 1914), p. 535.

26. Orage also published articles in the *New Age* as 'M. M. Cosmoi', which was the pseudonym of Serb prophet Dmitri Mitrinovic. See Paul Beekman Taylor, *Gurdjieff and Orage: Brothers in Elysium* (York Beach, ME: Weiser Books, 2001), p. 14.

27. R. H. C., 'Readers and Writers', *New Age*, 22: 14 (31 January 1918), p. 271.

28. R. H. C., p. 271.

29. Oxon replied to Alcock on 28 August; Alcock fired back on 4 September; Oxon reacted again on 18 September; Alcock wrote back on 25 September. The 23 October issue includes a letter on psychoanalysis by Alcock and another by Kenneth Richmond.

30. James Webb, *The Harmonious Circle: The Lives and Work of G. I. Gurdjieff, P. D. Ouspensky, and Their Followers* (London: Shambhala, 1987), p. 217. Psychoanalyst Barbara Low and Philip Mairet also contributed to the *New Age* debate. Mairet is also the author of *A. R. Orage: A Memoir* (London: Dent, 1936).

31. Webb, p. 217.

32. To understand the full import of this debate, let us remember that Jung's *Red Book* – a visionary inner journal, the manuscript of which dates back to 1914–17, after his break with Freud in 1913 – was not published until 2009.

33. James Young, 'The Psychology of Dreams', *New Age*, 25: 27 (30 October 1919), p. 438.
34. Young, p. 439.
35. Young, p. 439.
36. *Letters*, 4, p. 307. To John Middleton Murry, 23 October 1922.
37. In addition to Mansfield's major biographies, let me point readers to James Moore, *Gurdjieff and Mansfield* (London: Routledge & Kegan Paul, 1980). Also, in order to counter the wave of criticism that Gurdjieff and his community encountered after the death of Mansfield, various eye-witnesses published their memories of Mansfield's sojourn at Le Prieuré. See in particular A. R. Orage, 'Talks with Katherine Mansfield at Fontainebleau', *Century Magazine*, 87 (November 1924), pp. 36–40.
38. Webb, p. 228.
39. M. B. Oxon, *Cosmic Anatomy and the Structure of the Ego* (London: Watkins, 1921), p. 1. All further references to this book will be placed parenthetically within the text; for example, '(CA 1)'.
40. Far from being totally abstruse, these reflections anticipate Eder's influential essay, *The Myth of Progress* (1932), although of course the perspectives are different.
41. *Letters*, 1, p. 330. To Dorothy Brett, 11 October 1917,
42. *Letters*, 4, p. 69. To John Middleton Murry, 13 October 1920.
43. *Letters*, 2, p. 66. To John Middleton Murry, 10 and 11 February 1918.
44. David Daiches, 'Katherine Mansfield and the Search for Truth', in Rhoda B. Nathan, ed., *Critical Essays on Katherine Mansfield* (New York: Hall & Co., 1993), p. 170.
45. Katherine Mansfield, 'The Daughters of the Late Colonel', in *The Garden Party, and Other Stories* (New York: Alfred A. Knopf, 1922), pp. 113–14.
46. Gerri Kimber, *Katherine Mansfield and the Art of the Short Story* (Basingstoke: Palgrave Macmillan, 2015), pp. 70–1.
47. Andrée-Marie Harmat, '"Is the master out or in?" or Katherine Mansfield's Twofold Vision of Self', in Paulette Michel and Michel Dupuis, eds, *The Fine Instrument: Essays on Katherine Mansfield* (Sydney: Dangaroo Press, 1989), p. 117.
48. Mansfield, 'The Daughters of the Late Colonel', p. 115.
49. Harmat, p. 121.
50. John Middleton Murry, *Between Two Worlds* (New York: Julian Messner, 1936), p. 287.
51. Susan Reid, '"Children of the Sun": D. H. Lawrence, His Contemporaries and the Cosmos', in Nick Ceramella, ed., *Lake Garda: Gateway to D. H. Lawrence's Voyage to the Sun* (Newcastle: Cambridge Scholars Publishing, 2013), p. 101.
52. *Letters*, 5, p. 225. To S. S. Koteliansky, 17 July 1922.
53. Bruce Steele, Introduction to D. H. Lawrence, *'Psychoanalysis and the Unconscious' and 'Fantasia of the Unconscious'* (Cambridge: Cambridge University Press, 2004), p. xix.
54. D. H. Lawrence, *Psychoanalysis and the Unconscious* (London: Martin Secker, 1923), p. 41.
55. Lawrence, *Psychoanalysis and the Unconscious*, p. 46.
56. D. H. Lawrence, *Fantasia of the Unconscious* (New York: Thomas Seltzer, 1922), pp. vii–viii.
57. See Steele, pp. xix–liv; Fiona Becket, 'Lawrence and Psychoanalysis', in Anne Fernihough, ed., *The Cambridge Companion to D. H. Lawrence* (Cambridge: Cambridge University Press, 2001), pp. 217–34.
58. Lawrence, *Fantasia of the Unconscious*, p. ix.
59. *Letters*, 5, p. 326. To John Middleton Murry, c.24 November 1922.
60. See Meyers, p. 247.
61. *Letters*, 5, p. 303. To S. S. Koteliansky, 19 October 1922.

Mansfield's Psychology of the Emotions

Meghan Marie Hammond

A Curious Pain Somewhere

In one of Katherine Mansfield's early stories, 'In Summer' (1908), a young fairy child named Phyllis sits upon a hillside and sobs, 'Oh, I have never been so unhappy before. [. . .] I have a curious pain somewhere.'[1] It is an arresting and confusing moment. Phyllis, a child on the brink of adulthood, cannot name the unfamiliar and vaguely located pain. The nature of the pain is never clarified. It might be physical pain (for women's specific pains are often spoken of in oblique terms) or emotional pain, which plays out in the body but cannot be said to happen in any particular place. To read Mansfield is to reckon with such ambiguously embodied feelings – life for her characters is the experience of obtrusive and often unarticulated emotions. In her most memorable characters we observe emotion in the body: Ma Parker tries desperately to hold back her 'proper cry' (2: 297), Bertha Young has uncontrollable urges 'to run instead of walk' in her moments of bliss (2: 142), and the anxious Kezia tiptoes out of 'Prelude' feeling 'hot all over' (2: 92).

For Mansfield, manifest character emotion made literature valuable. In her letters, notebooks and published reviews, she often criticised modernist peers who, in her estimation, wasted their craftsmanship on characters with no apparent emotional life. Dorothy Richardson and Edith Wharton both received this charge from Mansfield, as did E. M. Forster, of whose *Howards End* she wrote, 'And I can never be perfectly certain whether Helen was got with child by Leonard Bast or by his fatal forgotten umbrella. All things considered, I think it must have been the umbrella.'[2] The long-suffering Bast, in Mansfield's opinion, is not present in Forster's novel as a human body with an emotional life and is therefore no better than an inanimate object. Mansfield's thoughts on

Bast are particularly important in that they directly discuss his physical abilities (in this case, sexual potency) in order to suggest indirectly a lack of interiority. If Bast had any perceivable *feeling*, Mansfield believes, we could certainly imagine him making love and procreating.

Today we are accustomed to understanding the emotions as a central part of psychology. Indeed, most of us encounter psychology primarily through psychotherapy and self-help discourses meant to help us deal with our emotions. But in Mansfield's early life, especially before the influence of Freud became particularly pronounced, the emotions were considered peripheral to many in the growing field of psychology. As William James wrote in the journal *Mind* in 1884, the 'aesthetic sphere' of the mind – 'its longings, its pleasures and pains, and its emotions' – had 'so far been ignored by empirical psychology'.[3] Carl Lange, producing similar work in Copenhagen in 1885, was more direct in his assessment, saying, 'it might be declared without exaggeration that scientifically we have absolutely no understanding of the emotions'.[4] More than a decade later in 1896, the French psychologist Théodule-Armand Ribot insisted that the emotions had gained little ground, estimating that of all the work published in psychology each year, 'less than the twentieth part, on an average, relates to the feelings and emotions. It is a very small part compared to the part played by the emotions and passions in human life, and this region of psychology is not deserving of such neglect.'[5]

Other important psychologists in the late nineteenth century focused the majority of their experiments on mental faculties like perception, attention and memory rather than on emotional states. It is easy to understand why this was the case in the early days of psychology: emotions are difficult to track, understand and quantify. They were risky subject matter for a new discipline looking to establish scientific legitimacy. Yet, as Lange insisted, 'Emotions are [. . .] the most important factors in the life of the individual human being.'[6] Lange's belief in the supremacy of emotion is certainly in keeping with the world of Mansfield's fiction.

Without making claims about direct influence, this essay lays out noteworthy connections between the work of James, Lange and Ribot and Mansfield's early fiction, suggesting that her *œuvre* is itself a psychology of the emotions, especially as they are embodied. Specifically, it examines how physical sensations show up in tandem with emotions in Mansfield's early stories about children and young people nearing adulthood. These particular stories pre-date the obvious cultural influence of psychoanalysis that we see in some of Mansfield's later work. Furthermore, they feature protagonists who, due to their young age, are likely to perceive and understand emotion in bodily rather than intellectual terms.

The James–Lange Theory of the Emotions

Working independently, James and Lange both reached the conclusion that the emotions are physiological in origin. Their similar, although not identical, arguments soon came to be collectively known as the James–Lange theory of the emotions. Ribot, a prominent figure in the early decades of experimental psychology, was one of the major champions of this theory. Just as James has often been called the father of American psychology, Ribot has frequently been named the father of French psychology. From the time of Mansfield's birth until the publication of her early short stories, James, Lange and Ribot were perhaps the most dominant theorists of human emotions in the field of psychology.

In his 1896 work, *The Psychology of the Emotions* (*La Psychologie des sentiments*), Ribot insisted 'the dominant prejudice which assimilates emotional states to intellectual states, considering them as analogous, or even treating the former as dependent on the latter, can only lead to error'.[7] Ribot's rejection of an approach that privileged intellectual states over emotional states was premised on James and Lange's belief that emotions came from our physical bodies, not from our intangible thoughts. As Lange put it, 'We owe all the emotional side of our mental life, our joys and sorrows, our happy and unhappy hours, to our vasomotor system.'[8] James was well aware that this idea ran counter to common wisdom but was adamant in his presentation:

> Our natural way of thinking about these standard emotions is that the mental perception of some fact excites the mental affection called the emotion, and that this latter state of mind gives rise to the bodily expression. My thesis on the contrary is that *the bodily changes follow directly the* PERCEPTION *of the exciting fact, and that our feeling of the same changes as they occur is the emotion.*[9]

Emotion, as conceived by the James–Lange theory, is a physiological process and experience through and through. To give an example, the common experience of being 'lovesick' is not the result of the emotion, love, producing the feeling, sickness. Rather, it is the odd, queasy sensation in the body itself that constitutes the state of being in love. As Ribot understood this physiological thesis, it meant our conscious thought processes might have little to do with our emotions, which he called 'primitive, autonomous, not reducible to intelligence, able to exist outside it and without it'.[10]

It is easy to see how the James–Lange theory would be threatening in the male-dominated world of early psychology: it indicates that our bodies, rather than our minds, are what determine our emotional experience. As Patricia Moran establishes at the start of her monograph on body language in Mansfield and Woolf, 'the man/woman opposition combines with the mind/body split to align man with mind and woman with body'.[11] James, for one, was famously against the idea of a mind/ body split. While his work has its fair share of embedded male bias, his basic tenet on emotion suggests that all humans, not just females, are first and foremost bodies. Notably, the first objection to his theory of the emotions, published by Edmund Gurney in the subsequent number of *Mind*, hinged on the firm belief that a man can control his body while feeling strong passions. Going to Shakespeare to illustrate his point, Gurney proclaimed, 'Iago did not go about habitually with a flushed face, dilated nostrils, and clenched teeth.'[12] Mansfield's characters, however, do often go about with flushed faces.

The James–Lange theory was based on both observation of everyday experience and experiment. James claims, for example, that episodes of 'precordial anxiety' (what we would today call panic attacks) are clear proof that 'our mental life is knit up with our corporeal frame'.[13] Additionally, in this era newly established psychological laboratories throughout Europe and the United States were providing the evidence utilized by James, Lange and Ribot. Physiological experiments showed that bodily reactions, often subtle ones like constricting blood vessels, accompany our mental states. James was sure that these reactions, while not yet completely understood, were extremely intricate and would prove to correspond to the entire range of human emotion: 'And the various permutations and combinations of which these organic activities are susceptible make it abstractly possible that no shade of emotion, however slight, should be without a bodily reverberation as unique, when taken in its totality, as it is the mental mood itself.'[14] Further experiment, James hints, would one day show us how the mechanisms of the body give rise to each emotion.

It would be tempting to misunderstand the James–Lange theory as one that robs the individual of agency, as Gurney did. Some of Ribot's statements about the primacy of the physiological processes in emotions risk such a reading. He declares, for example, that this theory 'connects all states of feeling with biological conditions, and considers them as the direct and immediate expression of the vegetative life'.[15] Such a statement is hard to accept when what we *feel* is so inextricably tied to what we *think*. Yet Lange and Ribot in particular leave room for the intellect when they clarify that 'emotion' and 'feeling' are not interchangeable concepts. According to Lange, the emotions (like fright, rage and joy) are 'simple, single phenomena'. Feelings (like jealousy, love and desire for freedom) are more complex phenomena in which various emotions mingle.[16] Ribot explains that complex feelings arise when our thoughts meet our emotions:

> the psychology of the emotions has its point of departure in those complex feelings which daily life brings beneath our eyes every moment. Their complexity is the work of our intellectual nature, which associates and dissociates, mixing and combining perceptions, images, ideas, each of which [...] produces in the organism variable effects which, translated into consciousness, impart an affective tone to intellectual states.[17]

The theory does not then relegate all human feeling to 'vegetative life'. Rather, it insists that feeling originates within our bodies, not within the easily accessible realm of our conscious thoughts. Emotions are biologically fundamental precursors to human thought that partner with human intellect but are not subject to it.

Perhaps the most fascinating thing about the James–Lange theory of the emotions from a historical perspective is that it implies that a subconscious realm is the foundation of human experience. As Ribot writes, this theory means that emotions are 'no longer a superficial manifestation, a simple efflorescence; they plunge into the individual's depths'. When we consider those emotions, superficial consciousness 'only delivers up a part of their secrets; it can never reveal them completely; we must descend beneath it'.[18] For those of us who study modernist writers, especially writers like Mansfield who were fascinated by 'descending beneath' the conscious mind and became adults in the era of early experimental psychology, the James–Lange theory is inarguably important.

At the same time, it is also appropriate to look at modernist literature in order to understand the psychological theories of the era. As Lange himself pointed out, it is to poetry that scientists often turn for the most vivid depictions of emotion. 'In articles on the bodily expression of the emotions,' he wrote, 'we usually find innumerable quotations from earlier and more recent poets.'[19] Indeed, we have seen that Gurney reached for Shakespeare when he hoped to contradict James. But Mansfield's body of work offers ready examples if one wants to illustrate Ribot's belief that 'certain sensations, images, and ideas awaken organic and motor states, and, consequently, emotion'.[20] In 'The Little Governess' (1915), for example, we see how Mansfield's young protagonist suddenly feels afraid after the 'warm rocking' of her boat ceases and 'a cold, strange wind [flies] under her hat' (1: 423). 'At the Bay' (1921) offers a more nuanced example in which Linda Burnell feels 'swept away' by life: 'And lying in her cane chair, Linda felt so light; she felt like a leaf. Along came Life like a wind and she was seized and shaken; she had to go. Oh dear, would it always be so? Was there no escape?' (2: 354). In the first example, the external stimulus causes a bodily reaction that gives rise to an emotion. In the second example, it is unclear where the feeling of lightness comes from. The sensation may be the result of sitting in the chair, but there is a clear possibility that it originates within Linda's body, before she articulates internal questions about it. The order of events – feeling before thought – is significant here, for it echoes the schema that Ribot offers in his psychology of the emotions.

Feeling is First

Mansfield's treatment of children, which consistently posits the legitimacy and worthiness of their emotional lives, is perhaps the most important site of contact between her fiction and the James–Lange theory. But here it is also worth noting that Mansfield's respect for the child's emotions is not always matched by early psychology. Lange grouped infants with 'primitive peoples' as good subjects in the study of emotions. He found that, with infants, the affections are 'undisturbed and uninterfered with by reason'. The opportunity to examine emotions without the diluting influence of civilised intellect, however, produced its own challenges in Lange's estimation: 'On the other hand, we meet with the same difficulties in dealing with infants and primitive peoples, as we do when we study animal behavior, namely the uncertainty of our psychological understanding, the inevitable consequence of the subject's reports.'[21] In so far as children are misunderstood in Mansfield's work, it is usually because adults make little effort to understand their way of feeling and thinking. Yet, as we will see in a number of Mansfield's early stories, Mansfield does privilege children as emotional beings in a physical, pre-rational state.

For Ribot, too, the evidence in favour of the James–Lange theory hinges on infancy. He contends that the place of feelings 'in the total psychic life' of the human is 'the *first*',[22] by which he means we have emotions before we have thoughts. As he explains, 'If the feelings appear first it is clear that they cannot be derived, and are not a mode or function of knowledge since they exist by themselves and are irreducible.'[23] Like Lange, he reasons that the earliest stage of human life is quintessentially animal: 'in man is not foetal life, and that of the first months after birth, much the same [as that of animals], almost wholly made up of satisfied or unsatisfied needs, and consequently of pleasures and pains?'[24] A child's early psychic life is 'purely affective' and 'rudimentary', especially in the early weeks when 'he learns to localize his sensations'.[25] In this context, the clear value of Mansfield's stories is that so many of her protagonists are in the early years of life, when they are transitioning from an infant's purely affective and sensory world to the adult's world, in which emotion and thought are inextricably tangled.

In Mansfield's early work we often find a child learning how to contend with or express emotions, given the strictures of the adult world. In the 1908 story, 'Juliette Delacour', for example, young Juliette has the traumatic experience of seeing her ill father die on her fourth birthday. Juliette reacts first to the sound of her teapot smashing when her father drops it: 'The child uttered a little cry of mingled disappointment and astonishment' (1: 108). Realising that something is amiss with her father, she tries to revive him by forcing a chocolate into his mouth and assuring him 'I'm not angry' (1: 108). Juliette, notably, has a physical reaction before she seems to have grasped quite what has happened: 'Suddenly she burst into a frightful passion of weeping, and so they found her, and carried her to her room' (1: 108). Her young body experiences the loss and expresses it with the appropriate passion, even though her young mind is still in the process of understanding. Her removal is both a kindness and an inadvertent censure of her untempered bodily emotion – such passions are natural but belong within one's own room.

In 'The Little Girl' (1912), the young protagonist Kass is unable to control her body sufficiently to please her father, 'a figure to be feared and avoided' (1: 302). Like Mansfield when she was young, Kass has a stutter. She is able to control this stutter around everybody except her father 'because then she was trying so hard to say the words properly' (1: 302). Kass's anxiety manifests in a bodily tremor and in a deeply worried facial expression that are bothersome to her father, who complains that her 'hands jog like an old lady' and that she 'appear[s] on the brink of suicide' (1: 302). Kass clearly does not yet have the capacity to negotiate the world with an adult's logic but is held to that standard anyway. After she shreds the pages of a speech her father was writing to gather material for his birthday present, he whips her hands. What is significant here is that Kass is obviously too young to read, so she is being punished for having a child's intellectual ability through harm to the body, the seat of her emotions. Her body remembers the emotional pain, so that 'Next time she saw him she whipped both hands behind her back, and a red colour flew into her cheeks' (1: 303). It is only through the body that this emotional pain can be healed, both in the short term, when her grandmother rocks her and Kass 'cuddle[s] close to her soft body' (1: 303), and in the long term, after her father lets her sleep next to him to recover from a nightmare. The bodily contact with her fearsome father cultivates tender feelings: 'Poor father! Not so big after all – and with no one to look after him. . . . He was harder than the Grandmother, but it was a nice hardness.' The story ends with Kass listening to the inner workings of her father's body and saying, 'my head's on your heart; I can hear it going. What a big heart you've got, Father dear' (1: 304). Even in the scary father, then, positive feeling (heart) can be verified through physical touch.

The role that affectionate physical contact plays in the emotional relationships between children and adults is featured in 'How Pearl Button Was Kidnapped' (1912). The story works with long-established tropes about the colonised racial other who experiences the world as a body rather than as a mind. The two women who encounter Pearl and bring her away with them are 'big' and walk slowly 'because they [are] so fat' (1: 286). These large feminine bodies are, like that of the grandmother in 'The Little Girl', extremely comforting for the young protagonist. Pearl 'nestles' into one woman's lap, where her physical sensations bleed into a contented emotional state: 'The woman was warm as a cat and she moved up and down when she breathed, just like purring [. . .] Pearl had never been happy like this before' (1: 287).

Throughout her 'kidnapping', Pearl experiences positive emotions that burgeon out of bodily experience. The women first see her in the joyful, childlike act of swinging on a front gate. They reciprocate her motions by 'waving their arms and clapping their hands together' (1: 286). Pearl's responsive laughter reveals that her primary means of experiencing the world is through reactive and embodied emotion. Later, she will cry when tired and confused, laugh when entertained by funny faces, and scream when she sees the ocean (1: 286–7). She learns to enjoy the sea by entering it with the trusted woman, whom she is hugging and kissing at the moment she sees the 'little blue men' coming to carry her back home (1: 287). It is in fact the sensory experience of the ocean that provokes the most feeling from Pearl. Its warmth, wetness and unique visual properties – 'it stopped being blue in her hands' – get her to shriek, exclaim and throw 'her thin little arms round the woman's neck' (1: 288). During this time away from the restrictive civilisation of the 'House of Boxes', Pearl, unlike young Kass, does not have to fight a natural order in which feeling comes first.

Thoughtful and Tired

There are some notable instances in which Mansfield's stories feature pre-verbal infants. One such instance is 'The Thoughtful Child' (1908), in which one of Mansfield's 'fairy' children is caught between the adult world of her parents and the 'purely affective' world of her baby brother. What we get to see through the eyes of the Thoughtful Child is in fact the loss of an infant to illness: 'Brother got something the matter with him. He cried all the day until the Thoughtful Child was cross' (1: 126). The brother is, at this early stage of life, incapable of understanding what is wrong with him – he can only cry out in pain. Ribot might suggest the crying infant is experiencing a 'pure state' of feeling: that is, one 'empty of any intellectual element, of every representative content, not connected with perceptions or images or concepts'.[26] Going over what he understands to be the evolution of the affective life, Ribot names four principal types of 'pure state': the agreeable state, the painful state, the state of fear, and the state of excitability.[27]

The Thoughtful Child, although young, is beyond Ribot's pure states or 'primitive emotions' and is moving on to 'that stable and chronic state which constitutes the passions'.[28] Her crossness signals her process of maturing, for she displays a typically adult frustration with the infant who cannot say what he feels, but rather can only let his body communicate it. Yet she is not so adult that she clearly understands the loss when it happens:

> One night she woke up and heard someone crying in her room. It was Mother. Father held a light and Mother took the Thoughtful Child to her arms, and said 'You are all that we have now, baby, baby'. Her face was very wet. (1: 126)

The child here is tasked with decoding both the passion of sadness as expressed through the body and the adult's act of making meaning out of the experience of emotion – what her body feels, the mother is saying, is her traumatic transformation from mother of two to mother of one.

Later, in 'The Child-Who-Was-Tired' (1910), Mansfield would give a much fuller treatment of the toll taken by a screaming infant. Of all Mansfield's early stories, this one is most keenly aware of the connection between the body and the emotions. The titular child, named for her exhaustion, works as a domestic servant and struggles to care for a difficult baby. As the story unfolds, Mansfield illustrates clearly the disconnect between the emotional world of the baby and the emotional world of the worn-out caregiver: 'She looked with horror at the one in her arms, who, seeming to understand the contemptuous loathing of her tired glance, doubled his fists, stiffened his body, and began violently screaming' (1: 159). Clearly, the baby understands nothing and is merely distressed, but in her own painful state the Child-Who-Was-Tired can only attribute his emotion to a thought process trained on her. She knows the key to calming his emotional turbulence is in fact physical attention, but also cannot help but bargain with him, saying, 'Just stop crying until I've finished this, baby, and I'll walk you up and down' (1: 161). This desperate utterance functions not as an actual proposition to the baby, but rather as a performance of adult negotiation that helps the Child-Who-Was-Tired soothe her own emotions.

It is clear from the story's opening lines that the Child-Who-Was-Tired is experiencing emotional and cognitive instability because of her bodily experience. While we are led to believe that she is 'half silly' (1: 162), it is stress to her body rather than feebleness of mind that eventually leads to the outburst in which she kills the baby. As she is woken from her bed with a barrage of physical and verbal abuse, she thinks, 'I'm sleepy. [. . .] That's why I'm not awake' (1: 158), showing that the fact of exhaustion is the only one she is capable of processing. Throughout the day, she remains focused on the inescapable pains of her body:

> Oh, how tired she was! Oh, the heavy broom handle and the burning spot just at the back of her neck that ached so, and a funny little fluttering feeling just at the back of her waistband, as though something were going to break. (1: 160)

Even when she experiences a positive emotion, it is in connection with her bodily experience and her need for rest. 'When she thought of the nearness of bedtime', we read, 'she shook all over with excited joy' (1: 163). It is the prospect of that joyful escape into sleep that prompts her 'beautiful, marvellous idea' to quiet the baby permanently and her subsequent bodily expression of happiness – laughter and hand clapping (1: 163). Her goal is in fact to return to a state of pure feeling that, as an adolescent with adult responsibilities and burdens, is no longer accessible to her.[29]

This last, dark, example from Mansfield's fiction also helps to illustrate a point on which her work is in opposition to the James–Lange theory. Although James believed firmly in the physiological origin of feeling, he also thought that emotions could be conquered by the intellect. He hints that even if we cannot stop emotions from coming to life within us, we can stop them from thriving by calming our bodies. 'Refuse to express a passion', he writes, 'and it dies.'[30] James is even certain, in a way that anticipates some of today's cognitive behavioural therapy, that we can actively induce emotions more appropriate to our situation. He explains, 'if we wish to conquer undesirable emotional tendencies in ourselves, we must assiduously, and in the first instance cold-bloodedly, go through the *outward motions* of those contradictory dispositions we prefer to cultivate'.[31] Mansfield's characters tend to show quite the opposite. Ma Parker's decades of refusing to express her passions do nothing to kill her painful emotions. And in the case of the Child-Who-Was-Tired, such cold-blooded performance of the proper outward motions is not possible – her exhausted body no longer has the power to act invigorated.

Here is the crucial point of difference between Mansfield's psychology of the emotions and the James–Lange theory. Mansfield's *œuvre*, while fictional, is not theoretical. James, Lange and Ribot wrote from positions of institutional and male privilege. Mansfield wrote from the embodied experience of a woman whose adult life was marked by physical challenges. If we are to consider fully how the emotions have been understood in relation to the body, a voice like Mansfield's is invaluable.[32]

Notes

1. Gerri Kimber and Vincent O'Sullivan, eds, *The Collected Fiction of Katherine Mansfield*, 2 vols (Edinburgh: Edinburgh University Press, 2012), Vol. 1, p. 113. Hereafter references are placed parenthetically in the text noting volume and page number, e.g. (1: 113).
2. Clare Hanson, ed., *The Critical Writings of Katherine Mansfield* (Basingstoke: Macmillan, 1987), pp. 74–5, 49–50, 28. Mansfield's critiques of Wharton and Richardson were published in the *Athenaeum*; her thoughts on *Howards End* were written in her private journal.
3. William James, 'What is an Emotion?', *Mind*, 9: 34 (April 1884), p. 188. James also wrote at length about the emotions in his vast *Principles of Psychology* (1890). My discussion of his work here is restricted to the *Mind* article, from which is derived his contribution to the James–Lange theory as it was widely understood.
4. Carl Georg Lange, 'The Emotions', in Knight Dunlap, ed., *The Emotions* (Baltimore: Williams & Wilkins, 1922), p. 38.
5. Théodule-Armand Ribot, *The Psychology of the Emotions*, trans. unknown (London: Walter Scott, 1897), p. v.
6. Lange, p. 34.
7. Ribot, p. vi.
8. Lange, p. 81. Similarly, James wrote that the emotions 'correspond to processes occurring in the motor and sensory centers' (James, p. 188).
9. James, pp. 189–90. Emphasis in the original.
10. Ribot, p. vi.
11. Patricia Moran, *Word of Mouth: Body Language in Katherine Mansfield and Virginia Woolf* (Charlottesville: University of Virginia Press, 1996), pp. 1–2. Moran's work highlights some of the problematic self-presentations in Mansfield and Woolf that are perhaps symptomatic of belief in 'patriarchal devaluations of femininity' (p. 3). Mansfield's treatment of the female body is certainly conflicted throughout her *œuvre*, but my purpose here is to concentrate on how her stories link emotion to the body in ways that undermine both the mind/body split and the hierarchical privileging of thought over emotion.
12. Edmund Gurney, 'What is an Emotion?', *Mind*, 9: 35 (July 1884), p. 424.

13. James, pp. 199, 201.
14. James, p. 192.
15. Ribot, p. vii.
16. Lange, pp. 35–6. Despite clarifying this difference between 'emotion' and 'feeling', both Lange and Ribot sometimes use the terms interchangeably – or at least their English translators do.
17. Ribot, p. 441.
18. Ribot, pp. vii–viii.
19. Lange, p. 39.
20. Ribot, p. viii.
21. Lange, p. 40.
22. Ribot, p. 438.
23. Ribot, p. 438.
24. Ribot, p. 439.
25. Ribot, p. 8.
26. Ribot, p. 7.
27. Ribot, p. 10.
28. Ribot, p. 3.
29. Ribot hints that certain drugs, like 'haschisch', might provide such an escape (p. 9).
30. James, p. 197.
31. James, p. 198.
32. And, it should go without saying, the voices of people with multiple kinds of embodied experience.

Feeling 'Like a Work-girl':
Class, Intimacy and Alienation in
'The Garden Party'

Rebecca Thorndike-Breeze

In a letter written on 13 October 1920, while Katherine Mansfield was living in Menton, she describes an exchange she had with a 'jardinier who comes here le vendredi', that anticipates a key scene of attempted cross-class intimacy in 'The Garden Party':

> This man drew a design of the flower bed on the gravel, & then after telling me the names of the flowers he described them. [. . .] In trying to describe the scent – c'est – un – parrr-fum – & then he threw back his head put his thumb & forefinger to his nose – took a *long* breath & suddenly exploded it in a kind of AAAHHH, almost staggering backwards – overcome – almost fainting. [. . .] To think the man *cares* like that – *responds* – laughs like he does and snips off a rosebud for you while he talks. Then I think of poor busmen & tube men and the ugliness of wet dark London. Its wrong. People who are at all sensitive ought not to live there.[1]

Mansfield may be hinting at her own feelings about the ease of breathing on the Mediterranean coast compared to the suffocations of London, but this letter also anticipates a pair of interactions between Laura Sheridan and working-class men in 'The Garden Party'. The first interaction resonates strongly with the text of this letter:

> Only the tall fellow was left. He bent down, pinched a sprig of lavender, put his thumb and forefinger to his nose and snuffed up the smell. When Laura saw the gesture she forgot all about the karakas in her wonder at him caring for things like that – caring for the smell of lavender.[2]

His love of lavender fills Laura with such homely comfort that she begins to feel 'just like a work-girl' (288). The second interaction, with Scott the carter's body, aligns with the 'poor busmen & tube men' of London. When Laura is invited, 'to her horror', deeper and deeper into the 'disgusting and sordid' sphere of the neighbourhood's working classes, she both confronts the unhomely abjection of working-class reality and intuits the inextricability of that reality from herself (297, 293).

The consequences of Laura's desire and failure to transcend what she calls 'absurd class distinctions' (288) are well established in Mansfield criticism, though this abundance of critical agreement does not diminish the intensity of Laura's cry, 'we can't possibly have a garden party with a man dead just outside the front gate' (293). Unlike her family, and despite her naïvety, Laura does not accept the dominant view of social class at the diegetic time of the story – she does not think the working classes are lower people. Sydney Janet Kaplan notes that Laura's protest, followed as it is by her sister and mother's attempts to divert it, aligns 'The Garden Party' with Mansfield's 'cry against corruption' stories. These convey 'outrage against a society in which privilege is so marked by indifference to the misery of others that it must demean or ignore any unmediated reaction to injustice'.[3] Clare Hanson and Andrew Gurr note the tense interplay between Laura's sense of suffering and the realities of social class around her; they explain that 'The Garden Party', like the other Sheridan stories, is keenly interested in 'human relationships, the impact of local conditions on the developing personality and how the present affects the past and future'.[4] More recently, Christine Darrohn has noted the absence of 'the war context' in readings of 'The Garden Party', and in her groundbreaking essay, '"Blown to Bits!" Katherine Mansfield's "The Garden Party" and the Great War', she interprets 'parallels between Mansfield's personal loss and the anxieties spawned by the war in the upper and middle classes' to illuminate our understanding of how gender and class shaped the experience of war.[5] And, most recently, as she traces parallels between the 'kind of fellow feeling Mansfield [. . .] cultivates' in 'The Garden Party' and contemporary psychology's taxonomies of tangled fellow-feeling, Meghan Marie Hammond argues that when Laura discovers 'how inaccessible the primary pain of [Scott's death] is for her, she realises she has trespassed on the community of feeling inside the widow's home [. . .]. Laura comes to see that she does not feel "just like a work-girl"'.[6]

These psychological readings of 'The Garden Party' rightly emphasise various ways in which the working-class Other influences Laura's subjectivity. In this essay, I will draw upon similar psychological frameworks to investigate how 'The Garden Party' deals with the idea of working-class characters not just as Others, but as selves. I contend that, though it does not render the inner experiences of these characters, 'The Garden Party' still raises important questions for its readers about the selfhood of the Other, and the uncanny, sometimes abject, sense of the Other within one's self.[7] This essay takes the self–Other relation between Laura and the working class as its starting place, but it emphasises how the overlap of middle and working classes generates Laura's increasingly abject experience throughout the story. Through Laura, the story confronts us with the everyday, simultaneous, uncanny intimacy and alienation inherent in class relations in the upper-middle-class household at the turn of the century. Through a series of uncanny parallels, 'The Garden Party' collapses the distance between Laura and the working class. As it does, it confronts us with questions about what it means to stare the Other in the face – as Laura stares into the swollen, grief-stricken face of Scott's widow – and to realise that the Other is at the core of the self.

In 1923, Virginia Woolf famously declared a major shift in human character 'on or about December 1910'. I refer to this now-clichéd declaration because the change in character she describes includes a change in upper- and middle-class understanding of human character in the working class, and thus a shift in society's structure of feeling. To illustrate her point, Woolf presents two caricatures of the same working-class icon – the cook:

> The Victorian cook lived like a leviathan in the lower depths, formidable, silent, obscure, inscrutable; the Georgian cook is a creature of sunshine and fresh air; in and out of the drawing room, now to borrow the *Daily Herald*, now to ask advice about a hat.[8]

Though Mansfield never went so far as to decree a shift in the structure of feeling, we can see some agreement among Woolf's 'Victorian leviathan', the Georgian 'creature of sunshine and fresh air' and Mansfield's sketches of the working class. For example, Woolf's dark and bright cooks parallel Mansfield's poor tube men and flower-sniffing jardinier; and we find reasonable facsimiles of Woolf's two cooks in Mrs Sheridan and Laura's very different perceptions of the cook in 'The Garden Party'. Mrs Sheridan asks Jose to 'pacify cook if you do go into the kitchen, will you? I'm terrified of her this morning'; whereas when Laura later finds Jose in the kitchen, the cook 'did not look at all terrifying' (291). In the story, Mansfield dramatises a commonplace contradiction of domestic life that Woolf would later caricature. Around the time Mansfield was writing 'The Garden Party', the uncanny feelings associated with the nested interdependence of middle-class and working-class selves had become obvious, if not universally acknowledged.

Of course, such shifts in human character and structures of feeling did not suddenly commence in 1910. For Raymond Williams, structures of feeling function 'in the most delicate and least tangible parts of our activity', and though 'communication depends' upon them, they 'can fail to be fully understood even by living people in close contact with [them]'.[9] Class feeling is, of course, inherent in a society's structure of feeling. A thorough discussion of the simultaneously intimate and alienated relation between the middle and the working class is beyond the scope of this essay, but it is still worthwhile to consider the confusing status of 'the middle class' and 'the working class' briefly. In the mid-1970s Raymond Williams observed, 'To this day this confusion reverberates';[10] in the twenty-first century, it has yet to be clarified. Throughout the Industrial Revolution, the terms 'middle class' and, slightly later, 'working class' took shape to differentiate among the common people according to their social and economic status. Increasingly, legal definitions of the 'working class' in England aligned it with manual work, 'any person who, being a labourer, servant in husbandry, journeyman, artificer, handicraftsman, miner, or otherwise engaged in manual labour . . . has entered into or works under a contract with an employer'; by 1890, the legal definition expanded to include 'all classes of persons who earn their livelihood by wages or salaries'.[11] This would place merchants, doctors and bank managers under the same class designation as servants, gardeners and delivery men. Official class distinctions continue to shift; because the middle class and working class both aligned themselves with 'useful or productive classes, [. . .] in opposition to the *privileged* or the *idle*' from the start, the boundary between working and middle class has always been muddled. [12]

Despite this overlap, class mobility was difficult, and despite the pervasive Victorian fixation upon the power of sympathy and the cultivation of moral perfection, throughout the period, as Williams observes, when it came to 'the lives and the problems of working people, [. . .] [r]ecognition of evil was balanced by fear of becoming involved. Sympathy was transformed, not into action, but into withdrawal.'[13] In 'The Garden Party', Mansfield also eventually withdraws from 'the lives and the problems of working people'; as Darrohn notes, she 'tries to imagine a moment when class and gender divisions cease to matter but [. . .] ultimately she cannot sustain this hopeful vision'.[14] Though Mansfield falters in her attempt at transcendence, she also grapples at length with the painful effects of the simultaneously intimate and alienated relation between working people and the middle class they serve. Though she ultimately withdraws, it is not without a fight.

Other stories published in *The Garden Party and Other Stories* (1922) also struggle with questions of class, intimacy and alienation. 'Life of Ma Parker' is particularly salient for its rendering of permeable class boundaries and their attendant tensions. In numerous ways, this London story of a cleaning woman grieving over the death of her young grandson can be read as a looking-glass companion to 'The Garden Party'. Ma Parker cleans for a 'literary gentleman' whose housekeeping philosophy – 'You simply dirty everything you've got, get a hag in once a week to clean up, and the thing's done' – creates a kitchen so filthy 'It would take a whole book to describe the state' (231). The state of this 'gigantic dustbin' of a kitchen, its floor 'littered with toast crusts, envelopes, cigarette ends' (231) and so forth, is far worse than the Scott's kitchen, which is only 'wretched', it seems, because it is 'low' and 'lighted by a smoky lamp' (297). We can assume that Mrs Scott, being of a similar class to Ma Parker, does her own cleaning, whereas such mundane tasks are beneath 'the literary gentleman'. He is a bachelor of the hazily defined artistic class; perhaps he is a true gentleman of the upper class with bohemian tendencies. But this 'literary gentleman' could also be someone like Murry, raised up from humble beginnings through education. Before she sets to work, Ma Parker rubs her aching knees, and eidetically experiences a memory of her grandson standing on her lap, insisting she give him a penny she 'ain't got' (230). In response to Ma Parker's playful riposte, 'Well, what'll you give your gran?', Mansfield renders a most gentle and intimate exchange: 'he gave a shy little laugh and pressed closer. She felt his eyelid quivering against her cheek. "I ain't got nothing," he murmured. . . .' (231). Such sweet, painful memories juxtaposed with the literary gentleman's perspective both jar the reader and emphasise the simultaneous physical intimacy and the wide gulf of class that defines this arrangement. Ma Parker has no self to the literary gentleman; 'a hag' to him, she has more in common with Virginia Woolf's 'Victorian leviathan' than the new Georgian cook 'of sunshine and fresh air'.[15]

'Life of Ma Parker' dramatises both the richness of working-class experience and the middle-class tendency to dismiss it. Regarding 'The Garden Party', even critical readings tend to neglect the significance of Scott's widow and her sister. Darrohn breaks from this trend and demonstrates the 'virulently classist' contrasts between the beautiful description of Scott, the carter's, corpse and the 'corporeal grotesqueness' that characterises his swollen-faced widow and oily-voiced sister-in-law.[16] But, through these contrasts in Laura's experience of the Scott family, I contend that we can also read Laura as *unheimlich*, an alien interloper within the Scott home.[17] Though the middle-class Sheridans accept the presence of the working class within their home as a given, the reverse situation is so unheard of it is unspeakable:

'Only the basket, then. And, Laura!' – her mother followed her out of the marquee – 'don't on any account –'
'What mother?'
No, better not put such ideas into the child's head! 'Nothing! Run along'. (296)

'The Garden Party' highlights the permeability of the classes, in particular the open secret of the simultaneous intimacy and alienation between them. I find Lacan's notion of *extimité*, or extimacy, a useful lens through which to understand how such permeability relates to subjectivity, the structure of feeling, and their expression in the fiction of 'inward-turning' modernists like Mansfield.[18] In *The Ethics of Psychoanalysis*, Lacan uses a Möbius strip to illustrate the intense, simultaneous intimacy and alienation of extimacy. The coincidence of two sides in one represents the position of the Other external to, yet at the core of, the self. '*Extimité*' is Lacan's attempt 'to find a French equivalent for *das Unheimlich*',[19] but its connotation differs somewhat from Freud's. For Lacan, the uncanny as extimacy is the 'intimate exteriority' of subjectivity.[20] In other words, extimacy is not so much the return of the repressed, but the uncanniness inherent in the 'internaliz[ed] otherness' that is the subject's very 'condition of possibility'.[21] As Mladen Dolar explains, such a coincidence of self with other and inner with outer 'becomes threatening, provoking horror and anxiety. The extimate is simultaneously the intimate kernel and the foreign body; in a word, it is *unheimlich*.'[22]

Extimacy's Möbius simultaneity of self and Other reworks conceptions of empathy circulating in philosophical and psychological circles at the time Mansfield was writing. Hammond cites philosopher Edith Stein's 1917 definition of empathy – 'the experience of foreign consciousness' – as 'the most germane' for thinking about 'inward-turning' literary modernism like Mansfield's. Though Mansfield did not herself use the word 'empathy', Hammond persuasively demonstrates how the author's modernism creates 'intersubjective experience' while also conveying ambivalence about the dangers of such intimacy of thought and feeling.[23] These dangers pre-figure a number of psychoanalytic themes that permeate the work of Mansfield and other modernists.[24] Angela Smith contends that Mansfield's fraught yet intimate friendship with Virginia Woolf was founded on their mutual sense of each other as 'the foreigner within', *à la* Kristeva, 'other but familiar, both frightening in her alien similarity and reassuring in her capacity to understand a shared obsession with writing'.[25] During their period of deepest intimacy, Mansfield encouraged Woolf to merge with her surroundings in the service of writing; in a diary entry of 25 August 1920, Woolf writes, 'I said how my own character seemed to cut out a shape like a shadow in front of me. This she understood [. . .] & proved it by telling me that she thought this bad: one ought to merge into things.'[26]

We can imagine that Mansfield's suggestion eventually led to Woolf's later insight, recorded in her diary on 18 November 1935:

> I see that there are 4? Dimensions; all to be produced; in human life; & that leads to a far richer grouping & proportion: I mean: I: & the not I: & the outer & the inner. [. . .] Very exciting: to grope on like this. New combinations in psychology & body – rather like painting.[27]

The pervasive colons in this passage create the appearance of perforated and thus permeable boundaries among the four dimensions. And we can imagine Mansfield being similarly struck, not least for the physical and psychological resonances she often noted between writing and painting. The interplay among these dimensions aligns with her 13 March 1922 letter to William Gerhardie, wherein she writes that she 'tried to convey in The Garden Party' the simultaneous

> diversity of life and how we try to fit in everything. Death included. That is bewildering for a person of Laura's age. She feels things ought to happen differently. First one and then another. But life isn't like that. We haven't the ordering of it. Laura says, 'But all these things must not happen at once.' And Life answers, 'Why not? How are they divided from each other.' And they *do* all happen, it is inevitable. And it seems to me there is beauty in that inevitability.[28]

It is inevitably beautiful but also dangerous; Laura's growing awareness and understanding of the permeable, simultaneous diversity of life are also a progressive confrontation with the sometimes abject foreigner within. As Kristeva writes, the abject is the 'massive and sudden emergence of uncanniness, which [. . .] now harries me as radically separate, loathsome. Not me. Not that. But not nothing, either. A "something" that I do not recognize as a thing.'[29] In 'The Garden Party', Mansfield closes the distance between self and Other, inner and outer, middle class and working class. As Laura interacts with different working-class people on her journey from her garden to Mrs Scott's kitchen, she experiences both cross-class recognition and its failure. Throughout, Mansfield expresses the extimacy and occasional abjection inherent in the luminous, simultaneous diversity of life.[30]

'The Garden Party' figures permeable boundaries on a number of levels, from the spaces within the home and throughout the neighbourhood, to spaces deep inside the realm of affect. In the Sheridan home, the private sphere of familial intimacy is also populated by a community of servants, workmen and delivery men, though class designations are usually left unsaid. The story never calls the Sheridans middle-class; it only mentions Laurie and Mr Sheridan 'brushing their hats ready to go to the office' (288). However, the biographical root of 'The Garden Party' and the parallels critics have noted between the Burnells and the Sheridans indicate that the Sheridans are a middle-class family on the rise.[31] As for the working-class characters, with the exceptions of Hans and Sadie, they are typically referred to by their job: gardener, marquee man, florist, Cook, Godber's man and carter.[32] In the midst of this labour force, the Sheridans must always be both mindful and ostensibly careless of the working-class gaze, even in their more intimate moments. When Laura expresses affection for her mother, once 'Sadie had gone' and 'the florist's man was still outside at his van', by playfully biting her mother's ear, 'gently, very gently', Mrs Sheridan quickly disentangles herself – 'Don't do that. Here's the man' (290). The homeliest expressions of intimacy are always implicitly bounded by invisible class distinctions.

The rhythm of the story conveys a sense of constant movement in and out of private spaces, all the while remaining largely within the intimate sphere of the home. Thus, the narrative insists upon the troubling proximity and interpenetration of the Sheridan home and the 'poky little holes' of the lane (294), which are an obvious abject 'Not me. Not that' to the Sheridans' lovely home.[33] In response to Laura's cry, 'But we can't possibly have a garden party with a man dead just outside the front gate,' the narrator archly responds:

> That really was extravagant, for the little cottages were in a lane to them-
> selves at the very bottom of a steep rise that led up to the house. A broad
> road ran between. True, they were far too near. They were the greatest
> possible eyesore, and they had no right to be in that neighbourhood at
> all. (293)

This passage of ostensible narrative self-contradiction underscores the simultaneous intimacy and alienation between the classes. At first, the cottages and the Sheridans' front gate are safely insulated by a 'steep rise' and a 'broad road'; but then again, they are 'far too near'. This oxymoron tensely signifies simultaneous feelings of social distance and physical intimacy, and contributes to the extimate picture of this neighbourhood.

Even in the most luminous moments of homely domesticity, some-thing uncanny moves through the Sheridan house. Early in the story, Laura takes a brief rest from party preparations and feels the energy of the house:

She was still, listening. All the doors in the house seemed to be open. The house was alive with soft, quick steps and running voices. The green baize door that led to the kitchen regions swung open and shut with a muffled thud. And now there came a long, chuckling absurd sound. It was the heavy piano being moved on its stiff castors. But the air! If you stopped to notice, was the air always like this? Little faint winds were playing chase in at the tops of the windows, out at the doors. And there were two tiny spots of sun, one on the inkpot, one on a silver photograph frame, playing too. Darling little spots. Especially the one on the inkpot lid. [. . .] She could have kissed it. (289)

Here Mansfield creates one of her classic moments of suspension in everyday luminosity. But she also weaves in the uncanny presence of invisible workers, who make much of the energy of the scene possible. Laura feels as though all the doors lie open, and thus boundaries between rooms – between family spaces and working spaces, like 'the kitchen regions' – become thoroughly permeable. Disembodied steps and voices bring the house to life. These could be the Sheridans' but they just as likely belong to servants, like Sadie and Hans. The latter, we learn, turns out to be the implied agent of the passive construction, 'it was the heavy piano being moved on its stiff castors' (289). But in this scene, the piano seems to move itself.

The lively buzz of the party preparations take on a ghostlier quality when read alongside the story's later description of the lane's cottages. Their 'low hum', 'flicker[s] of light' and 'crab-like' shadows moving across the windows (296) parallel the Sheridans' buzz of activity, 'Darling little spots' of sunlight, and 'Little faint winds [. . .] playing chase in at the tops of the windows, out at the doors' (289). At home, Laura loves the tiny sun spots; in the lane, the flickering lights and crab-like shadows make the cottages ghoulish and fill her with dread. Laura's suspended moment in her home is thoroughly permeated with the Other of the working class – the inhabitants of the abject lane.

We can see the intensity of the story's trajectory from homely, to uncanny, to abject as we narrow focus, turning from the uncanny parallels in external scenes to those within Laura's affective responses to cross-class recognition and its numerous failures. It is during breakfast that Laura begins a series of confrontations with what she considers to be 'absurd class distinctions' (288). As she does she also falters between different identities; her feelings of embarrassment, even shame, underscore the everyday habituality of extimacy. As she approaches the marquee men to give them instructions, Laura realises too late that she should have left her bread and butter at the breakfast table, instead of treating this as a good excuse to eat 'out of doors':

Laura wished now that she was not holding that piece of bread-and-butter, but there was nowhere to put it, and she couldn't possibly throw it away. She blushed and tried to look severe and even a little bit short-sighted as she came up to them. (287)

Too late, Laura realises that directing marquee men and breakfasting *al fresco* discord with each other; she attempts to cover over the evidence of her mistake by pretending it is not even there. She copies her mother's voice to help herself recover from the *faux pas*: 'But that sounded so fearfully affected that she was ashamed, and stammered like a little girl' (287).

Her awkwardness approaching the marquee men anticipates her later journey down into the dark lane with its poky little cottages.[34] But here the tall, lavender-loving marquee man assuages her embarrassment: 'His smile was so easy, so friendly, that Laura recovered. [. . .] And now she looked at the others, they were smiling too. "Cheer up, we won't bite", their smile seemed to say. How very nice workmen were!' (287). However comfortable the smiling workmen make her, the constant push and pull of recognition returns when a less cheerful workman interjects:

'H'm, going to have a band, are you?' said another of the workmen. He was pale. He had a haggard look as his dark eyes scanned the tennis-court. What was he thinking?
'Only a very small band', said Laura gently. Perhaps he wouldn't mind so much if the band was quite small. (287–8)

Here Laura is only somewhat discomfited because she cannot quite grasp how to behave or who to be as she talks to the hired help. But her embarrassment and frustration pre-figure, with less intensity, her sense of abjection as she walks through the lane in her fine hat and party dress.

Dressed in attire that unequivocally announces her class, Laura feels thoroughly alienated from the inhabitants of the lane:

Laura bent her head and hurried on. She wished now she had put on a coat. How her frock shone! And the big hat with the velvet streamer – if only it was another hat! Were the people looking at her? They must be. (296–7)

She recoils as much from her sense that the people perceive her as alien as she does from the squalor of the lane, and wishes 'to be away from those staring eyes, or to be covered up in anything, one of those women's shawls even', to hide but also to blend with the people of the lane and to subdue her feelings of abjection (297).

Then, once inside the Scott home, Laura confronts the ugly face of grief:

> the woman at the fire turned round. Her face, puffed up, red, with swollen eyes and swollen lips, looked terrible. She seemed as though she couldn't understand why Laura was there. What did it mean? Why was this stranger standing in the kitchen with a basket? What was it all about? And the poor face puckered up again. (297)

Laura reads Mrs Scott's 'terrible' face and bewildered expression and imagines the widow's inner experience. For an instant, Laura recognises herself as 'the stranger standing in the kitchen with a basket', the foreigner within, the Other. Laura experiences herself as *unheimlich* while also experiencing Mrs Scott's swollen, miserable face and her 'little low kitchen, lighted by a smoky lamp' (297) as the abject, 'Not me. Not that.' Here self and Other confront each other, face to face, and in a flash we can see both of them on both sides. They confront their own extimate relation, and it is terrifying.

We know that Laura's horror and abjection finally find relief in the story's epiphanic moment, as she gazes upon Scott, the carter's, beautiful, peaceful body. As numerous critics have noted, and as Mansfield herself indicates to Gerhardie, the beauty Laura finds in his repose allows her to reconcile the conflict she feels between the joy and frivolity of the garden party and the death outside her gates. But through this reconciliation, Laura also manages to dismiss her very recent horror and abjection:

> What did garden parties and baskets and lace frocks matter to him? [. . .] While they were laughing and while the band was playing, this marvel had come to the lane. Happy . . . happy. . . . All is well, said the sleeping face. This is just as it should be. (298)

Here, as Scott seems to speak using the narrator's voice, his apparent peace and happiness correspond to the rhythm of Laura's feeling at the garden party: 'Ah, what happiness it is to be with people who are all happy, to press hands, press cheeks, smile into eyes' (295). The echo indicates Laura's sense of recognition from Scott's body, not unlike her feeling with the lavender-loving marquee man. And yet, the story's enigmatic closing lines indicate the resolution, really, is that resolution cannot be maintained.[35] Laura's epiphany teaches her about the beautiful, bewildering inevitability of 'the diversity of life and how we try to fit in everything. Death included'; though she feels resolved, the story's struggle with class feeling extimates parallels, and moments of abjection are part of that diversity.[36]

When Mansfield describes the 'jardinier who comes here le vendredi' in the letter to Murry with which this essay opens, she presents a more polarised view. The letter conveys the sense that she and the jardinier live a world away from 'poor busmen & tube men and the ugliness of wet dark London'.[37] But in 'The Garden Party', idealised and abject workers live in the same neighbourhood. Workmen cannot help but stop and sniff up lavender, and yet, so close, 'far too near', people must find a way to 'keep alive in [. . .] poky little holes' (294). Both this letter to Murry and Mansfield's letter to Gerhardie illustrate a certain inattention to the extimacy of class; though she often cried against corruption, Mansfield was not actively political. Still, in the same letter with the jardinier, the busmen and the tube men, Mansfield credits 'the subconscious element' with developments of deeper insight in fiction:

> With an artist – [. . .] He writes he knows not what – hes *possessed*. I dont mean of course, always, but when he's *inspired* – as a sort of divine flower to all his terrific hard gardening there comes this subconscious . . . wisdom.'[38]

Mansfield's 'hard gardening' in this story grapples with a significant shift in the structure of feeling, and confronts the reader with difficult questions about the permeability and simultaneity of the classes, the self and the Other. She allows us to 'discover' a world where we can contemplate the Other at our core.[39]

Notes

1. Vincent O'Sullivan and Margaret Scott, eds, *The Collected Letters of Katherine Mansfield*, 5 vols (Oxford: Clarendon Press, 1984–2008), Vol. 4, p. 69. Hereafter referred to as *Letters*, followed by volume and page number.
2. Katherine Mansfield, 'The Garden Party', in Vincent O'Sullivan, ed., *Katherine Mansfield: Selected Stories* (New York: Norton, 2006), p. 288. All subsequent references to this edition are placed parenthetically in the text.
3. Sydney Janet Kaplan, *Katherine Mansfield and the Origins of Modernist Fiction* (Ithaca, NY: Cornell University Press, 1991), p. 192.
4. Clare Hanson and Andrew Gurr, *Katherine Mansfield* (New York: Palgrave Macmillan, 1981), p. 114.
5. Christine Darrohn, '"Blown to Bits!": Katherine Mansfield's "The Garden-Party" and the Great War', *Modern Fiction Studies*, 44 (1998), pp. 513–39 (p. 515).
6. Meghan Marie Hammond, *Empathy and the Psychology of Literary Modernism* (Edinburgh: Edinburgh University Press, 2014), p. 99. Other work on class and 'The Garden Party' includes William Atkinson, 'Mrs. Sheridan's Masterstroke: Liminality in Katherine Mansfield's "The Garden-Party"', *English Studies*, 87 (2006), pp. 51–63; and Thomas Day, 'The Politics of Voice in Katherine Mansfield's "The Garden Party"', *English: The Journal of the English Association*, 60 (2011), pp. 128–41. See also Jayne Marek, 'Class-Consciousness and Self-Consciousness in Katherine Mansfield's "The Garden Party"', *Postscript: Publication of the Philological Association of the Carolinas,*

7 (1990), pp. 35–43; and Maureen Murphy, 'The Image of Class in Mansfield's "The Garden Party": A Working-Class Critique', in *The Image of Class in Literature, Media, and Society*, ed. by Will Wright and Steven Kaplan (Pueblo, CO: Society for the Interdisciplinary Study of Social Imagery, University of Southern Colorado, 1998), pp. 139–44.

7. In a letter to Kotelianksy of 6 June 1919, Mansfield writes of Chekhov's view

> about the duty of the artist to *put* the 'question' – not to solve it but so to put it that one is completely satisfied seems to me one of the most valuable things I have ever read. It opens – it discovers rather, a new world (*Letters*, 2, p. 324)

8. Virginia Woolf, 'Character in Fiction', in *Selected Essays*, ed. by David Bradshaw (Oxford: Oxford University Press, 2008), pp. 37–54 (p. 38).

9. Raymond Williams, *The Long Revolution* (Swansea: Parthian Books, 2012), pp. 69, 70.

10. Raymond Williams, *Keywords: A Vocabulary of Culture and Society* (New York: Oxford University Press, 1985), p. 65.

11. 1875 and 1890 Acts of Parliament, quoted in Williams, *Keywords*, p. 65.

12. Williams, *Keywords*, p. 64. On these British class definitions, Hanson and Gurr note that though Mansfield has been criticised for inserting British class dynamics into New Zealand, the effects of the social world of the story on Laura's subjectivity are more important than the 'external realism' of class dynamics (p. 117).

13. Raymond Williams, *Culture and Society 1780–1950* (New York: Columbia University Press, 1983), p. 109.

14. Darrohn, p. 515.

15. Woolf, p. 38.

16. Darrohn, pp. 525–6.

17. On Mansfield's thematics of the uncanny, the abject and the foreigner within, see Clare Hanson, 'Katherine Mansfield's Uncanniness', in *Celebrating Katherine Mansfield: A Centenary Volume of Essays*, ed. by Gerri Kimber and Janet Wilson (Basingstoke: Palgrave Macmillan, 2011), pp. 115–30; Angela Smith, *Katherine Mansfield and Virginia Woolf: A Public of Two* (Oxford: Clarendon Press, 1999); and *Katherine Mansfield: A Literary Life* (New York: Palgrave Macmillan, 2001), pp. 54, 178–9.

18. Hammond includes Mansfield among 'the inward-turning branch of modernism', which sought to 'promote cognitive alignment between reader and character' in 'the tradition of the nineteenth-century psychological novel' (p. 3).

19. Ruth Parkin-Gounelas, *Literature and Psychoanalysis: Intertextual Readings* (Basingstoke: Palgrave Macmillan, 2001), p. 128.

20. Jacques Lacan, *The Seminar of Jacques Lacan: The Ethics of Psychoanalysis*, ed. by Jacques Alain-Miller, trans. by Dennis Porter (New York: W. W. Norton & Company, 1997), p. 139.

21. Elizabeth A. Grosz, *Jacques Lacan: A Feminist Introduction* (New York: Routledge, 1990), p. 43.

22. Mladen Dolar, '"I Shall Be with You on Your Wedding-Night": Lacan and the Uncanny', *October*, 58 (1991), pp. 5–23 (p. 6), cited in Hanson, p. 122.

23. Hammond, p. 9.

24. Hammond, pp. 9, 13.

25. Smith, p. 63.

26. Anne Olivier Bell, ed., *The Diary of Virginia Woolf*, 5 vols (New York: Harcourt Brace Jovanovich, 1977), Vol. 2, p. 61. Hereafter referred to as *Diary*, followed by volume and page number. For an example of Mansfield on merging, see her

11 October 1917 letter to Brett (*Letters*, 1, p. 330). See also Smith, *Literary Life*, pp. 9–13 and p. 124 on merging and Bergson's influence.

27. Woolf, *Diary*, 4, p. 353.

28. *Letters*, 5, p. 101.

29. Julia Kristeva, *Powers of Horror: An Essay on Abjection* (New York: Columbia University Press, 1982), p. 2.

30. On 'intimate exteriority' in Mansfield's luminous detail, see Josiane Paccaud-Huguet, '"By what name are we to call death?": The Case of "An Indiscreet Journey"', in *Katherine Mansfield and World War One. Katherine Mansfield Studies*, 6 (2014), pp. 13–25 (p. 20).

31. See Antony Alpers, *The Life of Katherine Mansfield* (New York: Viking Press, 1980), p. 46, and Hanson and Gurr, p. 113.

32. On the authoritarian quality of calling servants by their first names and how the working class is heard in 'The Garden Party', if heard at all, see Day, pp. 137 and 133.

33. Kristeva, p. 2.

34. Darrohn notes parallels between Laura's journey into the lane and 'imaginative geography by which the upper and middle classes imagined their separation from the working class', both before and after the war (p. 531).

35. See Hammond on how Mansfield's 'character minds always leave our readerly desire to empathise frustrated' (p. 91); see Josiane Paccaud-Huguet, 'A Remainder That Spoils the Ear: Voice as Love Object in Modernist Fiction', *English Text Construction*, 1 (2008), p. 159 http://dx.doi.org/10.1075/etc.1.1.12pac (last accessed 26 October 2015), on the extimate voice in these stammered closing lines; and Darrohn, pp. 524–5, on middle-class narrative ventriloquism that underscores Laurie's inability to grasp what life is.

36. *Letters*, 5, p. 101.

37. *Letters*, 4, p. 69.

38. *Letters*, 4, p. 69.

39. *Letters*, 2, p. 324.

Me or I? The Search for the Self in the Early Writings of Katherine Mansfield

Louise Edensor

At the end of the nineteenth century, enquiries into the nature of the self and the human psyche led to the development of two extensive and enduring psychological theories: those of William James and Sigmund Freud. James's theory has, at its base, the notion of a stream of consciousness, a phrase which would become almost an aphorism for modernism. His seminal work, *The Principles of Psychology* (1890), is said to have 'practically founded the modern science of psychology in America'.[1] Freud's topographical theory divides the human psyche into consciousness and the unconscious (later the Ego and the Id); he is considered the originator of psychoanalysis[2] and the reach of his work into other disciplines is, of course, extensive.[3] Whilst there is little evidence that Katherine Mansfield read either James or Freud,[4] her notebooks, letters and stories signify more than a passing interest into notions of the self. However, Mansfield was not a philosopher or scholar and, unlike Freud and James, her approach was intuitive rather than academic. The theories espoused by James and Freud are necessarily complex and seem at times at variance with one another; this speaks to the difficulties inherent in attempting to understand and express what makes up the concept of the human self. Mansfield's own thoughts and ideas about the self are equally complex and at times contradictory. In this essay, I want to show how she attempts to work through her personal deliberations about the self by drawing attention to some of her notebook entries and two very early short stories, 'Vignette: Summer in Winter' and 'The Education of Audrey'.[5] I do not propose that Mansfield absorbed the theories of James and Freud, or indeed offered any kind of theory herself. I wish only to show that the complexity of psychological theory is mirrored in Mansfield's conjecture about the self and to highlight affinities between the discourse of those theories and Mansfield's writing.

James begins with the statement that 'no psychology [. . .] can question the *existence* of personal selves'[6] because we are aware of our own existence, and aware of the thought process that tells us that we exist separately from the rest of the world. It is not *the* thought but *my* thought.[7] The states of consciousness in an individual that constitute the self are complex and made up of many impressions, thoughts, memories and sensory experiences in a variety of combinations and priorities which are constantly changing. James's rationale for describing human consciousness as a stream is therefore rendered thus:

> Consciousness, then, does not appear to itself chopped up in bits. Such words as 'chain' or 'train' do not describe it fitly as it presents itself in the first instance. It is nothing jointed; it flows. A 'river' or 'stream' are the metaphors by which it is most naturally described. *In talking of it hereafter, let us call it the stream of thought, of consciousness, or of subjective life.*[8]

In a letter to Koteliansky in 1915, Mansfield provides a very personal response to the nature of human experience, which has some affinity with James's description of the stream:

> But do you ever feel as though the Lord threw you into eternity – into the very exact centre of eternity, and even as you plunged you felt every ripple that flowed out from your plunging – every single ripple floating away and touching and roaring into its circle every slightest thing it touched.[9]

It is interesting to note that whilst Mansfield conjures the effect of James's theory of the stream, she nevertheless reconciles this with a Christian lexicon, marrying, for a moment, theories of science and theology. This speaks to the nature of her enquiries into the concept of the self and her experience of the world. I believe that she does not recognise, or wish to draw attention to, the dichotomy of scientific and theological theories, but merely responds in a personal way in order to depict the world as she experiences it. Her vocabulary does not deliberately suggest any kind of alliance with either science or religion but expresses poetically (and therefore with an element of poetic licence) how she perceives the world. With her use of the present continuous tense (plunging, floating, roaring), Mansfield gives a sense of the unceasing nature of the onslaught of perceptions that James conveys with his metaphor of a stream. Her response, however, is arrived at through personal intuition rather than philosophical enquiry and denotes her own need to grasp at ways to articulate her experience.

James's theory describes in some detail the nature of the self, and this is a subject that appears in Mansfield's notebooks almost as a preoccupation. James outlines how the stream is the basis for the construction of the self: a subjective selection of elements that create an inner construct:

> If the stream as a whole is identified with the Self far more than any outward thing, a certain portion of the stream abstracted from the rest is so identified in an altogether peculiar degree, and is felt by all men as a sort of innermost centre within the circle, of sanctuary within the Citadel, constituted by the subjective life as a whole.[10]

The 'subjective life', however, is not a fixed entity but an organic concept that 'changes as it grows and so the identity found by the *I* in its *Me* is only a loosely construed thing, an identity "on the whole"' from which we seek 'the true, the intimate, the ultimate, the permanent Me'.[11] The self is therefore a duality:

> Whatever I may be thinking of, I am always at the same time more or less aware of *myself*, of my *personal existence*. At the same time it is I who am aware; so that the total self of me, being as it were duplex, partly known and partly knower, partly object and partly subject, must have two aspects discriminated in it, of which for shortness we may call one the *Me* and the other the *I*.[12]

Mansfield's notebooks testify to her need to seek out, and to capture in writing, the exact nature of James's 'sanctuary within the Citadel', the inner 'me'. In an entry she writes:

> I positively feel, in my hideous modern way, I can't get into touch with my mind. I am standing gasping in one of those disgusting telephone boxes and I can't get through. 'Sorry. There is no reply' tinkles out the little voice. 'Will you ring them again, exchange? A good long ring. There must be somebody there.' 'I can't get any answer.' Then I suppose there is nobody in the building – nobody at all. Not even an old fool of a watchman. No, it's dark and empty & quiet, above all – empty.[13]

Her vocabulary bears witness to her unscientific, but nevertheless intuitive, approach to her enquiry. Throughout her notebooks and letters she experiments with the semantic field of the self: here she uses the word 'mind'; on other occasions she chooses from a lexicon that she uses interchangeably, such as 'one's nature',[14] 'inner life',[15] 'oneself',[16] 'a second you',[17] or the 'other self'.[18] The homologous way in which she uses the vocabulary resonates with her own level of understanding of a complex subject. Her expression is personal rather than scientific, and the metaphor in this example serves her well in expressing how the inner self is, at times, extremely difficult to grasp or to articulate. Whilst James's theory makes the suggestion that the duality of 'Me' and 'I' is interdependent and, therefore, represents a constant connection,

Mansfield's metaphor of a telephone line that cannot connect would appear to contradict this theory. However, James emphasises the mutability of the self, the 'loosely construed thing',[19] and Mansfield's lack of ability to grasp her 'mind' is perhaps symbolic not of a lost connection, but of a lack of clear vision or articulation of the self. Likewise, James's theory indicates that whilst the 'Me' and the 'I' exist, we have to seek the permanent Me, which would suggest that this is a constant struggle and something to be diligently pursued.

To add to this complexity, James identifies how 'A man has as many social selves as there are individuals who recognise him,'[20] and that 'from this there results what practically is a division of a man into several selves'.[21] Like James, Mansfield also expresses the self as a multiplicity. In a much-quoted passage she explains:

> Of course it followed as the night the day that if one was true to oneself . . . True to oneself! Which self? Which of my many – well, really, that's what it looks like coming to – hundreds of selves. For what with complexes and suppressions, and reactions and vibrations and reflections – there are moments when I feel I'm nothing but the small clerk of some hotel without a proprietor who has all his work cut out to enter the names and hand the keys to the wilful guests.[22]

Despite the idea that the outer self is a social construct, Mansfield nevertheless goes on in this notebook entry to highlight her conviction that we have a 'persistent yet mysterious belief in a self which is continuous and permanent'.[23] Again, her vocabulary betrays the contradictory nature of the issues she analyses: that it is possible for a sense of self to be simultaneously fluid and stable. Mansfield's treatment of the self in her writing has prompted comment by critics, particularly as to whether she commits to the idea of an essential or true self beneath the veneer of the everyday. Sydney Janet Kaplan identifies how 'Mansfield was already suspicious of the idea of the essential self. Her emphasis on roles and role playing reflects her sense of self as a multiplicity, ever changing, dependent on the shifting focus of relationships.'[24] Kate Fullbrook also suggests that

> Mansfield [has a] deep but resisted desire to believe in a continuous self that holds the possibility of release from roles, masks and fragmentation into a moment of pure being [. . .] But while she is attracted to the possibility of a unified self, even if knowable only in infinitesimal moments, there is a final hanging back.[25]

This lack of certainty highlights how the self is a question of subjectivity and therefore could be considered unknowable. The theories of James and Freud are equally subjective, given that, whilst they wrote concurrently, they did not express a shared viewpoint of the human psyche or of the self. Freud's topographical concept of the human psyche explores the schema of human consciousness as a structural entity which comprises consciousness and the unconscious. He posits that the unconscious contains our instinctual drives which, for the purposes of functioning in society, are held in check:

> the unconscious comprises, on the one hand, acts that are merely latent, temporarily unconscious but otherwise no different from conscious ones, and, on the other, processes such as repressed ones, which, if they were to become conscious, would contrast starkly with the other conscious ones.[26]

Freud provides extensive justification for the existence of the unconscious, concluding that 'it is nothing less than an *untenable presumption* to insist that everything occurring in the psyche must also be known to consciousness'.[27] Some elements of conscious knowledge 'exist for prolonged periods in a state of latency' and in this latent state 'are totally inaccessible to us'.[28] This echoes Mansfield's telephone booth metaphor of being unable to 'get through'. Whilst James acknowledges the existence of habits or conditioning that seem to take place below the level of consciousness, his concept of the human psyche as a duality is at the level of consciousness.[29]

Freud asserts that the conscious self believes that the body has submitted itself to socialisation, emphasising that this is a form of self-deception, the wearing of a mask.[30] This is something that Mansfield herself articulates in a letter to John Middleton Murry in July 1917, suggesting that the construction of the socialised self is deliberate and therefore exchangeable: 'It's a terrible thing to be alone – yes it is – it is – but don't lower your mask until you have another mask prepared beneath – as terrible as you like – but a mask.'[31] For Freud, what lies beneath the mask is his concept of the unconscious.

The unconscious is not subject to, and indeed cannot operate within the boundaries or rules of, socialisation because, according to Freud, this is in direct opposition to our primal instincts and impulses. Mansfield herself suggests not only that there is a more basic inner entity but also that this is something that, for her, it is important to maintain:

> No, no the mind I love must still have wild places – a tangled orchard where dark damsons drop in the heavy grass, an overgrown little wood, the chance of a snake or two (real snakes), a pool that nobody's fathomed the depth of, and paths threaded with those little flowers planted by the wind.[32]

Mansfield seems to be suggesting that this darker area of the 'mind' is important for artistic output. The entry in the notebook begins as a discussion of a 'cultivated mind', which has its 'shrubberies' where there is 'nothing to do but to trim & to lop and to keep back'. Her final statement, 'I loathe and detest shrubberies,'[33] proposes that this wild and uncultivated element of the psyche gives rise to artistic talent not expressed by someone with a more cultivated and, by implication, guarded outlook.

One of Mansfield's early stories, 'Vignette: Summer in Winter' (1907), has echoes of the Freudian theory of consciousness and the unconscious.[34] Much like a psychological sketch of the late nineteenth century, the narrative prioritises introspection over plot to explore elements of the psyche and how this relates to a questioning of the nature of the self. The narrator stands at a window looking upon the world outside and listening to the sound of Carlotta, who plays and sings at a piano inside. The story's title, the oxymoronic 'Summer in Winter', suggests a disjuncture in nature, a simultaneity that is incongruent, and this is symbolic of the character's interior struggle between the conscious self of the outside world and the unconscious inner self.

Mansfield often places characters at thresholds such as windows or on staircases.[35] Referred to as liminal spaces, these ordinary domestic places that are 'in between' position characters in a locus of reflectivity, allowing Mansfield to engage with different levels of interiority. In 'Vignette: Summer in Winter', Mansfield uses the liminal to give the reader direct access to the narrator's unconscious, giving the reader a deeper level of interiority than the first-person narration allows. Claire Drewery's recent work on the liminal is particularly useful in exploring Mansfield's use of these liminal spaces. Drewery defines the liminal as:

> a state signifying change from one place or state to another; a fleeting sense of being that renders all who experience it temporarily outside the strictures of social convention and the norms of measured space and time. Paradoxically however, whilst such a moment is apparently intangible, it is also simultaneously habitable.[36]

What is important in Drewery's definition is that the transitory nature of the liminal space, both spatially and temporally, allows for a moment of freedom from social censure. In a letter to Dorothy Brett in 1921, Mansfield muses on this freedom:

> Don't you think the stairs are a good place for reading letters? I do. One is somehow suspended. One is on neutral ground – not in one's own world nor in a strange one. They are an almost perfect meeting place. Oh Heavens! How stairs do fascinate me when I think of it. Waiting for people – sitting on strange stairs – hearing steps far above, watching the light *playing* by itself – hearing – far below a door, looking down into a

kind of dim brightness, watching someone come up [. . .] People come out of themselves on stairs – they issue forth, unprotected. And then the window on a *landing*. Why is it so different to all other windows?[37]

Stairs, she suggests, offer liberation, an opportunity to 'come out of' oneself. In many stories, Mansfield exploits liminal spaces to allow characters a moment of reflectivity; for example, Rosabel glances out of the window of the bus in 'The Tiredness of Rosabel' (1908), and in 'Vignette: Summer in Winter' the narrator considers her 'real self' hidden in her unconscious. Through a patina of discordant images the unconscious is explored through the lexicon of dream. Dream itself occupies a liminal space: between sleeping and waking, between fantasy and reality, where the dream work[38] is a collaboration between consciousness and the unconscious. In Freudian terms, the images and symbols of a dream are drawn from consciousness, whilst the impetus, the driving force of dream, is the unconscious.[39] In dream we believe the action and events are real; we think they take place in reality when they are, in fact, fantasy. An oneiric narrative, then, is an apt medium in which to present a narrator who, placed in a liminal space, exploits the unique vantage point in order to explore her own psyche and raise questions about her true self.

Mansfield depicts sights, sounds and smells as encoded symbols, like in dreams, presenting the imagery as contradictory, especially in 'Vignette: Summer in Winter'. For example, Carlotta at the piano is singing of love and she is framed by a bright 'daffodil silk' signifying both joy and opulence; by contrast, however, she wears a 'black frock' and a 'drooping black feather', and the faint scent of her perfume is mixed with the aromatic juniper wood being burned (67). The imagery of the external world outside the window is, however, far darker:

> The house opposite repelled me – it was like the face of an old man drowned in tears. In the garden below rotting leaves were heaped upon the lawns in the walls, the skeleton trees rattled together, the wind had torn a rose bush from the ground – it sprawled across the path, ugly and thorn crusted. Heavily, drearily fell the winter rain upon the dead garden, upon the skeleton trees. (67)

Redolent of Wildean symbolism, the pathetic fallacy portrays a gloomy outside world that represents the outer self of the narrator as onerous, the idea that the obligations of functioning outside of one's true self (the unconscious) are burdensome. What Mansfield depicts is two sides of one self: Carlotta, the 'summer' of the title, is the doppelgänger or the inner self of the narrator, who stands by the window looking out upon the 'winter' outside, the 'outer self'. Mansfield's employment of the liminal and dream states reveals the true consciousness of self and the wished-for unconscious self. Whilst Mansfield's story appears to depict two sides of one self as distinct, Freud's theory does not represent consciousness and the unconscious as a dichotomy. Consciousness is an aspect of, and can be found within, the outer circle of the unconscious.[40] Our unconscious, however, is '*as unknown to us in terms of its inner nature as the reality of the outside world and is incompletely rendered to us by the data of consciousness as the outside world is rendered by the information supplied by sense organs*' (Freud's italics).[41] But dream provides us with access to an unconscious 'form of expression' for ideas that have 'met with resistance from consciousness during the day'.[42] Mansfield's oneiric narrative, whilst clumsy in its approach to ideas about the unconscious mind, nevertheless expresses some affinity with Freudian theory. The narrator's feelings towards the nature of inner desires is mitigated by the ambivalent nature of the depiction of the inner self through contradictory imagery, suggesting that whilst the narrator acknowledges inner desires, there is also an element of fear involved. In Freudian terms, this internal dissonance in the narrator is the struggle between the reality and pleasure principles. In fantasising, we pay heed only to the pleasure principle; aberrance becomes acceptable, even normative. However, the incongruent imagery drawn from the narrator's unconscious gives rise to apprehension based on the underlying functioning of the reality principle, which governs our ability to 'protect ourselves from what is harmful'.[43] Although the reality principle does not occlude the pleasure principle, it safeguards us from it. A moment's pleasure with uncertain consequences can be circumvented to achieve a more 'secure' pleasure later on.[44]

The narrator's equivocation is mirrored in Drewery's identification of the liminal as being simultaneously emancipating and frightening. She observes how 'Thresholds are places of fear and ambivalence [. . .] [but] the schema of the rite of passage is also liberating, enabling the transgression of social boundaries, a confrontation with otherness, and a challenge to the limits of subjectivity.'[45] The acknowledgement by the narrator of the inner self, the self of the unconscious, is liberating but also contradicts the sense of the outer self, the self of consciousness. The disparity in the imagery becomes illustrative of this predicament. Both lexically and syntactically, the narrative evokes the fantasy/reality divide, suggesting uncanniness; shorter sentences give way to the longer, rambling syntax of discordant images:

> The walls were hung with daffodil silk – a faint golden light seemed to linger on her face. She wore a long black frock with a drooping black hat [. . .] the air was faintly scented with the perfume she loved that winter – peau d'Espagne. There was a little fire of juniper wood burning in the grate and the flames cast into the room strange grotesque shadows that leapt upon the walls, the curtains, that lurked under chairs, behind the lounge, that hid in the corners, and seemed to point long shadow fingers at Carlotta. (67)

The olfactory juniper wood, traditionally a symbol of strength or protection, gives rise to the anthropomorphic flames of the fire, which point their long fingers at Carlotta; its scent, often used to cleanse or bless a house, opposes Carlotta's sensuous perfume; daffodil silk is juxtaposed to black clothing; the renewal and growth of spring contrasts with images of death and dying (67). Each image of reality is countermanded by an image of fantasy, creating an environment where the everyday is infused with unreality. The uncanniness of the scene is a symbolic representation of the narrator's struggle with the self. As Freud explains, 'an uncanny effect often arises when the boundary between fantasy and reality is blurred, when we are faced with the reality of something that we have until now considered imaginary, when a symbol takes on the full function and significance of what it symbolises'.[46] The uncanny in the narrative symbolises the narrator's realisation of inner desires, of the inner self. The position at the window gives a unique glimpse of the inner world of the unconscious and this colours the perception of the outside world; the narrator is unable to view it as anything other than hostile. In a letter to Thomas Trowell in 1907, Mansfield similarly explains how

> this loneliness is not so terrible to me – because in reality – my outer life is but a phantom life – a world of intangible – meaningless grey shadow – my inner life pulsates with sunshine and music & Happiness – unlimited vast unfathomable wells of Happiness and *You*.[47]

Like the narrator, Mansfield views the obligatory self of consciousness that she is forced to wear as hostile, with the inner self existing beneath.

Carlotta entreats the narrator to join her, and in so doing she adopts the archaic language of fairy tale:

> Come, her voice cried to me, and we shall wander in a mystic garden filled with beautiful non-existent flowers. And I alone possess the key, I alone can search out the secret paths. Lo! There is a bower lit with the pale light of gardenia blossom, and the fountains are filled with laughing water. (67)

Mansfield's use of the discourse of fairy tale can be linked to Freudian theory and to the uncanny:

The world of the fairy tale abandons the basis of reality right from the start and openly commits itself to the acceptance of animistic beliefs. Here it is impossible for wish fulfilments, the existence of secret powers, the omnipotence of thoughts, the animation of the inanimate – all of which are commonplace in fairy tale – to produce an uncanny effect [. . .] a sense of the uncanny can arise only if there is a conflict of judgement as to whether what has been surmounted and merits no further credence may not, after all, be possible in real life.[48]

Mansfield's use of a fairy-tale lexicon could be considered pastiche, indicating perhaps her intuitive experimentation with writing in attempting to puzzle out issues of the self, rather than her affinity with Freudian theory. She employs a number of narrative techniques in this story in an attempt to unravel, and express linguistically, the nature of the human psyche. Oneiric symbolism, liminal spaces and fairy-tale language contribute towards her continued efforts to decipher the thoughts and feelings about her own self that she articulates in her personal writing. Like the use of liminal spaces, which allow for a freedom from social constraints, fairy tale is equally liberating. What is uncanny in reality can seem possible in the fantasy world of fairy tale. However, as Freud points out, uncanniness arises in conflict, and in Mansfield's story, whilst the narrator acknowledges that the outer world is unpleasant, the narrator simultaneously fears Carlotta's unconscious world and exhibits hesitancy. The narrator makes no move to join Carlotta when bidden but instead opens the curtains:

I drew back the heavy curtains from the window – the rain was splashing against the glass [. . .] heavily, drearily fell the winter rain upon the dead garden, the skeleton trees. I turned from the window and in the warm fire-lit room, with almost a noble defiance in her voice, Carlotta at the piano sang passionately of love. (67)

The curtains are heavy, signifying reluctance, and there is an element of realisation, a final resignation that what the narrator desires, to live as the unconscious self, is ultimately unachievable. There is hope, however, in the 'noble defiance' of Carlotta's singing tempered by the word 'almost', signifying Mansfield's reluctance to close the door completely on the possibilities she has explored in this story.

In this early short story, Mansfield demonstrates some affinity with Freudian thought, highlighting how it is possible that, beneath the 'outer' exhibited self, there may be an inner self related to the unconscious. Her 'final hanging back',[49] seen here in the narrator's reluctance, suggests that Mansfield seeks only to present her own personal interpretation, or to raise a question for which she has no definitive answer.

Whilst 'Vignette: Summer in Winter' gives credence to the possible existence of an inner self beneath the outer self of reality, Kaplan has highlighted how Mansfield's fiction often explores the difference between finding the self and creating the self. She notes that 'the nostalgia for an essential, original self alternates with the defiant – and at times triumphant – admission of self generation'.[50] 'The Education of Audrey' (1908), written a year later than 'Vignette: Summer in Winter', extends Mansfield's exploration of the outer self, but this time the emphasis is on the fragile nature of the self as a deliberate construction, or mask. The narrative features a woman, Audrey, who has not seen her lover, Max, for four years. She receives a note bidding her to call upon him. This narrative is indicative, again, of the struggle between two distinct personas or selves; however, instead of giving the reader direct access to the protagonist's unconscious through dream or fantasy, a catoptric experience serves to illustrate both the construction and the disintegration of the self.

As in 'Vignette: Summer in Winter', Audrey stands by the window and reads the note from Max bidding her to go to him. The description of the view from the window is focalised through Audrey:

> It was Saturday morning, and full of sunshine. She watched the fugue like course of hansoms, and four wheelers and automobiles. A man wheeling a barrow full of shining, waving palms in terra-cotta jars, passed by. Just under her window a boy was singing [. . .] in a fresh, rough, vigorous voice. His basket was full of little bunches of the fragrant dainty blossom. Audrey felt she would like to buy it all, crush it in her hands, bury her face in it, absorb it. (102)

The description of the scene outside the window evokes her state of consciousness, which is exultant and joyful. This is enveloped in symbolic detail and synaesthesia: the 'fugue like course of hansoms' is polyphonic and contrapuntal, suggestive already of the delicate nuances of self that will be drawn out over the course of the narrative. What Audrey sees is beauty and happiness when, in fact, the scene is of ordinary people going about their daily toil. Sounds, smells and sights mingle together to form a coherent whole, tempered by Audrey's mood; she sees what she wants to see. This almost breathless outpouring of description typifies Audrey's joy, but at the same time the structure guides the reader to suspect that Audrey's sense of herself here is fragile. The short sentences and fast pace serve to underscore the sense of joy, but the hyperbole is reminiscent of the way a child might describe something in excitement; the simplicity and effusion suggest fragility and naïvety. Mansfield provides little interiority in the narrative, instead relying heavily on Audrey's words and symbolism to exploit the difference between showing and telling, and using this difference ironically. Symbols indicate to the reader that the telling is unreliable because Audrey deludes herself, creating incongruity between what we are being told and what we are being shown. The hyperbolic description is focalised through Audrey, who tells us of 'sunshine', of 'shining palms', of a boy whose voice is 'vigorous' (102), when in fact what the reader sees is an ordinary, everyday scene, and Audrey's naïvety ironically suggesting that she really is the child, as suggested by the sentence's syntax. This is further reinforced when Audrey, on her walk, remarks how 'It is an uncomfortable thing [. . .] to possess a spirit that persists in hoop-bowling at my mature age, when the flesh must plod the pavestones of convention' (103). One of Mansfield's notebook entries from 1907 echoes Audrey's sentiments. Mansfield explains, 'I lean out of the window – the breeze blows, buffeting and friendly against my face, and the child spirit, hidden away under one thousand and one grey City wrappings, bursts its bonds & exalts within me.'[51] In 'Vignette: Summer in Winter', Mansfield's use of an oneiric narrative gave rise to disparate images, signalling the narrator's ambivalent feelings towards the 'inner' self of the unconscious. In this story, however, the incongruity of symbolic and linguistic detail operates at an ironic level, instinctively causing us to question Audrey's words and thereby her sense of self.

When Audrey glances down at the note again, 'a faint flush spread over her face' and she goes to the mirror, taking comfort in the catoptric reassurance of the self. She speaks to the mirror image: 'We'll go, my dear, and enjoy ourselves,' and reinforcing her sense of herself she says, 'I am the happiest woman on this earth [. . .] I have youth – oh, divine youth [. . .] and my beautiful voice, and freedom, absolute liberty' (102–3). Jenijoy La Belle's revealing work on the role played by mirrors in women's self-conceptions gives some insight into Mansfield's use of the catoptric trope in this short story. La Belle highlights how mirror scenes often reveal 'an intimate and significant relationship between the mirror and a woman's conception of what she is [. . .] creating the self in its self-representations to itself.'[52] This suggests that both the inner and the outer self are represented in the mirror: both subject and object, both of James's 'Me' and 'I'. Audrey observes herself, but is also the one being observed. La Belle further emphasises how, 'since the self is never fully achieved, it is necessary to look in the glass to see how one is doing in the process of constantly reinventing the self'.[53] For Audrey, the mirror provides the reassurance of her sense of self that has been disturbed by the note from Max. The reader is directed to see how fragile Audrey's sense of her self is in the face of this disruption. At the liminal space by the window she feels protected by being inside her own room, where she can be assured of her own sense of self, but the imma-turity implied by the structure of Audrey's thoughts steers the reader towards uncertainty. As readers we are invited to question Audrey's effusion of happiness and to look at what lies beneath. Audrey's con-structed outer self is very fragile and she lacks confidence in her ability to maintain her persona, illustrated here by the disturbance she feels at being faced with seeing Max again.

The continued effusive description causes the reader to question what is being focalised through Audrey: 'For days rain had been falling over London with a steady monotonous persistence. Now, in this sun-shine, she felt intoxicated. It was sparkling and golden, and enchanting, like champagne' (103). Mansfield shows us that this is where liminality provokes the visceral, in both Audrey and the reader, giving us the sense of something seething beneath the surface, visible because of the freedom provided by the liminal space. At a narrative and syntactic level through the use of symbolism, Mansfield elicits a sense of the inner/outer dichotomy of the self, which Audrey is able to observe in the liberating intangibility of the liminal space of the window. There is no one here to question her sense of self. The narrative, however, with its hyperbolic description, suggests to the reader that the self-assured musician that Audrey has become is merely a façade or a mask. What lies beneath, indicated by the childlike structure of the narrative, is the 'child spirit' of Mansfield's notebook entry. This is reinforced by structural irony. Mansfield tells us that Audrey has a 'wonderful sense of power, of complete confidence in herself' (103), but by the end of the narrative we realise that Audrey's sense of her self is easily broken.

La Belle refers to the mirror as oxymoronic, 'a mode of figuration or figuring forth an image which, like metaphor, is inscribed with both identity and difference'.[54] For Audrey, it is both the inner and the outer self as it becomes both the Jamesian knower and the known. Audrey speaks to her mirror image as if she is speaking to her inner self, but what she sees in the mirror is the outer self, what others see. This is the duplicitous nature of the mirror image: it is both subject and object but at the same time it is neither, and in that sense it represents a liminal space whose power of reassurance is delusory. In Audrey's case it allows her to deceive herself on both levels: what she sees as her outer self in the mirror is the accomplished musician, which Max will later sweep away very quickly, but she also sees the confident and independent inner self that Max reveals is also false – she is, in fact, still a little girl, whose outlook on life is based on 'a little literature and a great deal of morbid imaginings' (106). Mansfield here suggests that, for Audrey, the inner and outer self are mutually dependent. Audrey's sense of her self is contingent upon her own subjectivity; she is relying on the reassurance provided by the perceived objectivity of the catoptric experience. The mirror therefore represents a polarity: both the inner and the outer self, both the knower and the known, question whether Audrey is assured of her own sense of either.

Mansfield stalls the narrative briefly after Audrey's journey to Max's house, suspending Audrey in another liminal space, the flight of stairs she must climb:

> A sudden breeze in the Square caught the leaves of the plane trees, burnt a bright golden and a dull brown, and whirled them in the air like a flock of magic birds. Two floated onto her muff, and she held them against her cold face as she mounted the steep flight of stairs. (103)

The suggestion of magic and Audrey's exclamation to Max, 'I am bringing you summer,' when her fur coat indicates clearly that is it autumn, reinforces the sense that Audrey is deluded. Magic is fallacious and Audrey's conjuring of a sense of fantasy by carrying the 'magic' leaves into Max's flat suggests that the sense of self she carries is also illusory. When Max opens the door, the narrator tells us that 'the room was full of gloom, but the vivid yellow curtains hung, straight and fine, before the three windows' (103). Inside Max's flat it is dull and the only brightness comes from curtains against the window: against the outside world where Audrey was settled in her sense of herself. When she steps into Max's room she takes the first steps towards her realisation that her sense of self is as fragile as the leaves she carries. Mansfield is leading the reader towards the final denouement: the sexually charged 'Teach me, Max,' when Audrey's sense of her self is finally broken down.

Max immediately sees through Audrey's persona and, quoting from Oscar Wilde, he tells Audrey that 'the time has come to realise one's nature perfectly' (105–6). Max does not want the newly created, confident woman that Audrey has convinced herself she has become. He wants the Audrey of four years earlier: the childlike Audrey who worshipped him. He systematically breaks down Audrey's sense of herself to achieve that by showing her that her self-conception is self-deception. Throughout the narrative, Audrey's goal has simply been reification of her own sense of self, not Max's. In the safety of her room she sought reassurance from her mirror self. Her continued sense of herself is contingent upon Max's concurrence, which he does not give. He becomes her mirror,[55] but instead of reflecting back the self that Audrey saw in the mirror in her home, he reflects back his interpretation of Audrey, the one he knew four years earlier. Mansfield links the two places in the story spatially and psychologically through the catoptric trope; Max's house stands as the mirror of Audrey's true inner self.

This story serves to show how Mansfield illustrates the fragility and mutability of the self. As in James's theory, the self is not a fixed entity but an organic entity, subject to the delicate nuances of personal perception, but here Mansfield shows that it is also contingent upon the reification provided by others. Audrey's catoptric experience appears to enable her to view herself as both subject and object, to provide reassurance from the inner to the outer self. The narrative, however, shows this to be fallacious; both inner and outer selves are contingent upon Audrey's subjectivities, demonstrating that neither is durable.

Through this brief examination of some of Mansfield's writing, I have shown how she raises questions about the nature of the self. Whilst her writing has clear affinities with the work of James and Freud, Mansfield scrutinises the issues without recourse to any specific theories; nor does she advocate a theory of her own. In a letter to Virginia Woolf in 1919 she writes:

> Tchekov has a very interesting letter published in next week's A . . . what the writer does is not so much to *solve* the question but to *put* the question. There must be the question put. That seems to me a very nice dividing line between the true & the false writer.[56]

The editor's note to the letter quotes Chekhov's point:

> You are right in asking from an artist a conscious attitude to his activity, but you are mixing up two things: the solving of the question and the correct putting of the question. It is the latter only which is obligatory upon the artist. There's not a single question solved in 'Anna Karenina' or 'Onyegin', but they satisfy completely, because all the questions are correctly put.[57]

These two stories by the young Katherine Mansfield are illustrative of her ability to put the question correctly. It is not her intention to provide definitive answers to psychological issues of the self, but simply to question what the self means in order to deal with the enquiries she expresses in her personal writing. Mansfield shows how the true nature of the self is difficult to grasp, and her fiction bears this out by placing her characters in situations of self-exploration or self-creation and self-delusion. She shows that not only is the self constituted of an inner and outer, but also that the relationship between the two is interdependent. Whilst Mansfield seems to seek the inner or true self, and explores the concept linguistically, her narratives nevertheless raise the question of the nature of this interdependence. By showing that the outer self is a veneer, a self-directed construct capable of both disintegration and mutability, it is not unreasonable to conclude that this applies equally to the inner self. Fullbrook highlights how Mansfield's

> pessimism, her sense of fixed social forms as laughably flimsy and arbitrary and yet powerful as the sources of an otherwise unattainable communal illusion of certainty about individuals, and the sudden shifts in tone that emphasise discontinuity of vision are all, in their different ways, related to her ideas regarding the self.[58]

The inability to find the true inner self leads to self-doubt and self-creation: a 'loosely construed' state of being. Inevitably, then, this leads to 'uncertainty about individuals'. The inability to know one's own true nature suggests that we cannot know each other's, and Mansfield illustrates this in many narratives. Additionally, the ambivalent nature of the imagery in 'Vignette: Summer in Winter' reinforces Fullbrook's earlier assertion that with aspects of the self, Mansfield exhibits a 'final hanging back'. Whilst she questions the concept of the self as a conflict between unconscious desires and an outer persona, the desire to live out life as one's unconscious self is depicted as fearful. Finally, the idea that the self is an intangible concept which gives rise to 'discontinuity of vision', as Fullbrook asserts, suggests that the ability to represent this in fiction is equally problematic. Mansfield herself acknowledged this difficulty in a letter to Bertrand Russell:

> it's true that my desire is to bring all that I see and feel into harmony with that rare 'vision' of life of which we spoke, and that if I do not achieve this I shall feel that my life has been a fault at last, and it's my God terribly true that I don't see the means yet – I don't in the least know definitely *how* to live.[59]

Notes

1. 'William James Dies; Great Psychologist', *The New York Times*, 27 August 1910 <http://www.nytimes.com/learning/general/onthisday/bday/0111.html> (last accessed 1 November 2015).
2. '1939: Sigmund Freud, Psychoanalyst, Dies Refugee in England at 83', *International Herald Tribune*, 25 September 1939 <http://ihtretrospective.blogs.nytimes.com/2014/09/23/1939-sigmund-freud-psychoanalyst-dies-refugee-in-england-at-83/> (last accessed 4 November 2015).
3. 'Obituary: Dr Sigmund Freud', *The Guardian*, 25 September 1939 <http://www.theguardian.com/books/1939/sep/25/scienceandnature.booksonhealth> (last accessed 4 November 2015).
4. Mansfield quotes from *The Principles of Psychology* in a review of Hugh Walpole's *The Captive* in 1920. See Gerri Kimber and Angela Smith, eds, *The Collected Works of Katherine Mansfield* (Edinburgh: Edinburgh University Press, 2014), Vol. 3, pp. 672–3. She refers to Freud's work in a letter to Beatrice Campbell in 1916, saying

'and I shall *never* see sex in trees, sex in the running brooks, sex in stones & sex in everything. The number of things that are really phallic from Fountain pen fillers onwards!' Vincent O'Sullivan and Margaret Scott, eds, *The Collected Letters of Katherine Mansfield*, 5 vols (Oxford: Clarendon Press, 1984–2008), Vol. 1, p. 261. Hereafter referred to as *Letters*, followed by volume and page number. Both of these references suggest that Mansfield was at least aware of the work of both Freud and James.

5. Gerri Kimber and Vincent O'Sullivan, eds, *The Collected Fiction of Katherine Mansfield*, 2 vols (Edinburgh: Edinburgh University Press, 2012), Vol. 1, pp. 66–7, 102–7. All subsequent page references from this volume are provided parenthetically in the text.

6. William James, *The Principles of Psychology* (New York: Dover Publications, 1918 [1890]), p. 226.

7. James, p. 226.

8. James, p. 239; author's italics.

9. *Letters*, 1, 17 May 1915, p. 192.

10. William James, *The Principles of Psychology: Briefer Course* (Toronto: General Publishing Company, 2001 [1892]), p. 297.

11. James, *Briefer Course*, p. 71.

12. James, *Briefer Course*, pp. 42–3.

13. Margaret Scott, ed., *The Katherine Mansfield Notebooks*, 2 vols (Minneapolis: University of Minnesota Press, 2002), Vol. 2, p. 134. Hereafter referred to as *Notebooks*, followed by volume and page number.

14. *Notebooks*, 1, p. 97.

15. *Notebooks*, 1, p. 104.

16. *Notebooks*, 1, p. 284.

17. *Letters*, 2, 17 August 1919, p. 350.

18. *Notebooks*, 2, p. 209.

19. James, *Briefer Course*, p. 71.

20. James, *Briefer Course*, p. 45.

21. James, *Briefer Course*, p. 46.

22. *Notebooks*, 2, p. 203.

23. *Notebooks*, 2, p. 204.

24. Sydney Janet Kaplan, *Katherine Mansfield and the Origins of Modernist Fiction* (Ithaca, NY, and London: Cornell University Press, 1991), p. 37.

25. Kate Fullbrook, *Key Women Writers: Katherine Mansfield* (Bloomington and Indianapolis: Indiana University Press, 1986), p. 19.

26. Sigmund Freud, *The Unconscious* (London: Penguin Books, 2005 [1911]), p. 55.

27. Freud, p. 50; my italics.

28. Freud, p. 51.

29. Eric Thomas Weber, 'James's Critique of the Freudian Unconscious – 25 Years Earlier', *William James Studies*, 9 (2012), pp. 94–119. See also James's chapter, 'The Mind Stuff Theory', *Principles*, pp. 145–82.

30. Freud, pp. 3–9.

31. *Letters*, 1, late July 1917, p. 318.

32. *Notebooks*, 2, p. 163.

33. *Notebooks*, 2, p. 163.

34. Sigmund Freud, *The Interpretation of Dreams* (London: Penguin Books, 2006 [1899]), pp. 630–3.

35. Alpers notes how this is particularly evident in Mansfield's early stories. He says that

'she is constantly inhabiting one space while observing another, and has her characters doing the same'. Antony Alpers, *The Life of Katherine Mansfield* (Oxford: Oxford University Press, 1982), p. 43.

36. Claire Drewery, *Modernist Short Fiction by Women* (Farnham: Ashgate, 2011), p. 1.
37. *Letters*, 4, 29 July 1921, p. 256.
38. Freud, *Dreams*, p. 559.
39. Freud, *Dreams*, p. 558.
40. Freud, *Dreams*, p. 628.
41. Freud, *Dreams*, pp. 628–9.
42. Freud, *Dreams*, p. 629.
43. Freud, *The Unconscious*, p. 7.
44. Freud, *The Unconscious*, p. 7.
45. Drewery, p. 2.
46. Sigmund Freud, *The Uncanny* (London: Penguin, 2003 [1919]), pp. 150–1.
47. *Letters*, 1, 11 August 1907, p. 24.
48. Freud, *The Uncanny*, p. 156.
49. Fullbrook, p. 19.
50. Kaplan, p. 179.
51. *Notebooks*, 1, p. 135.
52. Jenijoy La Belle, *Herself Beheld: The Literature of the Looking Glass* (Ithaca, NY, and London: Cornell University Press, 1990), p. 2.
53. La Belle, p. 17.
54. La Belle, p. 42.
55. La Belle highlights how 'Sometimes, as in Dreiser's *Sister Carrie*, the male becomes a mirror, telling the female how to compose her outer self' (p. 27).
56. *Letters*, 2, 27 May 1919, p. 320.
57. *Letters*, 2, 27 May 1919, p. 320.
58. Fullbrook, p. 17.
59. *Letters*, 1, 17 December 1916, p. 287.

'Jigging away into nothingness': Knowledge, Language and Feminine *Jouissance* in 'Bliss' and 'Psychology'

Allan Pero

'There is something profound and terrible in this eternal desire to establish contact.'[1]

'You can invent anything you like, but you can't invent psychology.'[2]

'Language operates entirely within ambiguity, and most of the time you know absolutely nothing about what you are saying.'[3]

One of the hallmarks of Katherine Mansfield's work is its uneasy relationship to knowledge. Her characters stumble about, trying to narrate what they know, or hope to know, even as they just as regularly misunderstand not only their desire, but also the desire of others. In a letter of 1918 to John Middleton Murry, Mansfield describes what she refers to as 'two "kick offs" in the writing game', in which writing, as a form of knowledge, reveals itself to her. The first is marked, coincidentally enough, by a kind of peaceful bliss in which 'something delicate and lovely seems to open before my eyes, like a flower without thought of a frost or a cold breath'; the second is much more sinister, born of 'an *extremely* deep sense of hopelessness – of everything doomed to disaster, almost willfully, stupidly'.[4] A crucial dimension of the difference between these forms of knowing, of writing, is less Mansfield's attitude than the shape the writing takes. She insists that the former is conditioned by humility, to express what she witnesses during the act of writing, whilst the latter is '*a cry against corruption* that is *absolutely* the nail on the head'.[5] When one considers these two forms of knowledge, the first is a revelation that must be approached cautiously, humbly, for fear that the act of writing itself might inadvertently misconstrue or mar the beauty of its truth; the second takes a violent stand against that which threatens to corrupt knowledge or truth itself. Although each form of knowledge is shaped

100

by a desire to know, one is structured by submission and the other by resistance. Fittingly, both submission and resistance inform the strange knowledge, the strange desires, that the character Bertha encounters in Mansfield's short story, 'Bliss'.

For Jacques Lacan, desire searches for objects to fill, however provisionally, the fundamental lack that constitutes desire; we should recall that desire is meant to be sustained, that it cannot be ultimately or completely fulfilled because every object of desire is a substitute for the lost Thing, the primordial object which castration denies to us.[6] As Kate Fullbrook has argued, 'Mansfield sees desire as diffuse and unpredictable, and in the story ['Bliss'] shows her awareness of the fine mesh of social definition that is supposed to contain, express, and control the desires of an advanced, western woman.'[7] The vehicle of knowledge is language, but Mansfield quickly disabuses us of the notion that either knowledge or language is transparent. As tools of desire, they are often maddeningly unwieldy, resisting and thwarting the blandishments of desire itself. One reason for their ungainliness is that, as a psychoanalytical reading of Mansfield will show, there is a split in knowledge and language; as her letter to Murry shows, knowledge operates in different registers for both the ego and the subject, while language operates both at the level of conscious speech (for Mansfield, a cry against corruption) and at the level of unconscious enunciation (the expression of a revelation). But what are the differences? For Lacan, knowledge in the imaginary register, or *connaissance*, emerges from the formation of the ego. It is the false knowledge that comes not from ignorance, but from the illusion of self-mastery or self-understanding. Ultimately, *connaissance* is, for Lacan, necessarily a form of *méconnaissance*, or misrecognition of oneself as self-identical, coherent.[8] As a fantasy, the knowledge of the ego has a price; it is perforce paranoiac, imaginary. Paranoia hopes always to be the last word in certainty. In an important sense, the knowledge the ego possesses is structured by a paranoiac avoidance of a particular bit of knowledge – the very split between the ego and the subject. In other words, in privileging the fantasy of self-mastery, self-identity, the ego disavows the other form of knowledge – the knowledge of the subject, or, in Lacanian terms, *savoir*. Unlike *méconnaissance, savoir* is symbolic knowledge; it is the unconscious knowledge the subject does not know that she knows, but may come to know. *Savoir* emerges from the subject's relation to the symbolic order, to the other; in sum, it is the truth of one's unconscious desire.[9] The experience of this truth, this symbolic knowledge, is a form of enjoyment, or *jouissance*. For Mansfield, it is the stuff of 'Bliss'.

Bliss can be a kind of knowledge, but knowledge of a special type; that is, given its overwhelming nature, how it defies definition, it cannot be reduced to mere trivia. It is the knowledge *of jouissance*, which refers not to mere pleasure, but to a kind of suffering that attends the experience of bliss. This particular kind of enjoyment implies that there is something about the experience of bliss that somehow defies internalisation. In any encounter with *jouissance*, there always remains some residue that renders the experience 'senseless', an indigestible experience which resists meaning. But what I will suggest, and I think Mansfield's eponymous story is proof of, is that the apparent senselessness of enjoyment does not hinder our submission to its status as a symbol or meaning; indeed, it is the very basis of our submission. We work very hard to make *jouissance* make sense.

Let us now turn to Mansfield's story proper. As Patricia Moran has persuasively argued, 'Bliss' is not a neat story of O. Henryesque reversal, and thus cannot be reduced to 'merely a result of the author's quick sleight of hand'.[10] The reason is that the text 'offers no such satisfactory reversal', but instead produces nothing but questions. As Moran reminds us, Bertha's 'utter unreliability as a narrator makes this particular plot impossible to decipher'.[11] In Lacanian terms, Bertha's unreliability is, at the level of language, both an effect of the gap between *méconnaissance* and *savoir*, and of the experience of *jouissance* itself. There is a strange temporality which inheres in Bertha's bliss. The opening paragraph suggests that her bliss has a stuttering, immature quality, as if it could be explained away as simply the vestigial joy of youth, one which continues to press itself intermittently upon a thirty-year-old woman. (It also implies that her life otherwise gives her no reason to feel such bliss.) Her body is seized by an unaccountable ecstasy – marked by dancing, throwing, playing and laughing – all of which point to the uncanny absurdity of a body in *jouissance*. This somatic ecstasy is an experience beyond language, beyond sense and meaning. In its sublimity, bliss is compared to having 'suddenly swallowed a bright piece of the late afternoon sun [which] burned in your bosom, sending out a little shower of sparks into every particle, into every finger and toe'.[12] But in its narration, bliss quickly becomes the opposite number of 'idiotic civilisation' itself, as if the symbolic order, the seat of law, were in contradistinction to the body's freedom to enjoy itself.

In this regard, we are tempted to place her bliss squarely within the realm of transgression, of that which, in Freudian terms, is beyond the pleasure principle. Freud famously talks about the body as a space of hydraulics – of flows, affects, discharges, regulatory structures – that work toward achieving or maintaining a kind of stability in the level of excitation or pleasure. The level of excitation must be regulated because of the consequence of overwhelming unpleasure – in other

words, *jouissance* – that will result in transgressing the pleasure principle. For Lacan, desire *is* the pleasure principle, a regulatory force inau-
gurated by symbolic law, one that permits us to desire certain things,
to have and rationalise certain pleasures, but deny or interdict others.
Bertha's bliss would seem to transgress this model of desire. Her bliss
resists being domesticated into particular forms of pleasure, exceeds
them, and strangely is supplementary to them. However, an important
clue about the nature of her bliss is provided by her chafing against
enclosing her body 'in a case like a rare, rare fiddle' and then dismissing
the simile: 'No, that about the fiddle is not quite what I mean' (111).
If we compare the 'little shower of sparks into every particle, into every
finger and toe' and shutting up the body 'in a case like a rare, rare
fiddle', we not only confront an infelicitous admixture of metaphor
and simile, we also encounter the difference between two forms of
enjoyment: the first is, I will suggest, akin to what Lacan calls feminine
or Other *jouissance*, while the second is analogous to what he names
masculine or phallic *jouissance* (or enjoyment). Part of the narrational
problem Mansfield presents us with is that knowledge can be a form of
enjoyment, but what form of enjoyment does this knowledge evoke?

Before I can answer this question, I will first explain the difference
between phallic and feminine *jouissance*.[13] However, we must keep in
mind that when Lacan uses the terms masculine and feminine to refer to
jouissance, he is not referring to gender or gender assignment. Instead,
he is referring to a particular identification with the phallus. Another
way of putting it is to say that one can be a woman and identify with
phallic *jouissance*, and be a man and identify with feminine *jouissance*,
and so on. For Lacan, phallic enjoyment is marked by sexuality (but not
sexual orientation), and as such is genital. It is governed by the phallic
function, by the law or interdiction of the father. Feminine *jouissance*
is a state of exception, outside the phallic function, outside genital or
sexual enjoyment. Woman, as a cultural idea, throws the universality of
the phallic function into question because there is no exception in her;
in other words, she resists nothing. One way of capturing this idea is to
say that the limitation of the phallic function coincides symptomatically
with Woman, producing a non-phallic exception. The masculinist fascination with Woman as symptom of Man then resides precisely in this
absence, and helps explain why there are sexist and misogynist fantasies
about the concept of Woman, fantasies which are meant to confine
and define her. She is enigmatic in so far as she is the exception that
manifests itself within the symbolic order. In order for a particular man
to submit to the phallic function, then, Woman is the other who points
to that very submission, rendering Woman as 'marked' and Man as

'unmarked' (since castration is the mark that is taken for granted, and is naturalised by the symbolic order). Since Woman is radically excluded from the universality of the phallic function, 'she has a supplementary jouissance compared to what the phallic function designates by way of jouissance'.[14]

By way of example, Lacan's discussion of feminine enjoyment centres upon Saint Teresa of Avila. More specifically, he looks at Bernini's famous sculpture of Saint Teresa in a state of religious ecstasy. If one looks at the sculpture, one notices that, as the golden metal beams surrounding – indeed, radiating from –Bernini's Saint Teresa suggest, it is the result of a feminine *jouissance*, a staging of the Other *jouissance* in the body of Saint Teresa. This example is uncannily paralleled in Mansfield's description of Bertha's own bliss. Her enjoyment is not phallic, not sexual in nature; it is not governed by the logic of phallic finitude, but rather one of feminine infinitude. W. H. New has noted that Bertha's actions are described, at least in the story's first sentence, as 'verbs in the infinitive form – concepts more than actions – and that the sentence closes with "nothing, simply," as though (whatever freedom Bertha might dream of in the present moment) her expressed desires at least will be shown to be insubstantial'.[15] This is one reason why Bertha intuitively dismisses the simile of the fiddle case; her bliss is not one of confinement, of limitation, but one of freedom, one which she imagines radiates from her fingers and toes. Like Saint Teresa, Bertha 'experience[s] it, but knows nothing about it'.[16] Her body's enjoyment cannot be compared to an instrument precisely because it is outside the phallic function. Her body, and its bliss, cannot be reduced to a tool of masculine enjoyment; it is a *jouissance* of being, not of the body. In this respect, feminine *jouissance* is literally epiphanic; it brings a sublime experience of being to light. What that experience will yield is another matter.

But the problem is that Bertha's enjoyment may be supplementary (and not complementary) to phallic *jouissance*, yet she is absolutely bound to masculine desire in so far as she identifies with the phallic function. That is to say, her troubled identification with the phallic function prompts her to seek a form of knowledge, of epiphany that is ultimately phallic rather than feminine in nature. The simile of the 'rare, rare fiddle' surfaces again in its conflation with 'Little B', who is confined, kept from her by the unyielding arms of Nanny, even as the baby's 'exquisite toes as they shone transparent in the firelight' evoke the sparks infusing Bertha's 'every finger and toe' (113). Together, they suggest confusion between forms of knowledge, between forms of enjoyment that will persist as the story proceeds.

For example, Mansfield draws our attention to how paltry Bertha's vocabulary for expressing her feelings is. She is obviously excited by seeing her child, yet all she can say, once she has prised Little B from the nanny's jealous arms, is "'You're nice – you're very nice!" said she, kissing the warm baby. "I'm fond of you. I like you"'; in effect, there is a significant gap between what is felt and what is said. The woeful inadequacy of her words points to the experience of enjoyment being akin to feeling like an object out of place, and that she does not know 'what to do with it' (113). It is as if her desire and her enjoyment are not working in concert with each other. One has the impression that she generally does not really care that much for her child at all, and that she suddenly desires her child merely because Nanny is so jealous of the baby's affection. But the indeterminate nature of her enjoyment makes it possible for it to attach itself to different objects. At different moments, we discover that her enjoyment wanders, attaching itself to different people, identifying with Miss Fulton and desiring Harry, and later identifying with Harry and desiring Miss Fulton. In sum, Bertha attempts to manage her enjoyment or bliss by appropriating the desires of other people and by identifying with them. We are invited, in other words, to view Bertha as a hysteric – she herself characterises her virtually uncontrollable laughter as a symptom of her 'getting hysterical' (112). Certainly, she exhibits symptoms of hysteria, but that would mean that we utterly dismiss Bertha's enjoyment or bliss as pathological, as simply another hysterical symptom. Such a move would be hasty. I think there is something more subtle going on in the text than diagnosing Bertha with hysteria will explain; the problem is that hysteria is predicated on the deferral of enjoyment, that every object of desire placed in her path will be dismissed as hopelessly inadequate, yet with one proviso. The hysteric will happily work to sustain the desire of the other on the condition that she is not the object of that desire.[17] What, then, are we to make of her bliss, if we take it seriously, and if we resist adding it to the laundry list of hysterical symptoms? That is to say, how can a hysteric experience enjoyment without an object of desire? In answering this question, we encounter the important difference between knowledge that knows itself (conscious knowledge) and a knowledge that does not know itself (unconscious knowledge). Her bliss is a form of knowing that does not know itself; as the narrative proceeds, this knowledge does the 'work' of coming to consciousness. For Lacan, the latter, a knowledge that does not know itself, is the engine of the hysteric's discourse.[18]

More bluntly, Mansfield's story becomes much more productive, and much more interesting, once we turn away from the notion of hysteria as pathology and toward the idea of hysteria as a discourse. The hysterical dismissal of different objects of desire – the logic of 'That's not it!' – becomes more useful if we instead understand it as a search for knowledge. By way of a productive digression, and a better understanding of the difficulty in conflating knowledge with language, with our ability to nominate different objects as the 'truth' of our desire, let us turn briefly to Mansfield's brilliant story, 'Psychology'. What is fascinating about the story is how she handles two apparently opposing narrative stratagems: the first obviously pokes fun at a particular kind of intellectualism, of a kind which we should distinguish from analysis proper. It is the kind of intellectualising that works to avoid thought, to avoid confronting what one does not want to know. In other words, one does not use one's intellect to know, but to avoid knowing. The second stratagem involves a complex psychological representation of the couple's relationship. Two conversations are apparently going on – one at the level of fantasy, and the other at the level of reality. But what is even more interesting about this narrative device is that, on the surface, the 'fantasy' conversation, what the narrative refers to as their 'secret selves', speaks their desire for each other more truthfully, more forcefully than their flaccid conversation about the psychological novel (125). Of course, their nervousness and their fear of rejection drive their intellectual posturing, yet the narrative is even more complex than that. It demonstrates the important distinction between *méconnaissance* and *savoir* I discussed earlier. How? We see their mutual investment in this self-knowledge – that they are so frank, so modern, such 'eager, serious travellers' that they imagine it is this very attitude that 'made it possible for him to be utterly truthful to her and for her to be utterly sincere with him' (126). Yet this fantasy, that they can engage in this kind of travel 'without any stupid emotional complication' (127), is of course the stumbling block that this fantasy of self-knowledge misrecognises, refuses to acknowledge –that this journey is littered with stupid, emotional complications. What is more, they are ensnared in just such a complication at this moment! Truth and sincerity cannot operate at the level of *méconnaissance*, only in the hard-won knowledge of *savoir*. But this failure is mirrored in the strange, contradictory temporality of their fantasy of themselves. At one instant, the male character is a traveller; the next, he imagines that he has arrived, 'already, at the journey's end' (127). Again, we see that his (and her) inability to travel the road of their mutual desire, that they insist that they are always already at their destination, permits them to avoid the anxiety and excitement of the actual journey. As a result, we discover a third level of conversation, one punctuated by silences – the uncomfortable gaps in which their present, pressing desire demands to be known and said. It is thus especially ironic that he invokes psychoanalytical jargon to mistake psychology for literature, to insist that today's writers are, in their diagnosis of society's ills, 'just wise enough to know that it is sick and to realise that its only chance of recovery is by going into its symptoms – making an exhaustive study of them – tracking them down – trying to get at the root of the trouble' (129). In this passage, we discover that the discourse of psychology, of psychoanalysis, is not in itself sufficient to diagnose and uncover symptoms. As Mansfield's narrative deftly shows, this very discourse can become the means by which to disavow, to corrupt all the more forcefully the knowledge or truth of one's desire. As the story proceeds, we come to see not that it is their speech, their fantasy of 'complete surrender' that lies, and that the discourse of 'their secret selves' is the truth; rather, the truth resides precisely in what they know without knowing it – the 'solemn music' that informs the silences between them (129).

This is why the two conversations converge with the silent, third conversation at an interesting moment – in the invocation of the term 'symptoms'. Even as he asserts that this is literature's task in the future, of 'trying to get at the root of the trouble', we recognise that this is exactly what Mansfield is doing, but in a more complex, satisfying way. We are witnesses of the spectacle of two people 'enjoying their symptom': that is, the painful pleasure, the enjoyment they receive from avoiding the truth of their desire for each other by boring themselves to distraction. You will recall the moment when it appears that, at least by her smile, they 'have won' (129). But the question arises: won what? They have sustained their desire by deferring its enunciation; they are able to continue speaking to each other, to remain friends, but only by keeping the terrifying declaration of love at bay. But what is the effect? We see it the moment when the silence ceases interrupting speech and interrupts thought itself: '"What have we been talking about?" thought he. He was so utterly bored he almost groaned' (129). What becomes clear is that he is not bored by her; rather, he is bored by their own fantasy, that they speak, but cannot enunciate their desire. At the same time, the prospect is so terrifying that the painful boredom of holding on to this manner of talking is preferable to the unconscious silence which all the while demands enunciation. That is why he makes his sudden, symptomatic choice: he, to his own horror, leaves.

We see the result. She is devastated, bereft, but is saved by the bell. She answers the door, hoping that it is he, but no. It is only the pathetic, sweet, older woman who continually announces her arrival with the words, '"My dear, send me away!"', which, of course, is clearly not what she wants to hear, only that she always anticipates rejection, and hopes to forestall it (131). She, too, longs for connection, affection, but cannot be direct. However, unlike the 'serious travellers', she is more vulnerable. She leaves herself open to rejection in a way that the young man and woman cannot. The silence that falls between the two women, 'like a question' (131), receives a very different answer from the one the young man offers a few moments before. The young woman embraces her, thanking her for the flowers, and they are both overwhelmed by the happiness of the gesture. After saying good night to her, the young woman writes to the young man, but she cannot name her desire. Although she can write only of their boring conversation about the psychological novel, she maintains, at least, the possibility of intimacy. We see this in her signing off the letter, in the repetition of what she has learned from her encounter with the older woman: 'Good night, my friend. Come again soon' (132). It is a knowledge that does not yet know itself, but is perhaps coming to know itself.

If we turn back to 'Bliss', this search for knowledge manifests itself in a different way. Bertha nominates different objects as the possible source of her enjoyment, but each of them, in turn, presents different forms of knowledge from what she first expects. In this sense, part of the brilliance of the story lies in the way Mansfield combines the two forms of knowledge she describes to Murry. By way of example, let us consider the pear tree. Clearly, the tree evokes the interdicted tree of knowledge, one that Bertha decides, at one juncture, to see 'as a symbol of her own life' (115). Yet the symbol does not adequately fulfil its function. That is to say, the tree does not permit Bertha to make sense of her bliss, to calm down its curious eruption in her life. It is not a symbol but a symptom; it is symptomatic of her identification with the phallic function. However clichéd it might be, it is understandable that one would, in a psychoanalytical reading, suggest that the tree is a symbol of the phallus. But again, I would argue that Mansfield is doing something more subtle. Bertha identifies with it, even as she resists it. What we discover is that the symptom is not simply a bothersome enigma that refuses symbolisation; rather, it is a point of knowledge, of epiphany, in her ongoing search for self-knowledge. In other words, as a symptom, the pear tree is not absolutely 'negative'. Her attempts to symbolise, to represent, to know are productive: that is, produced by her relation to the different symptoms, different objects of desire which appear in the narrative.

Interestingly, the figure of Miss Fulton is intuited as a possible source, not of the bliss or enjoyment, but of a kind of vocabulary or speech for it. In this respect, there seem to be two mysteries in the story: one, of course, is the source of the bliss itself; the second mystery is, at least from Bertha's perspective, Miss Fulton's own elusive, silent, ineffable bliss. Her expression 'has something behind it' and Bertha 'must find out what that something is' (114). This particular search for knowledge creates the sexual ambiguity of the scene in the garden later in the text, when the two mysteries come together. The pear tree, nominated as the symbol of Bertha's own life, fails to sustain itself as symbol precisely when the women stand together gazing upon it. Otherwise, the story would have ended there; the tree would have, in a sense, provided a path for Bertha's enjoyment, and brought her to Miss Fulton. But as I have already noted, when Bertha identifies with Miss Fulton, she desires Harry, and when she identifies with Harry, she desires Miss Fulton. At that moment the tree is nominated as the source of her bliss. Her enjoyment is given yet another object. But Miss Fulton and the tree are, in turn, identified with each other, since the tree, in the moonlight, would be 'as silver as Miss Fulton, who sat there turning a tangerine in her slender fingers that were so pale a light seemed to come out of them' (119). The symbols, the objects of identification, seem to pile on themselves; it is not only that the tree and Miss Fulton are now conflated as objects of desire, but also that Miss Fulton herself embodies the kind of feminine enjoyment that Bertha describes in referring to both herself and Little B earlier that day. Miss Fulton holds the tangerine, that 'piece of the late afternoon sun' that Bertha contrives to have swallowed. Her fingers radiate light in a similar way. Yet Bertha herself acknowledges that this form of knowledge is utterly without evidence, that Miss Fulton's mood (here cast as enjoyment) is commensurate with Bertha's: 'For she never doubted for a moment that she was right, and yet what had she to go on? Less than nothing' (119). In other words, she is confronted yet again with the nothing that provoked her laughter in the story's first sentence. What I would contend is radical about 'Bliss' is that it shows marvellously how hard Bertha is working to sustain her desire, to sustain what she permitted to desire; she turns to her baby, her house, her garden, her husband and, unconsciously, her husband's mistress to keep desire going – but as Colette Soler reminds us, 'from the moment desire becomes a defense, wherever it falls, jouissance rises'.[19] This is one of the many insights which emerges from reading Mansfield's work; the tidy distinctions between desire and its object, between the object of desire and enjoyment, are productively undermined.

When the women stand together in the garden, the phallic symbolism of the pear tree, which has already failed to calm her hysterical discourse, becomes absurd, comically tumescent: 'Although it was so still it seemed, like the flame of a candle, to stretch up, to point, to quiver in the bright air, to grow taller and taller as they gazed – almost to touch the rim of the round, silver moon' (120). But the stability of the symbol is thrown into flux; this phallus is both masculine and feminine; this phallus bears fruit. Even if we were to shift interpretative gears and look instead to the consummation suggested by the image, the penetration of the moon by the tree, it remains silent, mysterious, producing more questions than answers. Gazing upon the tree, bathed in moonlight, produces this strange misrecognition: the two women 'understanding each other perfectly, creatures of another world, and wondering what they were to do in this one with all this blissful treasure that burned in their bosoms and dropped, in silver flowers, from their hair and hands?'(120–1). Even as Bertha fantasises about their communion, that they together bask in feminine enjoyment, she cannot hold on to the illusion. Did it happen, 'Or did Bertha dream it?' (121). Again, the knowledge fails her; she can only try to accommodate the feeling to phallic desire by hoping to tell Harry about it that night in bed. Yet that hope prompts another hysterical disavowal; she is shocked by a knowledge she had never known before – that she, 'for the first time', actually desires her husband, but this knowledge, which would seem to threaten her enjoyment, to domesticate it as phallic enjoyment, however 'modern', is pushed aside by the cry 'What a pity someone does not play!' (122). Unlike the 'solemn music' of the silences in 'Psychology', here music is invoked as a distraction from the knowledge she has come to possess, but hysterically fears may destroy her own enjoyment.

Although the story seems to move toward the possibility that the unnameable bliss of the title is lesbian desire, the possibility becomes lost in the series of objects that Bertha comes upon in search of a symbolic knowledge that will accommodate her bliss but not snuff it out. As it turns out, the moment of bliss Bertha supposes exists between them is not about their sexual desire for each other. It has always already been compromised, spoiled, by the prerogatives of phallic enjoyment. In another irony, it is her husband's duplicitous boredom and annoyance with Miss Fulton that leads her to confront, as we have seen, the truth of her desire, her sexual desire for him, which terrifies her. Here we see what distinguishes feminine from phallic *jouissance*; her *jouissance* is a an enjoyment of being that can only manifest itself, be granted legitimacy, as a series of semblances, as appearances of feminine desire through marriage, motherhood and masculine desire. If Bertha's enjoyment is real (and I think it is), her hysteria emerges from the fact that her enjoyment is not a bodily, sexual enjoyment, but an enjoyment of being that has no place in the domestic sphere. Because she can only address her enjoyment to semblances, to symbolically sanctioned objects of desire of the kind listed above, she has no choice but to follow the logic of hysterical desire: she must operate within the economy of desire, help to maintain it, even as she moves from object to object, as each of them fails to give her what she really wants. When she discovers that Miss Fulton and Harry are having an affair, it is merely another instance of an object or semblance having failed her, of making her defer yet again finding the truth of her desire. In realising that Harry has betrayed her, in realising, perhaps even more to her horror, that Miss Fulton has betrayed her, Bertha can only ask, 'Oh, what is going to happen now?' (124). Her enjoyment has been stained by her husband's obscene enjoyment, by his summarily and brutally revealing her debased position in relation to his desire. In answering her own question, she turns vainly back to the 'symbol', which, as we have seen, is her symptom. She looks to the pear tree, 'as lovely as ever and full of flower and as still' (124), to see that she is condemned to repeat, to know only in part, to be plagued by the nothing which fuels her enjoyment. This time, though, she has been able to answer a question that had been dogging her: she wanted to know just what that *something* in Miss Fulton's face signified. Now, she knows.

Notes

1. Margaret Scott, ed., *The Katherine Mansfield Notebooks*, 2 vols (Minneapolis: University of Minnesota Press: 2002), Vol. 2, p. 231.
2. John Middleton Murry, ed., *The Scrapbook of Katherine Mansfield* (New York: A. A. Knopf, 1940), p. 170. Mansfield is quoting from a letter from Tolstoy to Chekhov.
3. Jacques Lacan, *The Seminar of Jacques Lacan. Book III: The Psychoses: 1955–1956*, trans. by Russell Grigg and ed. by Jacques-Alain Miller (New York: Norton, 1993), p. 115.
4. Cherry A. Hankin, ed., *Letters Between Katherine Mansfield and John Middleton Murry* (London: Virago Press, 1988), p. 107.
5. Hankin, p. 107.
6. Jacques Lacan, *The Seminar of Jacques Lacan. Book VII. The Ethics of Psychoanalysis: 1959–1960*, trans. by Dennis Porter and ed. by Jacques-Alain Miller (New York: Norton, 1992), p. 57.
7. Kate Fullbrook, *Katherine Mansfield* (Brighton: Harvester Press, 1986), p. 96.
8. Jacques Lacan, *The Seminar of Jacques Lacan: Book I. Freud's Papers on Technique, 1953–1954*, trans. by John Forrester and ed. by Jacques-Alain Miller (New York: Norton, 1991), p. 167.
9. Jacques Lacan, *The Other Side of Psychoanalysis: The Seminar of Jacques Lacan, Book XVII*, trans. by Russell Grigg (New York: Norton, 2007), p. 13. Hereafter cited as *Seminar XVII*.
10. Patricia Moran, *Word of Mouth: Body Language in Katherine Mansfield and Virginia Woolf* (Charlottesville and London: University Press of Virginia, 1996), p. 40.
11. Moran, p. 41.
12. D. M. Davin, ed., *Katherine Mansfield, Selected Stories* (Oxford: Oxford University Press, 1998), p. 111. Hereafter page numbers are cited parenthetically within the text.
13. Much of Lacan's seminar *Encore* is occupied with the task of exploring and explicating the differences between phallic and feminine *jouissance*. For the sake of brevity

and clarity, I have condensed a great deal of abstruse material. See *The Seminar of Jacques Lacan: Book XX Encore, 1972–1973*, trans. by Bruce Fink (New York: Norton, 1999), pp. 7–10, 64–77, 78–89. Hereafter cited as *Encore*.

14. Lacan, *Encore*, p. 73.
15. W. H. New, *Reading Mansfield and Metaphors of Form* (Montreal and Kingston: McGill–Queen's University Press, 1999), p. 74.
16. Lacan, *Encore*, p. 76.
17. Jacques Lacan, *Écrits: The First Complete Edition in English*, trans. by Bruce Fink, Héloïse Fink and Russell Grigg (New York: Norton, 2006), p. 222.
18. Lacan, *Seminar XVII*, p. 23.
19. Colette Soler, *What Lacan Said about Women: A Psychoanalytic Study*, trans. by John Holland (New York: Other Press, 2008), p. 99.

'For the life of him he could not remember': Post-war Memory, Mourning and Masculinity Crisis in Katherine Mansfield's 'The Fly'

Avishek Parui

The First World War had an understandable and immediate impact on the lives and works of all contemporary European writers, but Katherine Mansfield's experiences during the war were perhaps more personal and dramatic than those of most of her peers. Having lost her brother, Leslie, who died in a grenade explosion in the war, and having had a stormy love affair in February 1915 with Francis Carco – a French poet and soldier – while illegally travelling to the occupied zone at Grey, Mansfield's existential experiences of loss emerging out of the war throw significant light on the craft and content of her short fiction.[1] Her experience of trauma at the heart of a city is evinced in many accounts. In a letter written to John Middleton Murry on 2 April 1918 from Paris, Mansfield described the visual and auditory effect of gunfire in the street and the grotesque spectacle that followed:

> Gunfire last evening – and at 3:15 this morning one woke to hear the air screaming. That is the effect of these sirens; they have a most diabolical sound. I dressed and went down to the *cave* . . . I got up again and went to look. Very ugly, very horrible. The whole top of a house as it were bitten out – all the windows broken, and the road of course covered with ruin.[2]

The description underlines the increasing internalisation of trauma and nervous anxiety at the heart of a wartime city. As Mary Burgan argues in an analysis of Mansfield's literary representation of war à propos her personal loss and existential mourning, the wartime horrors 'actually enabled her to rework the past out of fragments of memory, dreams, and an eventual understanding of the origins of her destabilizing anxieties'.[3] Such modes of representation, with their liminality and psychological intensity, were perhaps best suited to the formal quality

113

of the short story, which can crystallise memory and embodied experiences in episodic and epiphanic narrative frames.

Written in February 1922 during a sojourn at the Victoria Palace hotel in Paris, where Mansfield had gone for X-ray treatment with Dr Ivan Manoukhin, 'The Fly' is widely regarded as one of the most psychological representations of repression and loss in First World War fiction, and as a story which also approximates Mansfield's own complex relationship with her father and her response to her brother's death in the war.[4] A condensed narrative about death, decadence and denial, 'The Fly' is a depiction of post-war mourning and the masculinity crisis at the heart of the modern metropolis, and at the same time an exploration of the ritual of memory preservation inside the closeted space of the modern office. The effort of resistance to trauma in the story is enacted by an authoritative figure who wants to preserve the phallogocentric order through a strategic system of remembrance and orchestrated rituals of pseudo-hysterical mourning. 'The Fly' probes into the privilege of the pseudo-hysteric, who attempts to maintain the phallogocentric economy with its triumph over time by seeking to relive and replay the original moment of loss. Like the erotic economy of male homosexuality that is anxiously articulated in *fin-de-siècle* fiction on the perceived masculinity crisis, evinced in texts such as *The Picture of Dorian Gray* (1890), the pseudo-hysteria of the boss in 'The Fly' emerges as a psychological drama and a failure of the ritual of remembrance and retention. The hysteria at the end of the short story is paradoxically constituted by its absence and the failure of the masculinist memory-project of preservation.

It may be argued that the mode of mourning that the boss in Mansfield's story seeks to enact by locking himself up in his office space and staring at his dead son's photo is essentially masturbatory, with its compulsory economy of secrecy, shame and satisfaction. The erotic economy of release informing the pseudo-hysterical performance is hinted at by the sadomasochistic pleasure the boss initially derives during the fly episode after his last attempt at weeping. The emasculation that the boss experiences at the end of the story corresponds to his current inability to weep at will because of the loss of his son, an inability that corresponds paradoxically to an inability to assert his masculinity through a strategic mode of memory and mourning. The lack of grief in the boss's masculinist economy thus corresponds to a failure of phallic performance. Thus, 'The Fly' may be considered as a complex depiction of pseudo-hysteria and the failed possibilities of cathartic mourning in a post-war metropolis. It emerges as an entanglement of public architectures of post-war memory and private strategies of self-preservation. It dramatises the masculinity crisis it conveys by juxtaposing women who travel to the memorials of loss and move on, and men who cannot and do not.

Jay Winter's study of the culture of remembering through the construction of memorials examines how the commercially shared architecture of loss addresses the mourner, who is also the consumer. The vocabulary of collective mourning through public memorials is constituted by the emotional, as well as the commercial, orders:

> Despite powerful currents of feeling about the need to express the indebtedness of the living to the fallen and the near-universality of loss in many parts of Europe, commemoration was and remained a business, in which sculptors, artists, bureaucrats, churchmen, and ordinary people had to strike an agreement and carry it out.[5]

Specific pilgrimages to the sites of mourning were co-terminous with the culture of tourism that emerged at the end of the First World War as more and more women travelled on their own to the sites of loss and memorials of mourning. The ritual of mourning-travel, swiftly transforming into the discourse of commercial tourism, connected the economy of the emotions to the traffic of commerce after the war. The site of death and the site of tourism conflate and mingle seamlessly in Mansfield's 'The Fly' as symptomatic of the contingent totems of loss and leisure in a decadent demography of dead sons and mourning fathers. As Eric Leed argues in his work on post-war rituals of remembrance:

> the earliest tours to the front in 1919 and 1920 were sold as opportunities to visit the site of destruction and chaos, while through the 1920s touristic pilgrimages to the front were organized to visit the graves of the fallen. The memory of the dead replaced the memory of the war, the human relations that killed them.[6]

In its dramatisation of post-war memory, mourning and masculinity crisis, 'The Fly' depicts old Woodifield, whose 'girls' keep him 'boxed up in the house every day of the week except Tuesday' and travel on their own to visit the dead son's grave in Belgium, haggle over the price of jam in the hotel, and bring back the jam pots 'in order to teach them a lesson' because the hotels with their prices are felt to 'trade' on the women's feelings.[7] The trade-off between tourism and post-war mourning is mediated through a network of rituals that preserved the memory of loss, as well as changing it into a consumable commodity. Thus Woodifield gives his description of the graves to the boss: 'There's miles of it, and it's all as neat as a garden. Flowers growing on all the graves. Nice broad paths' (530). The endlessness indicated in the description emerges as the dead soldiers' graves merge seamlessly with the scenery and the memorials that are the focus of tourist visits.

As Ariela Freedman argues in her analysis of the epistemology of tragedy in the post-war imagination,

> For the early twentieth century, tragedy wears a male face. The face of the disaster is the face of a dead young man: with a cap and a uniform, he is a soldier, with a crown of thorns, he is a God. He is the culmination of masculinity, and at the same time, the sign of its decline.[8]

The trauma of the First World War transformed hysteria from a commonly conceived female malady to a form of masculinity crisis often embodied by soldiers: a condition which had to be differentiated from hysteria by the pseudo-medical term 'shell shock'. Post-war trauma and experiences of loss reconfigured the received notions of manly strength and feminine weakness, of male control and female anxiety. The women in Mansfield's 'The Fly' appear as enterprising travellers reporting on the memorials of mourning to fathers who are 'boxed up' in houses and unreal offices. If the 'boss' appears misogynistically manly and in control at the beginning of the story – passing condescending comments on the ability of women to understand while pouring whisky with a wink for the senile and shaken Woodifield – he becomes increasingly unsettled and defeated in the course of the narrative. His symbolic emasculation is enacted through the failure of his private mourning-project to re-live the loss of his son's death in the war. It is rendered clinically complete with his inability to remember his thoughts, an experience of emptiness with which the story ends.

Travelling to Belgium to see the 'boys' graves' (530), the women in Mansfield's story are external to the space of loss that consumes the nervous men who have inherited death from their sons. 'The Fly' thus presents a paradigm of hysteria through a reconfiguration of received notions of gender. The figure of the boss – the strong, silent man, embodying the Victorian and Edwardian ideal of masculinity – exists on the same map of loss as that of 'old Woodifield', who shakes and develops patches above his beard in his struggle to remember the news of his dead son. The experience of loss is re-articulated and remembered by the women, who travel together and visit the sites and memorials of mourning, while the men inhabit an entanglement of denial and forgetfulness. The language of loss and the vocabulary of shock are thus symptomatic of a broader narrative of melancholia and post-war masculinity crisis.

'The Fly' opens with the voice of senility that carries an almost grudging admiration for a man who, despite his age, seems to have perpetuated his manly control by constructing a space of machines that ritualise efficiency and newness:

> 'Y'are very snug in here', piped old Mr Woodifield, and he peered out of the great, green leather armchair by his friend the boss's desk as a baby peers out of his pram.
>
> [. . .]
>
> 'Yes, it's comfortable enough,' agreed the boss, and he flipped the *Financial Times* with a paper-knife. As a matter of fact he was proud of his room; he liked to have it admired, especially by old Woodifield. It gave him a feeling of deep, solid satisfaction to be planted there in the midst of it in full view of that frail old figure in the muffler. (529–30)

The opening thus reveals a solid bourgeois space that exhibits its signifiers of control and newness. With the new carpet, new furniture and new electric heating in his office, the masculine authority of the boss stands in stark and deliberate contrast to the feeble senility of Woodifield, who embodies the infantilisation of the castrated male through the continuous connections the narrative makes with the baby image. The phallogocentric economy in the opening of the story is neatly localised in the body of the boss – who is five years older than Woodifield but 'still at the helm, still going strong' (530) – and accentuated by the signifiers of the paper-knife, the electric heating and the *Financial Times*.

The narrative voice then sharply and almost surreptitiously draws attention to the close-up on an object that is not displayed by the self-congratulatory voice of masculinity: a photograph of a grave-looking, uniformed young man that has been on the table for over six years, the photograph that emerges as a signifier of loss and its corresponding masculinity crisis in the story. The photograph carries the characteristic setting of 'the spectral photographers' parks with photographers' storm clouds' (530) to dramatise the darkness of the war, for which it was supposed to stand as a formal and iconic signifier. It is interesting to observe that Mansfield described the photo studios in her journal as 'the most *temporary shelters* on earth'.[9] The temporality and constructed quality of the photo studio and the permanence of the photograph produced out of it both become bearers of the endless entanglement of loss and replication in an age of mechanical reproduction where the 'technological recording of the real entered into competition with the symbolic registration of the Symbolic'.[10] As revealed to the reader soon enough, the photograph of his dead son embodies the traumatic memory of the boss, hidden among the objects of compulsive newness in his office, as the strategic signifier of 'that unwitting re-enactment of an event that one cannot leave behind'.[11]

The image of castrated masculinity in 'The Fly' not only is evident in the character of Woodifield, who is allowed to go to the City only on Tuesdays, according to the rules set by his wife and daughters, but also is seen in the boss, who uses the privacy of his office space to ritualise his mourning through the totem of his dead son's photograph. The boss's 'Ah, that's where we know a bit more than the ladies' (530) emerges as a presumptuous and preposterous statement of superiority in a culture of mourning where senile survivors inherit loss from their dead sons. In effect, the 'boss' and Woodifield in Mansfield's story embody the *Menschenleere*, the German term that entered the war vocabulary to denote a sense of being utterly abandoned through an experience that is a combination of resignation, renunciation and humiliation.[12] In a letter written to Sydney and Violet Schiff in May 1920, Mansfield describes the dweller in the post-war metropolis in an image reminiscent of the crowds of undone faces in Eliot's *The Waste Land*: 'Yesterday I drove down to the city to my Bank. It was almost terrifying to see such blank strained faces – moving in the fog.'[13] The disorder and the numbness characteristic of the city after the war can be read as signifiers of the collective neurosis born out of the war itself. The memory of Woodifield emerges as functional only under whisky-induced stimulation as he struggles to remember the scene of his son's grave. In its entanglement of forgetting and selective remembering, memory in 'The Fly' becomes a signifier of a decadent recall and a failed project of private mourning.

In his case study of hysteria through the figure of Irene, the French neurologist Pierre Janet distinguished two modes of memory: the traumatic memory that is essentially non-adaptive and non-integrative to the daily discourses around one's life, and the narrative memory that proceeds and functions as a social act integrating and incorporating the social phenomena around the remembering subject. While the normal narrative memory operates in continuation with the temporality and the narrative of logic around oneself, the traumatic memory is triggered by a particular object or act that replicates the original horror of the loss. The first to introduce the term *traumatic memory* to medical parlance, Janet classifies the triggering object or situation that produces traumatic memory as *restitutio ad integrum*, the objective correlative to the original experience of horror.[14] Eric Leed's analysis of the difference between traumatic and narrative memory underlines the voluntary and involuntary processes informing the nature of recall:

The traumatic memory recurs involuntarily against the wishes of the rememberer, in contrast to our studied efforts to remember what we have forgotten or dreaming reverie. In the traumatic memory the past defines and determines the present actions and thinking of the rememberer, whereas in normal remembering the needs of the present determine what is called up associationally from the past.[15]

'The Fly' exhibits Janet's descriptions of traumatic and narrative memory in its depiction of two male figures – the boss and Woodifield – and eventually dissolves away the borderlines between the two. Thus while Woodifield revisits his son's death with a nonchalant narrative that describes the price of jam in the hotel and the scenic quality of the war graves in Belgium, the boss's negotiations with his son's death and his refusal to remember the same except as a traumatic memory emerge as an arrogant and masculinist preservation project through which his ego is sustained and perpetuated.

Mansfield's story makes continual connections between the social position of the boss and the perverse privilege he associates with his traumatic memory: 'Other men perhaps might recover, might live their loss down, but not he' (532). The boss in Mansfield's story, in effect, tries to ritualise and remember his experience of loss by shutting himself in the enclosed space of his office, covering his face with his hands, uttering his chosen vocabulary – 'My Son!' – and lastly, by staring at the photograph of his dead son. The narrative dramatises the ritual of conjuring up his traumatic memory and the constructed quality that goes into its making: 'The door shut, the firm heavy steps recrossed the bright carpet, the fat body plumped down in the spring chair, and leaning forward, the boss covered his face with his hands. He wanted, he intended, he had arranged to weep . . .' (532).

The almost automatic causal connection between the reified rhetoric and the privileged position in grief is neatly asserted in the boss's mind, for earlier 'he had only to say those words to be overcome by such grief that nothing short of a violent fit of weeping could relieve him' (532). The politics of precision and the strategy of catharsis that the boss follows to hystericise himself systematically are in sharp contrast to the spontaneity and involuntary quality of traumatic memory. 'The Fly' is a scathing critique of orchestrated and arrogant attempts at self-preservation, attempts which are not discursively dissimilar to the phallogocentric principles of control and expansion that had historically informed the war. Thus the traumatic memory of the boss, one which he seeks to internalise permanently as a perverse pointer to manly strength and status, emerges as increasingly effaced in a symbolic castration process that adversely affects his private and practised rituals of memory and mourning. This dramatises an erasure of the traumatic memory and a fall in the emotional register from the truly tragic order of experience to the pathetically overdone orchestra of repetition.

Like the erotic economy of male homosexuality that is anxiously closeted and articulated in *The Picture of Dorian Gray*, which uses the liminality of the attic space to preserve the politics of masculine beauty and control, the hysteria of the boss emerges as a secret drama and a ritual of retention that is used to perpetuate the phallogocentric principle. The closeted space, where the boss shuts himself in for a satisfactory recall of his traumatic memory, becomes what Slavoj Žižek describes as the 'hysterical theatre',[16] a space where the pseudo-hysterical subject dramatises his position in order to articulate the rhetoric of his loss for a cathartic and masturbatory release. By locating himself inside a private space in order to enact his grief, the boss appropriates, as well as mimics, the vocabulary of the hysteric through the constructed quality of his performative mourning. Like the decadent portrait of Dorian Gray, the picture of the dead son in the boss's office serves as a signifier of loss that is revisited privately in order to retain and reify his phallic authority in the public space of significations. The anxiety in the boss's politics of preservation emerges as a post-violence discourse of remembrance that is threatened only when the subject fails to hystericise himself through his reified rituals. The position of privilege is problematised in Mansfield's story through post-war mourning and the anxiety of remembering and retention, issues which inform the masculinity crisis in the post-war metropolis.

Unsurprisingly, the disclosure of the traumatic memory of loss in Mansfield's story is described in characteristically Freudian metaphors:

> It had been a terrible shock to him when old Woodifield sprang that remark upon him about the boy's grave. It was exactly as though the earth had opened and he had seen the boy lying there with Woodifield's girls staring down at him. For it was strange. Although over six years had passed away, the boss never thought of the boy except as lying unchanged, unblemished in his uniform, asleep for ever. (532)

The image of the grave opening up and the female gaze directed towards the dead male may be read as the visual horror of the masculinity crisis at the end of the war that appropriates a necromantic order of mourning, the Medusa stare at castrated masculinity. But what emerges as more significant in the description is the fixation with the unchanged and unblemished body of traumatic memory that corresponds to the fixity of the photographic body of the dead son. In effect, the boss in 'The Fly' orchestrates a ritual of his loss by constructing his private cult of mourning, enacting what Derrida defines as an attempt to 'ontologize remains, to make them present'.[17] Mansfield's story is an unsettling narrative of the failure of such a process of ontologisation that appropriates masculinist rituals of control and containment.

In *Inhibitions, Symptoms and Anxiety* (1926), one of his late works on trauma, Freud analysed Janet's notion of traumatic memory and the compulsive nature of the traumatic mind, whose desire to repeat the original trauma was, in Freud's view, in itself a function of repression. The 'various reasons' why the boss had not been to see the grave of his son correspond to Freud's analysis of repression in the traumatic mind that refuses to encounter the loss in its consciousness:

> We found that the perceptual content of the exciting experiences and the ideational content of pathogenic structures of thought were forgotten and debarred from being reproduced in memory, and we therefore concluded that the keeping away from consciousness was the main characteristic of hysterical repression.[18]

The citadel of newness the boss has constructed around himself in his office corresponds to his refusal to visit the geographical site of his loss, the miles of graves in Belgium that mingle seamlessly with the signifier of tourism and its associated commodities in the public discourses of post-war Europe. The boss's refusal to remember the loss of his son except in its original experience of trauma also corresponds to an order of repression, as analysed by Freud, as a state whereby the mind 'is obliged to repeat the repressed material as a contemporary experience, instead of [. . .] remembering it as something belonging to the past'.[19]

The fly episode in the story, where the boss drops a blot of ink on a fly three times and also helps it dry itself, may be read as a classic Freudian drama of projection and transference. But it also emerges as a scene of closet hysteria, whereby the discourse of destruction enacted by the war enters the private bourgeois space and deconstructs the division between the subject and the object. This is done by an endless entanglement of machines of destruction and machines of reproduction that blur the borderlines between preservation and violence, informing the nervous condition that characterises modern metropolitan man. The telegram that had conveyed the news of his son's death to the boss is itself a construct of the typewriter that Friedrich Kittler classified as a 'discursive machine gun. A technology whose basic action not coincidentally consists of strikes and triggers proceeds in automated and discreet steps, as does ammunitions transport in a revolver or machine gun, or celluloid transport in a film projector.'[20] The anonymous urban citizen thus enacts the trauma of the trench on an object that also becomes the subject enacting his own ego. An inset drama within the decadent drama of hystericisation, the fly episode emerges as a sadomasochistic show whereby the Lacanian *fundamental fantasy* that Žižek classifies as inter-passive is enacted through the contingent space where a 'scene of passive suffering (subjection) is staged which simultaneously sustains and threatens the subject's being'.[21]

The fly episode enacts a Freudian shift from mourning to melancholia that constitutes an exhaustion of the subject's ego through a failed fixation on an object that eventually subsumes the ego of the subject.[22] Having failed to attain his cathartic weeping despite looking at his dead son's photograph and groaning at it, the boss notices a fly struggling to emerge out of his inkpot. He helps it out with his pen and places it on a piece of blotting paper. After the fly wriggles itself dry, he drops a blot of ink on it to test if it will survive. It does through a laborious process; the imagery used by Mansfield here is deliberately Sisyphean, with the fly's leg moving along its wing in the way that a stone goes over and under a scythe till it 'was ready for life again' (533). The boss finds himself admiringly attracted to the fly's ability to survive shocks, in a perverse imaginary where he is both the victim and the cruel god. He drops another blot of ink on the fly after it dries itself for the second time. He waits with anxious suspense till the fly begins to dry itself again in a way that appears visibly weaker and more timid. In keeping with the dual role of torturer and sufferer, the boss actually breathes on it in order to help its drying process while addressing it as an 'artful little bastard' (533). In a psychological sadomasochistic drama of simultaneous projection and internalisation, the boss establishes empathy with the 'plucky little devil' in its manly spirit to survive the shocks in life. The third blot of ink that the boss drops on the fly kills it and, as it lies dead, the boss makes a desperate attempt to bring it to life: '"Come on", said the boss. "Look sharp!" And he stirred it with his pen – in vain. Nothing happened or was likely to happen. The fly was dead' (533).

The fly episode may be read as a desperate attempt on the part of the boss to reassert and recover his masculine control, with the fly emerging as a metonymic projection of his manly struggle to survive his son's death and move on through a strategic method of memory and pseudo-hysterical mourning. The failure of the fly appears totemic in relation to the failure of the boss, and thus the boss emerges after the death of the fly with an experience of emptiness characterising the Freudian melancholic subject: 'such a gnawing feeling of wretchedness seized him that he felt positively frightened' (533). The telos of torture that the boss enacts on the fly may be read as a pathetic attempt to regain an existential control whose closure corresponds closely to the experience of masculinity crisis and loss of privileged traumatic memory. The effect of the episode comes to assume the political contingency of its time and may be read along the lines of Žižek's analysis of the shift from perversion to hysteria. Examining the experiential difference between hysteria and perversion, Žižek argues that

> the pervert precludes the Unconscious because he knows the answer (to what brings *jouissance*, to the Other); he has no doubts about it; his position is unshakeable; while the hysteric doubts – that is, her position is that of an eternal and constitutive (self) questioning: What does the Other want from me? What am I for the Other?[23]

The practised ritual of hysteria that the boss has enacted thus far can be seen as a performance in perversion, of a position of certainty enacted by the rituals of remembrance. The failed pseudo-hysteria thus emerges as a paradoxical move into the true hysterical space with the uncertainty and ambivalence that accompany the process.

The failure of the boss to remember the original trauma of his loss despite the perfected rituals inside his private space is a pointer to the paradigm shift in memory. The hysteria at the end of 'The Fly' is thus paradoxically constituted by its absence and the failure of its programmed performance. The politics of remembering and the politics of gender (re)formation are complexly welded in Mansfield's story through the contingent location of the masculinist hysterical performance. The entanglement of hysteria and private remembrance is inflected by the contingency about gender roles in the post-war metropolis. The failed preservation project of the boss to retain the masculinity of his private and privileged grief extends on to 'the struggle of memory against forgetting'.[24] The fly dies with the boss's ego, which had retained the privileged position of the traumatic rememberer; at the end of it all, the boss cannot relocate or recall his remembering self, which is now permanently lost to him. Along with his closely guarded and protected traumatic memory, the boss also seems to have lost his ordinary narrative memory as he struggles to remember what it was he had been thinking of before he spotted the fly in the inkpot. A perfect little piece on post-war memory, mourning and masculinity crisis, as well as a critique of the hubris of the phallogocentric order of reified self-preservation and systematic denial, Mansfield's short story draws to a close with a psychological and existential entanglement of confusion, contingency and closure as the boss awakens, shaken and emptied out after the death of the fly: 'For the life of him, he could not remember' (533).

Notes

1. See Mary Burgan, *Illness, Gender and Writing: The Case of Katherine Mansfield* (Baltimore: Johns Hopkins University Press, 1994); and Patrick Morrow, 'Katherine Mansfield and World War I', in *Literature and War* (Amsterdam: Atlanta, 1990), ed. by

David Bevan, pp. 39–44. For a biographical account of Mansfield's affair with Carco, see Gerri Kimber, *Katherine Mansfield: The View from France* (New York: Peter Lang, 2008), pp. 63–75.
2. C. K. Stead, ed., *The Letters and Journals of Katherine Mansfield* (London: Penguin, 1977), p. 108.
3. Burgan, p. 90.
4. It may be argued that the imperious and overly masculine 'boss' and his dead son in 'The Fly' are thinly disguised descriptions of Mansfield's banker father, Harold Beauchamp, and her brother, Leslie Heron Beauchamp.
5. Jay Winter, *Sites of Memory, Sites of Mourning: The Great War in European Cultural History* (Cambridge: Cambridge University Press, 1995), p. 86.
6. Eric Leed, 'Fateful Memories: Industrialized War and Traumatic Neurosis', *Journal of Contemporary History*, 35 (2000), pp. 85–100 (p. 93).
7. Katherine Mansfield, 'The Fly', in Antony Alpers, ed., *The Stories of Katherine Mansfield* (Oxford: Oxford University Press, 1984), pp. 530–2 (p. 530). Hereafter page numbers are placed parenthetically in the text.
8. Ariela Freedman, *Death, Men and Modernism: Trauma and Narrative in British Fiction from Hardy to Woolf* (New York: Routledge, 2003), p. 3.
9. Stead, p. 199.
10. Friedrich Kittler, *Discourse Networks 1800/1900*, trans. by Michael Metteer and Chris Cullens (Stanford: Stanford University Press, 1990), pp. 229–30.
11. Cathy Caruth, *Unclaimed Experiences: Trauma, Narrative and History* (Baltimore and London: Johns Hopkins University Press, 1996), p. 2.
12. Eric Leed, *No Man's Land: Combat and Identity in World War I* (Cambridge: Cambridge University Press, 1981), pp. 19–20.
13. Stead, p. 174.
14. Pierre Janet, *L'Évolution de la mémoire et la notion du temps* (Paris: Cahine, 1928), pp. 207–8.
15. Eric Leed, 'Fateful Memories', p. 87.
16. Slavoj Žižek, *For They Know Not What They Do: Enjoyment as a Political Factor* (London: Verso, 1991), p. 143.
17. Jacques Derrida, *Spectres of Marx: The State of the Debt, the Work of Mourning and the New International*, trans. by Peggy Kamuf (London and New York: Routledge, 1994), p. 30.
18. James Strachey, ed., *The Standard Edition of the Complete Psychological Works of Sigmund Freud*, 24 vols (London: Hogarth Press, 1957), Vol. 20, p. 163.
19. Strachey, Vol. 18, p. 18.
20. Friedrich Kittler, *Gramophone, Film, Typewriter*, trans. by Geoffrey Winthrop-Young and Michael Wutz (Stanford: Stanford University Press, 1999), p. 191.
21. Slavoj Žižek, *The Ticklish Subject: The Absent Centre of Political Ontology* (London: Verso, 2000), p. 265.
22. Sigmund Freud, 'Mourning and Melancholia', in Peter Gay, ed., *The Freud Reader* (New York and London: Norton & Company, 1989), pp. 584–8.
23. Žižek, *The Ticklish Subject*, p. 248.
24. Milan Kundera, *The Book of Laughter and Forgetting*, trans. by Aaron Asher (London: Faber & Faber, 1996), p. 4.

CREATIVE WRITING

SHORT STORY
Isn't It
[after 'The Garden Party']

Paula Morris

At first people thought Uncle Jack had been killed in a hit-and-run, mowed down crossing the road near the May Road dairy. That was what Lorenzo heard in the first delirious phone calls from his mother: Uncle Jack had been mown down, and it was a brutal, heartless and sadistic act, no doubt perpetrated by someone twenty-one and Chinese in a brand new car with a learner's licence and no insurance.

In fact, Uncle Jack had just collapsed while crossing the street and died from a heart attack. This was explained in the second wave of phone calls. Cigarettes killed him, and cream on his porridge, and old age. He was eighty-six, and on his way to buy a Lotto ticket.

'Thinking of us', said Lorenzo's mother, 'right to the end.'

'What do you mean?' asked Lorenzo. He imagined murmured last words, overheard by Good Samaritans kneeling at the side of his great-uncle's frail, crumpled body.

'Well, he didn't need the money, did he?' said Lorenzo's mother. 'What would he have done with it, if he'd won?'

Gone to Bali, Lorenzo suspected. Last year one of Uncle Jack's RSA friends had gone to Bali for the first time, aged seventy-eight, and returned with news of a much younger girlfriend. He'd sent her and her family almost ten thousand dollars before his grown-up children got wind of it, and changed his mobile phone number so the girlfriend in Bali had no way of tracking him down.

'Uncle Jack was always thinking of us,' said Lorenzo's mother. She was ringing Lorenzo from the big New World because they would be needing food, huge amounts of it, when the undertakers brought Uncle Jack back to the house. He would lie there in his coffin for three days, and people would need to be fed.

'Why was he walking all the way to the May Road dairy?' asked Lorenzo,

127

because part of him still wanted to believe there was something suspi-cious about all this, something needing investigation and possibly a visit from TV3 News.

'We'll never know,' said his mother. 'This trolley squeaks. Why do I always get the bad trolleys? They spend all this money on a big new supermarket, and the trolleys are already useless.'

She seemed to be crying, or else holding the phone to the trolley so he could hear it squeaking. Lorenzo did what he always did when his mother – or anyone, really – started to cry during telephone conversa-tions. He'd tell her that her voice was breaking up, or that he was walking or driving through a tunnel. Then, mid-sentence, he'd disconnect the call. That way it would seem as though they'd been cut off. His mother never rang back, as though she knew the truth, that he'd hung up on her. Hung up on himself, really. Lorenzo often hung up on himself.

He'd never hung up on Uncle Jack, or hung up on himself while talking to Uncle Jack, and this was a relief right now. He wouldn't have to go through life tormented with guilt because he had betrayed Uncle Jack with phone-call deceit. This was mainly because Uncle Jack was too deaf for phone calls. Even if he'd won Lotto and gone to Bali and found himself a much younger girlfriend, she'd never have been able to ring him in New Zealand to arrange a ten-thousand-dollar money transfer.

Lorenzo reported his mother's side of the conversation to his cousin, May, who was driving him home from the airport. He'd been down in Wellington for two days of meetings and he could have paid for a taxi home on expenses, but May had insisted on picking him up.

'Your mum's in an emotional state,' May told him. 'It's a very emotional time.'

'What does that even mean?' Lorenzo asked. All times were emotional for his mother.

'You know she always gets anxious when lots of people are coming over. Death is much worse than a marriage, say, or even a new baby. Everyone turns up pretending to pay their respects, wanting a massive feed. And there's no garden any more, so everyone'll be squeezed into the house, getting on her nerves.'

This was true. Lorenzo's mother had rented the small brick-and-tile house in Mt Roskill for five years, ever since his father had moved to the Gold Coast with a woman named Vicky. Relatives over sixty referred to Vicky as Lorenzo's father's Fancy Piece, but she was, in fact, his Life Coach and now – as Lorenzo's father insisted on calling her – his Life Partner.

Two years ago, the owner of the Mt Roskill house subdivided the garden so another, bigger house could be built at the back. This new house was 'Tuscan', according to Lorenzo's mother and her landlord, maybe because it was painted the colour of an apricot or an orange or a peach – naming colours wasn't Lorenzo's strong suit – and because its roof was flat, as though the weather in Mt Roskill was sunny and dry like the weather in Tuscany. It was a stupid and stupidly expensive house, in Lorenzo's opinion, with a big garage and high walls. The looming presence of the House Behind, as they called it, meant that Lorenzo's mother only got sun after three in the afternoon, and her back garden was barely deep enough for a washing line.

'Speaking of babies,' said May, though nobody had been speaking at all for several minutes. 'I went to see the doctor again about why we're not having them. You know, me and Tony.'

'You don't have to tell me anything personal,' said Lorenzo. This was not the kind of anecdote he wanted to hear from anyone – not a cousin or sister, not a girlfriend. No woman at all needed to confide such a thing in him, at any point. He knew he should have caught a taxi home.

'Because there's nothing wrong with me and there's nothing wrong with Tony,' May continued, changing lanes in her usual erratic way. 'According to the specialists.'

'It's a very emotional time,' Lorenzo said, and hoped that would be the end of it. Agreeing with people, he found, sometimes shut them up.

'Well, this has been going on for two years,' said May. 'So I went back to see my doctor, and you know what he said? That I may have a womb that repels sperm.'

Lorenzo said nothing. He'd remembered, too late, that agreeing with women just encouraged them to divulge more.

'I kind of like that,' May said. 'A sperm-repelling womb! I've had a superpower all these years and never realised it.'

Lorenzo still said nothing. You couldn't hang up on yourself when you were sitting next to the other person in the car. For the first time in his life, he wished he was in a meeting in Wellington.

'A sperm-repelling womb,' May said again, lingering over every word, and he realised she was saying all this to wind him up.

'I guess I'm still really preoccupied with Uncle Jack,' he said, looking straight ahead. 'I'm just really . . . sad.'

'Liar,' said May. 'Uncle Jack had a good run. It was amazing he lasted as long as he did, with all that smoking and drinking. Not to mention the dairy products.'

She swerved into Lorenzo's street, and he gripped the handles of his bag, ready to leap out.

'He looked pretty good, really, all things considered,' May was saying.

'According to Mum, it's because he never had children. Children age you, apparently. Not that we'll ever know, eh? Me and you. Though it's not too late for you. Biologically, men can go on until – '

'Thanks for the lift!' Lorenzo said, opening the door even though the car was still in motion. 'See you tomorrow.'

'I'll be dressed as Wonder Woman,' May called after him. Her voice was clear and loud, so she must have buzzed the windows down. That was always the thing with May: she didn't care who heard things. If Uncle Jack were still alive, she'd be shouting away at him tomorrow about her sperm-repelling womb, determined that he heard every word, not content until she made him choke on his tea.

Uncle Jack was lying in his coffin on the spare bed, looking small and spindly. He didn't smell of smoke any more, and he didn't look anything much like the framed old pictures of him arranged around the spare room. He'd looked so wily and nimble, once upon a time, Lorenzo thought. He'd looked like a man of the world. In three of the old photographs, he had slicked-back hair and was wearing tennis whites, in the manner of some European playboy. Lorenzo tried to imagine the photos they'd pick if Lorenzo himself were laid out on the spare bed. He'd be dressed in a rumpled suit in most of them, pictured with long-forgotten colleagues while attending a product launch or strategic away-day. His shoes would be unpolished. He'd be wearing a lanyard or name badge. He'd probably have red-eye.

May was talking to someone in the hallway, offering up her car as coffin transportation on Monday. A hearse was unnecessary. A rip-off, she announced, and Lorenzo agreed. It was bad enough that the under-taker appeared to be holding the coffin lid to ransom. Lorenzo wasn't sure why. Couldn't their family be trusted with the lid? Hadn't they paid a large sum of money for it?

'He'll bring it round on Monday,' said Lorenzo's mother. He'd sought her out in the kitchen, where she was rearranging the freezer to accommodate a tinfoil pan of lasagne from Mrs Devich across the road. 'We don't need it until then. You always worry about the wrong things.'

What he should be worried about, according to his mother and the huddle of hairsprayed aunties monopolising the kettle, was the party going on that day at the House Behind.

'They've got a sign up on the driveway! With balloons!' This was Auntie Joan, May's mother. She was morally opposed to the subdivision of sections, and had written various letters to the *Herald* advocating a high-speed commuter train to Whangarei and/or Hamilton, effective immediately, to relieve the housing crisis in Auckland.

'It says "This Way to the Garden Party",' said Auntie Sila, who wasn't a relative but had lived two doors down from them in the street where Lorenzo had grown up. 'While we've got a funeral on here, the curtains drawn. It's disrespectful.'

'The funeral's not until Monday,' Lorenzo pointed out, and the aunties rose up, bristling like furious sparrows, and told him not to split hairs. They were all getting smaller as they aged, he'd noticed, but they were also louder and fluffier, inflating with every new small outrage.

'You need to go up there and tell them that we've had a tragic loss here, that a respected kaumatua has died, and that –'

'Yes, yes,' said Lorenzo. 'It's an emotional time.'

'It's Wellington that's done this to him,' one of the aunties complained to the others, and he left the room.

Lorenzo stood for a while on the front steps, blinking in the sun. He wasn't sure what he was supposed to say to the people in the House Behind. He couldn't ask them to cancel their garden party because Uncle Jack had keeled over en route to the dairy, in an unsurprising and non-tragic way, and was lying in the spare room until Monday, being visited by everyone they'd ever known, as well as a Ratana minister and a cluster of watchful Mormons. Probably the House Behind people – not neighbours exactly, not yet – had planned this party for weeks or even months. They would be happy that the weather was so good, that it was as sunny and cloudless today as it was, presumably, in Tuscany all the time.

But the aunties were right, in a way. Lorenzo saw the new houses of the neighbourhood, hidden away like citadels at the end of long, secretive driveways, as inhabiting an entirely different place. Those people drove different cars, ate different food, sent their children to different schools. They weren't so much joining the community as colonising it. Soon all the little houses would be bulldozed and a new Tuscany would rise up in its place, dreamy pastel townhouses encircling the scrubby green maunga like some medieval hill town. And all the aunties and uncles and cousins, their superettes and fabric stores and takeaways, their schools and churches and mobile health centres, would be packed into the high-speed trains to Whangarei and/or Hamilton, where land cost less and people were still allowed to have gardens and low wages.

May emerged from the open front door, pulling on her shoes. She wasn't dressed as Wonder Woman after all; she was all in black, the clothes she wore every day.

'If you're going up there, I'll come with you,' she told him. 'I'd like to have a nose around that place.'

'It's not an Open Home,' he said, but he didn't really object to May coming along. When they were growing up, she'd always been the tough one, protecting him from the attacking batallions of other cousins. Recently she'd started studying part-time to get a Legal Executive Diploma, and he'd tried a couple of times to talk her into going to university instead, to become an actual lawyer. It was too much money, May said; she and Tony were saving to buy a home unit like the one they lived in now, except in a neighbourhood that was even scruffier and further away.

'We could rip down their sign and the balloons,' she suggested. 'Or I could cry. Do some keening and wailing. Collapse on their doorstep.'

'No crying,' Lorenzo said, though he had no better ideas. He stepped out of the way so eight members of the Tigafua family could make their way up the stairs and through the front door. His mother would be pleased, because they were carrying a large amount of food, because they'd left the smallest children at home, and because their presence here today, a delegation from all the way around the corner, was a sign of respect to Uncle Jack.

Someone else was lingering in the wake of the Tigafua family, a tall blonde girl clutching a fabric shopping bag from Nosh.

'Hi,' she said, looking from Lorenzo to May. 'I live – up there. Round the back.'

The House Behind, Lorenzo wanted to say, but he said nothing, and neither did May. The girl was in her twenties, he guessed, but she was dressed like someone from a World War II movie, in a tailored floral dress, her fair hair in smooth waves the shape of sausage rolls. Her lipstick was bright red.

'We heard about your – uncle, is it? The undertaker was blocking our driveway. I mean, it wasn't a problem.'

'Great-uncle,' said May. 'Our great-uncle Jack has died.'

The tone of her voice made it sound such a dignified thing. Lorenzo was impressed.

'Really, so sorry.' The girl was flushed. 'It's awful. Very sad. And I just wanted to say, I'm sorry that today of all days we're having a party. A stupid garden party. Themed. You know, vintage.'

She gestured at her hair. Lorenzo still said nothing. Women's hairstyles were not something he liked to discuss. In his experience, they were a minefield, like height, weight, the use or absence of make-up, and all items of clothing.

'I'm Laura,' she said, still pink-cheeked.

'I'm May. And this is my cousin, Lorenzo. This is his mother's house.'

'Lorenzo?' Laura seemed startled. 'Are you Italian?'

132

'From Tuscany,' said Lorenzo.

'He's Maori and Dutch,' May told her. 'And maybe a bit of French as well, going back.'

There was something doll-like about Laura – her pink cheeks and red lips, her dress – and Lorenzo almost felt sorry for her, venturing down from the House Behind into the low-lying, dank marshes where the peasants still lived. But why had she wandered in here with her Nosh bag and her fancy dress? To let them know that the undertaker had blocked her driveway? To explain to them what the sign and balloons had already announced?

Inside, the Tigafua family was singing a hymn. Lorenzo remembered it from school: 'Pe a Faigata Le Ala, Taumafai! If the Way be Full of Trial, Weary Not.' He wasn't sure why the Samoan version had an exclamation mark and the English version didn't. It was just one more unanswered question in a life of small, niggling anxieties.

Uncle Jack's way may or may not have been full of trial; Lorenzo wasn't sure. Uncle Jack never seemed to weary, at least, but Lorenzo felt exhausted most days. He'd wanted to fall asleep on the plane yesterday, coming back from Wellington, but the flight was too short: by the time the shouty All Blacks safety video was over, and someone had demanded he choose between a savoury or a sweet snack, it was time to land. He wouldn't mind lying down on the spare bed next to Uncle Jack's coffin right now, just to close his eyes for ten minutes, though people kept trooping in and out, telling stories about Uncle Jack's exploits and rude sayings.

May stood on the steps humming along with the hymn. The Tigafuas' voices rose, rich and swaying, above the sound of distant traffic and the whining lawnmower down the street. Laura, the Nosh bag clasped in her arms, stared down at the cracked concrete of the path. When the hymn ended, she looked relieved, and something else as well. Trapped, maybe.

'It's a very multicultural neighbourhood, isn't it?' she said.

'It was,' said May, her tone pointed, and Lorenzo folded his arms, suppressing a smile. This was so much better than the two of them creeping along the driveway, knocking on the other front door like salesmen, like service-providers. Laura had come to them. They could have their way with her, whatever their way might be.

'I brought you some food,' Laura said, squeezing the Nosh bag. 'Some things from our party. Just little sandwiches and cakes. It's not much. I'm sorry.'

She looked defeated. And she was quite right, Lorenzo thought; compared with the formidable vats and trays borne by the Tigafua delegation, this bag of fancies wasn't much at all. Once Lorenzo had brought Uncle Jack some miniature croissants, leftovers from an office lunch, tucked with limp triangles of ham and lettuce. Uncle Jack had laughed so much, he'd started coughing. He'd spat out one of his fillings.

'It's just a little, you know, a koha,' Laura continued, and this seemed to soften May.

'You better come in.' She reached out to take the Nosh bag. 'Pay your respects.'

'Really, I don't want to intrude.' There was panic in Laura's voice, but if May heard it, she was ignoring it. Lorenzo followed them inside, lingering on the doormat because Laura was blocking the narrow hallway, straining to unbutton the straps on her shoes.

'These are Mary-Janes,' she told Lorenzo, sounding apologetic, and he shrugged, as though she was speaking a foreign tongue. He walked her to the spare room and May disappeared to round up aunties. Lorenzo's mother came in, dabbing at her eyes with a tea towel.

'I find that hymn very moving,' she said.

'I'm so sorry,' Laura said, and she certainly looked very sorry. 'I don't mean to intrude at such a private family moment.'

'Nothing private about it,' said Lorenzo's mother. She glanced up and down at Laura, at her strange floral dress and sausage-roll hair, and then at Lorenzo. He was leaning against the candlewick cover, one proprietary hand on the coffin. He still couldn't understand why they couldn't be trusted with the lid. It was *their* lid. What if the undertaker brought the wrong lid on Monday? Uncle Jack would have a two-tone coffin. 'Lorenzo didn't mention anything about a girlfriend.'

'She's not my girlfriend,' he said.

'You met at work, I suppose. Are you the reason he's always going down to Wellington?'

'She's not my girlfriend.'

'I live here,' said Laura, pointing at the floor. Lorenzo's mother frowned. 'I mean, up the back. The house behind yours – you know, sixty-two A. We're having a garden party today. My parents.'

'Lorenzo never mentioned he knew you,' said his mother.

'He's a dark horse,' said Auntie Joan, who had materialised along with other aunts and female cousins, all crowding around the narrow bed, dislodging pictures, giving Lorenzo long, accusing looks. 'Just like his Uncle Jack.'

'Not one word,' said his mother, addressing Uncle Jack in his lidless coffin. 'He tells me nothing about his life.'

'Well, it's a very emotional time,' said May, slinging an arm around

Lorenzo's mother. She winked at Lorenzo, which he didn't appreciate at all. No doubt she'd been spreading misinformation in the kitchen.

Laura had started to cry.

'I'm sorry,' she said in a small, high-pitched voice. Lorenzo tried to edge away from the coffin and the bed, but the room was a thicket of bristling sparrows. 'I didn't know your Uncle Jack, but he looks so peaceful here, doesn't he? So still and calm. Surrounded by everyone who loved him.'

'And the Mormons,' said May, sidling close to Lorenzo. He wanted to think she was coming to his rescue, but experience told him the opposite was almost certainly true.

Laura was sobbing now, her thin body shuddering.

'Ah, your little girlfriend is crying,' said Auntie Sila, and lines from the All Blacks' safety video pounded through Lorenzo's head. *All lighted signs and placards too.* His mother was crying and Laura, who was not his girlfriend, was crying. In the living room the Tigafua family was cranking up another hymn.

'Please stop crying,' he said to Laura, but she just gripped Uncle Jack's coffin and sobbed.

'Shall I tell her about my superpower?' May whispered.

'Not now,' he said.

Laura turned to him, her cheeks even more pink, her eyes blurry with tears.

'Isn't life just . . . ' she began, and Lorenzo wanted to tell her that her voice was breaking up, that he was entering a tunnel. 'I mean, isn't life –'

'Isn't it,' said Lorenzo, and he pushed his way out of the room, hanging up on himself the way he always did, just as Uncle Jack had done by dropping dead in the middle of the road, so people would think it was someone else's fault.

POETRY

The Portrait

Anne Estelle Rice, Portrait of Katherine Mansfield, *1918*

Te Papa Museum, Wellington

A flare of red and there you are in your bright dress
the colour of pōhutukawa flowers.

Huge blooms burst out of the frame
into the air that separates us, their petals like gasps of light.

Your eyes blaze towards a point in the distance,
past everything in the room around you,

past me standing here in the half-moon circle
of your ruby luminescence,

as if you have just seen straight down
into the core of the dark pink light,

pulling the colour apart,
splitting it open.

NINA POWLES

Fever Dream

Bavaria, 1910

a stinging fever
dream scorching up
along the nerves
skin simmers in the hot
drench of rain inside
the lightning-struck air
wind tearing teeth
bones cracking under
a New Zealand sky
and she is the wave
rising to meet it

NINA POWLES

Silver Dream

London, 1915

In the garden
beneath the pear tree,

her brother hands her a yellow pear
and she bites into it.

It tastes like jam sandwiches
and sunshine on her mother's hair.

It tastes like the warmth
of his hand in hers,

like the light that falls
in dream places,

where everything is silver
and he is alive again.

*

Later she plants a pear tree
in one of her stories,

makes it glow in the window,
makes it touch the moon.

NINA POWLES

These three poems are from a longer sequence of biographical poems
about Katherine Mansfield, her work, and her presence in my life.
The sequence is titled 'Sunflowers' and forms part of a series of poetic
biographies of five New Zealand women: early pioneer Betty Guard,
cosmologist Beatrice Tinsley, dancer Phyllis Porter, writer Katherine
Mansfield and an unnamed school ghost. **NINA POWLES**

CREATIVE NON-FICTION
Katherine Mansfield, in the Archive and the Hereafter

Eve Lacey

I found Katherine Mansfield in the archives, and it was through Persephone Books, named for a chthonic goddess, that I came to her swansong works – those stories written in Switzerland in the months before her death. As I train to become a librarian at Newnham College, Cambridge, my first task has been to catalogue, classify and exhibit a Persephone collection that was donated to the college library. Encountering the stories in this context, I was intrigued by the Publisher's Note in *The Montana Stories*, and particularly the editorial admission that

> [f]or several reasons publishing her work as 'The Montana Stories' is unlikely to have been how Katherine Mansfield herself would have wanted to be read. Few short story writers arrange their work chronologically, preferring to intersperse moods and themes. [. . .] Nor would Katherine have wanted fragments included – yet these unfinished pages can give just as much insight into her mind as a fully completed and polished story . . . .[1]

It struck me as brazen to go so explicitly against the author's imagined wishes. Posthumous publications tend towards eulogy in their introductions and often bury all trace of editorial interference in an effort to preserve the author's reputation. The ordering of the text within a posthumous collection is usually presented as the gathered but untouched remains of the writer's work, a mausoleum of their final words. *The Montana Stories* marks a bold addition to Mansfield's afterlife – it favours the archive over the art and takes its order from all that is extant, rather than what the writer herself might have deemed worthy.

I liked the editorial intervention. Having spent years studying the beauty in things, I was now being trained to see how that beauty was stored, learning the housekeeping behind the party and the technical legwork behind cultural heritage. Chronological order aims to leave nothing out but this particular hubris of the archive meets its downfall at the end of a well-stocked shelf; space is limited, even if time is not.

For institutions that aim to conserve and chronicle, libraries often display an astonishing lack of foresight. The classification system at Newnham, for example, has one number – 673 – assigned to English novels of the twentieth century. There are eight decimal points chosen for the most prominent authors of the time, or the personal favourites of the librarians who created the system. All other writers from 1900 onwards are squeezed under 673.9, including all twenty-first century novels. This curious miscalculation is a telling error and reveals the unpreparedness of the archive. In a system so fundamentally concerned with retrospection, futurity remains an afterthought.

As a librarian-in-training, I decided to prize the archive above the author in my reading. The books I was cataloguing were not yet ready to borrow, so I gathered a series of older editions: *The Collected Stories*, *The Garden Party and Other Stories* and *The Doves' Nest and Other Stories*. I jumped to and fro, within and across these books, sticking strictly to the order stated in *The Montana Stories*, and broke my reading up further by returning to the Persephone publisher's commentary after each story. This commentary records Mansfield's letter to Lady Ottoline Morrell:

> [We] have occasional lovely talks which are rather like what talks in the after-life will be like, I imagine . . . ruminative, and reminiscent – although dear knows what it is really all about. How strange talking is – what mists rise and fall – how one loses the other and then thinks to have found the other – then down comes another soft final curtain . . .[2]

Mansfield's ruminations here do away with time constraints but there is a clear tension between the notion of an endless afterlife and the traditional framework of storytelling. Within the limited span of a book, problems must be raised, wrought and resolved, whereas with all the time in the world, a plot will lose its urgency. Continuing discussion past the point of death leaves narrative in crisis: talks in the afterlife teeter on the brink of fiction's own vanishing point.

Mansfield's inclination is to play around with time, yet time has since played a trick on her. As I read on, it became increasingly apparent that her stories are conversations in the afterlife, both in their conception and more so in their posthumous publication. Mansfield expertly incorporated a sense of the hereafter into her writing, but she could not anticipate the extent to which the forced inclusion of her unfinished work would enhance that 'ruminative, and reminiscent' style after her death.

Once again, order proves crucial. Most of Mansfield's stories begin in the wake of a passing; her characters' lives only get going after a death. Persephone honoured this tradition in the timing of their collection – the death of the author came first. The location of her sickbed became the eponymous focus of *The Montana Stories*, and the sequence of its contents charts the countdown of her life.

There is a causality in Mansfield's priorities – death does not so much precede life as give rise to it. She reverses the normal chronology of a lifetime and, in a phoenix-like literary trick, positions death as the dust from which her stories will rise. Figuratively, too, she uses the spectre of death to cultivate the epiphany trope of short stories. For example, in 'Taking the Veil', it takes an imagined afterlife in which Edna sees her fiancé in mourning at her own funeral for her to realise that she does love him after all. The story entails a coming-to-her-senses by way of a fantasy demise; death throws life into stark relief and a play at the brink is what drags the dreamer home.

The brink, as ever, is the sea. Mansfield's stories read as a litany of waves and shores, seas as beach holiday and seas as death. She has a littoral preoccupation with mortality – most evident in 'At the Bay' – and the sea becomes shorthand for an undulating, limbo-like style. The flickering of dark and light has a similar effect. In the unfinished manuscript of 'A Married Man's Story', images flare with religious luminescence, then fade: 'She sits, bent forward, clasping the little bare foot, staring into the glow, and as the fire quickens, falls, flares again, her shadow – an immense Mother and Child – is here and gone again upon the wall . . . .'[3] Conversations in the afterlife require the incorporation of absence into the story, and Mansfield crafts a prose shot through with loss until, as the Married Man muses: '"The darks stretches, the blanks, are much bigger than the bright glimpses."'[4]

The archive encounters a similar predicament. The attempt to include everything requires the incorporation of unfinished work – the blanks. Rather than stopping at the blanks, both the story and the library must continue, heedless of the gaps, until each dark stretch speaks volumes. In 'Six Years After', this compulsion to carry on beyond absence manifests as social etiquette in conversations with the bereft: 'As a rule men were not fond of chat as Mother understood it. They did not seem to understand that it does not matter very much what one says: the important thing is not to let the conversation drop.'[5] Mother's sentiment here may be read as the fundamental intention of the archive – if it must acknowledge its failure, it will, but that will not stop its accumulation.

'The Garden Party' takes place against the backdrop of a neighbour's death. Laura, the daughter of the host, leaves the party to take some food to the newly widowed woman who lives down the road. Death proves difficult to stomach, and her sandwiches are left untouched at the end of the story. Through Laura and her chronically bad taste, Mansfield teaches the reader a lesson:

> She feels things ought to happen differently. First one and then another. But life isn't like that. We haven't the ordering of it. [. . .] And they do all happen, it is inevitable. And it seems to me there is beauty in that inevitability.[6]

It is the chaos of life and death that Mansfield wishes to stress, the synchronicity of the two states, and the fact that, like the archive, *we haven't the ordering of it.* These are states which refuse separation, or cataloguing, or even effective description. And yet, they go on. Without sufficient words to describe or stories to order, life and death persist and the archive continues to grow. All this production will not cease, Mansfield suggests, but we would do well to heed its intermingling. And so her stories conclude with the uneasy sense that the party, and the conversation, will not be dropped, but that all our fêting is held in the shadow of death.

Publishers were including Mansfield's side-lined stories long before the Persephone edition. Her widower, John Middleton Murry, began the tradition just one year after her death, confessing that 'I have no doubt that Katherine Mansfield, were she still alive, would not have suffered some of these stories to appear.'[7] The title of that collection – *Something Childish and Other Stories* – resonates with Mansfield's unsettling depictions of family life; there is indeed something child-ish about the stories she left behind, in the sense that they are legacy-like. The written word becomes an heir of sorts, which can subsume the will of the deceased. Jurisdiction over a body of work expires on the author's deathbed, when they are forced to relinquish absolute control. This is a surrender to chronology, which must always win at the long game, and such a surrender allows the will of the archive to take over.

This difficult relationship with, and dubious control over, creative offspring is evident throughout Mansfield's work, and might explain why children – 'unaccountable little creatures' – so often appear as uncanny.[8] In 'An Ideal Family', Mr Neave 'stared at his youngest daughter; he felt he had never seen her before'.[9] Of his older daughter, he observes: 'Strange! When she was a little girl she had such a soft, hesitating voice; she had even stuttered, and now, whatever she said – even if it was only "Jam, please, father" – it rang out as though she were on the stage.'[10] In Mansfield's prose, the process of growing up is a process of becoming strange and, in this case, the distancing is paralleled with a kind of publication. The daughter seems further from her father because she has moved from the home to the stage. In projection, her voice acquires an uncanny tone and rings with the shrill discomfort of children who masquerade as grown individuals with impetuous lives of their own.

Again, Mansfield taps into the disquiet of a child outside the home in 'A Married Man's Story':

> A queer thing is I can't connect him with my wife and myself; I've never accepted him as ours. Each time when I come into the hall and see the perambulator, I catch myself thinking: "H'm, someone has brought a baby!" Or, when his crying wakes me at night, I feel inclined to blame my wife for having brought the baby in from outside.[11]

The narrator struggles to determine whether his son belongs within or without the house, and his distress emphasises the unhomeliness of the child. With an unfamiliar heir, the boundaries of inside and out, self and other, are blurred. It is this troubled lineage of the separate self that situates Mansfield's story firmly in that unsettling place she prefers, at the point of surgery, somewhere between domesticity and the wild limbo of the afterlife.

'The Fly' contains Mansfield's most explicit projection of an afterlife on to a text, and her most stark conflation of literary and biological progeny. Until his son's grave is mentioned in passing, the protagonist had 'never thought of the boy except as lying unchanged, unblemished in his uniform, asleep forever'.[12] From this fantasy of imagined stasis, the bereaved father turns his attention to a fly that has fallen into his inkpot:

> For a fraction of a second it lay still on the dark patch that oozed around it. Then the front legs waved, took hold, and, pulling its small, sodden body up it began the immense task of cleaning the ink from its wings. [. . .] The horrible danger was over; it had escaped; it was ready for life again.[13]

He repeats the process over and over, continually resurrecting and eventually killing the insect. For the span of his cruel experiment, the protagonist discovers the magic of ink. It allows a creature to be killed off and brought back, only to survive another drowning. The weapon becomes the salve and the writing instrument the gift of life. But the narrator who could see his son in a fly could not recognise him in a photograph. It is perhaps the stasis of a published self that makes one's legacy uncanny – the further an idea gets from its conception, the more static it becomes.

Librarians study this evolution from the cerebral to the physical. The theory behind cataloguing returns to the fundamentals of intellectual property and relates to what Mansfield called 'the strange barrier to be crossed from thinking it to writing it'.[14] Broadly speaking, it makes a distinction between the Work – an artistic endeavour; the Expression – the form in which this endeavour is realised; the Manifestation – the physical exemplar of that expression; and the Item – the single entity on the shelves. However uncanny this travel from concept to product may be, it is a necessary distancing if the author wishes to see her work embodied. Mansfield recognised this distinction and transition: 'This is a proof (never too often proved) that once one has thought out a story nothing remains but the labour.'[15] For the living, work is effort and toil; for the dead it settles into an œuvre. The archive is clinical, it flattens, and works can grow macabre when reduced to just their itemised remains.

Death is incorporated into publishing as a nuisance; 'widows' and 'orphans' are a burden to typesetters and editors alike. Incomplete stories and multiple drafted endings undermine the authority of a tale. In *The Montana Stories*, the unfinished works often unfinish at the point of death. 'A Married Man's Story' ends when the speaker 'did beyond words consciously turn towards [his] silent brothers . . . '.[16] 'Six Years After' concludes with the description of another falling curtain and, in 'Widowed', the final sentence describes a head injury: 'For there was nothing to be seen of Jimmie; the sheet was pulled right over . . . .'[17] Each of these stories stops abruptly, with a truncated sentence and ellipses. Repeatedly, Mansfield interrupts her own party with the kind of unfinishing that runs syntax-deep and falls short of a certain end.

There is an admission of powerlessness in such an ending, as though the story ran away from the author right in the middle of things. Mansfield wrote in her diary on 17 January 1922: 'Chekhov made a mistake in thinking that if he had had more time he would have written more fully [. . .]. It's always a kind of race to get in as much as one can before it disappears.'[18]

A sense of belatedness pervades Mansfield's work and the urgency is palpable because these texts lost their endings to her illness. The Persephone edition records how she abandoned her preferred stories in favour of the more commercial texts, whose magazine publication would pay her medical bills.[19] So, even before she died, her editorial decisions were subject to morbid compromise. But the unfinished text lingers longer than those stories with a definite end. Syntactically they are forever marked by the author's death, yet they need never yield to that final act of punctuation; they never have to die.

In Mansfield's work, death disturbs the normal passage of time. In *The Montana Stories*, chronology is meticulously restored. This strict adherence to the precise sequence of her final writings lends the collection an asynchrony all of its own. Each story is subject to temporal disruption because each was punctuated by illness and composed beneath the looming spectre of death. However, custodians of the archive will observe that the only curator left is time, the only order, chronology, and that the important thing is not to let the conversation drop.

Today is 14 October 2014, Mansfield's 126th birthday, and three days after my own twenty-fifth. I finish this essay ninety-three years, to the day, after she finished 'The Garden Party'. There again, time performs its trickery, organising coincidence, and prompting identification with the past. As readers, we are compelled to meaning-making – that is the pleasure of the text – and chronology, it turns out, can be an aesthete after all. I am halfway through cataloguing the Persephone collection at Newnham. The archive remains, though we haven't the ordering of it, and all that survives must be stored. The work will go on without end.

Notes

1. Katherine Mansfield, *The Montana Stories*, Introduction by Nicola Beauman (London: Persephone, 2001), pp. vii–viii.
2. Mansfield, *Montana Stories*, p. 309.
3. Katherine Mansfield, 'A Married Man's Story', in *The Doves' Nest and Other Stories* (London: Constable, 1923), p. 61.
4. Mansfield, 'A Married Man's Story', p. 76.
5. Mansfield, 'Six Years After', *Doves' Nest*, pp. 107–8.
6. Letter to William Gerhardi, 13 March 1922, quoted in *Montana Stories*, p. 318.
7. Katherine Mansfield, *Something Childish and Other Stories* (London: Constable, 1924), p. ix.
8. Katherine Mansfield, 'Sixpence', in *The Collected Stories of Katherine Mansfield* (London: Constable, 1945), p. 687.
9. Katherine Mansfield, 'An Ideal Family', in *The Garden Party and Other Stories* (London: Constable, 1922), p. 262.
10. Mansfield, 'An Ideal Family', p. 263.
11. Mansfield, 'A Married Man's Story', p. 64.
12. Mansfield, 'The Fly', *Doves' Nest*, p. 50.
13. Mansfield, 'The Fly', p. 52.
14. Mansfield, *Montana Stories*, p. 323.
15. Mansfield, *Montana Stories*, p. 323.
16. Mansfield, 'A Married Man's Story', p. 83.
17. Mansfield, 'Widowed', *Doves' Nest*, p. 197.
18. Quoted in Beauman, Commentary, *Montana Stories*, p. 326.
19. Beauman, Introduction, *Montana Stories*, p. viii.

CRITICAL MISCELLANY

Figure 1. Photo of Katherine Mansfield and John Middleton Murry.
Ref: 1/2-028635-F. Alexander Turnbull Library, Wellington, New Zealand,
with kind permission.

Poise

Angela Smith

On 12 May 2015, *The Telegraph* carried the following piece, written by Colin Gleadell, asserting that 'the sitter in J D Fergusson's Poise is revealed':

> A portrait of a beautiful young woman by the Scottish colourist J D Fergusson that was discovered in an attic in France last year is now thought to depict the celebrated author, Katherine Mansfield. Dr Gerri Kimber, senior lecturer in English at the University of Northampton and chair of the International Katherine Mansfield Society, says she is almost certain it is a missing portrait of Mansfield. She sent me a photograph of the author, who knew the artist well, with the same bob hairstyle, jacket lapels and doll like facial expression as in the painting, entitled Poise.[1]

A 'missing' portrait implies that Fergusson was known to have painted a portrait of Mansfield. This was an intriguing prospect which had first been indicated to Gerri and me by Rachel Boyd Hall, the enterprising researcher at the Richard Green Gallery in New Bond Street where the painting was exhibited, though she only suggested that the picture might depict Mansfield, not that there was known to have been a portrait of Mansfield by Fergusson. I have looked through all the sketchbooks belonging to Fergusson that are now in the Fergusson Archive in Perth and have never found what might be a line drawing of Mansfield, so I was keen to see the painting.

It was certainly not a disappointment. Its powerful presence dominated the room of the gallery in which it was hanging. Rachel had kindly sent me an image of the painting by email but nothing could have prepared me for its vitality, the intensity of the sitter's gaze (doll-like?), the dense vibrancy of the colour, and the rhythm created between the strong triangular shapes and the curving dish, fruit and leaves. The sitter leans over the back of a sofa towards intimacy with the viewer. But is this vigorous blue-eyed woman Mansfield? Both Ida Baker and Anne Estelle Rice refer to Mansfield's eyes: Baker writes that 'Katherine looked at me steadily with calm, deeply dark eyes'[2] and Rice, in her famous portrait of Mansfield, depicts them as dark brown. Mansfield herself lists them as brown in her passport.[3] In the years before *Poise* was painted, Mansfield, in a letter to one of her sisters, refers to symptoms such as 'a small attack of flue and then – familiar ailment – a touch of congestion. It is this last which "clings so fond"'[4] and develops into tuberculosis. She also has difficulty in walking because of what she takes to be rheumatism, though she is not yet 30. The healthy young subject of the painting looks to me much more like a member of Margaret Morris's dance company. Morris became Fergusson's life-long partner, ending his relationship with Anne Estelle Rice, in 1913. One of Margaret Morris's dancers, Kathleen Dillon, was the subject of a painting called *Rose Rhythm* in 1916. Fergusson described admiring her hat:

> It was just like a rose, going from the centre convolution and continuing the 'Rhythm' idea developed in Paris and still with me. Looking at K I soon saw that the hat was not merely a hat, but a continuation of the girl's character, her mouth, her nostril, the curl of her hair – her whole character.[5]

As he does here, Fergusson and Morris celebrated physical vigour, Bergson's *élan vital*, in their art and in their lives, as the extraordinary photographs of their beautiful bodies when he was in his eighties show. The title *Poise* surely indicates the painter's admiration for the sitter's qualities of grace and confidence. When he painted portraits, he often named the sitters: *Portrait of Jean*; *Grace McColl*; *Anne Estelle Rice*; *Self-Portrait*. When he wanted to capture a quality or an abstraction through figures, the titles signalled that purpose: *Rhythm*; *La Force*; *Les Eus*; *Megalithic*.

Gerri Kimber has suggested that the well-known passage in which Mansfield describes her visit to Fergusson's studio on 25 April 1918 may contain a memory of a sitting rather than the actual event since the painting in question was completed in 1916. On 12 April 1918, the day after her arrival in London, Mansfield wrote to Ida Baker: 'Johnny came in last night – God! – He gave me such a welcome. Before I knew where I was we had hugged & kissed each other & Johnny kept saying "this is a great success".'[6] What she is celebrating is her escape from three weeks' entrapment in Paris during the bombardment by the Kanon, the long-range gun with which the Germans shelled the city. Her friendship with

Fergusson had developed during their involvement with *Rhythm* before the Great War. She wrote to him from Bandol early in 1918, when a vase of roses caused her to recall *Rose Rhythm*, saying that 'your rose picture was vivid before me – I saw it in every curve of these beauties – the blouse like a great petal, the round brooch, the rings of hair like shavings of light'.[7] The bond between Fergusson and Mansfield as the practitioners of different arts became as strong as that between John Middleton Murry and Fergusson, as Mansfield realised in 1917 when Fergusson called on her at her home in Chelsea:

> This man is in many ways extraordinarily like me. I like him so much; I feel so *honest* with him that it's simply one of my real joys, one of the real joys of my life, to have him come and talk and be with me. I did not realise, until he was here and we ate together, how much I cared for him – and how much I was really at home with him. A real understanding. We might have spoken a different language – returned from a far country. I felt all was well, and we understood each other. Just that. And there was 'ease' between us.[8]

My reading of Mansfield's description of Fergusson's studio is not that it is a memory of having sat for a portrait two years earlier but an expression of the relief and joy she feels at having escaped from the devastation and danger of Paris to the relative peace of London. On her arrival in London, she and Murry took a flat at 47 Redcliffe Road opposite Fergusson's flat. Margaret Morris writes that all

> the time they were in Redcliffe Road, Fergus dined with them once a week. They never asked me, but I understood and did not resent this. They wanted to re-live those wonderful years in Paris before the war when they started Rhythm.[9]

Bearing in mind that Mansfield had crossed the Channel only two weeks earlier and then had the diagnosis of tuberculosis confirmed, it is possible to see that she might regard her friend Fergusson's studio, with his egalitarian use of her surname, as a sanctuary. I quote the passage from the notebook in full:

> 'Well sit down Mansfield, and reposez-vous' said Ferguson, 'and I'll get on with my dressing.'
> So he went into his bedroom & shut the door between, and I sat on the end of the sofa. The sun came full through the two windows, dividing the studio into four – two quarters of light and two of shadow. But all those things which the light touched seemed to float in it, to bathe and to sparkle in it as if they belonged not to land but to water; they even seemed, in some strange way, to be moving. When you lean over the edge of the rock

and see something lovely and brilliant flashing at the bottom of the sea it is only the clear, trembling water that dances – but – can you be quite sure? ... No, not quite sure, and that little Chinese group on the writing table may or may not have shaken itself awake for just one hundredth of a second out of hundreds of years of sleep. Very beautiful, oh God is a blue teapot with two white cups attending, a red apple among oranges addeth fire to flame – in the white bookcases the books fly up and down in scales of colour, with pink and lilac notes recurring until nothing remains but them, sounding over and over.

There are a number of frames, some painted and some plain, leaning against the wall, and the picture of a naked woman with her arms raised, languid, as though her heavy flowering beauty were almost too great to bear. There are two sticks and an umbrella in one corner, and in the fireplace – a kettle, curiously like a bird.

White net curtains hang over the windows. For all the sun it is raining outside. The gas in the middle of the room has a pale yellow paper shade and as Ferguson dresses he keeps up a constant whistling.

Reposez-vous.

Oui, je me repose . . .[10]

Mansfield paints her own still life, with an element of cubism and a gesture towards Fergusson as a colourist. One art becomes another as the colours of the books become musical scales. Fergusson's private space is like hers, using simple objects such as a kettle and a cup to focus the pleasure that can be gained from uncluttered domestic design. It stirs memories of childhood, of leaning over a rock on the sea-shore, and throughout there is the comfort of Fergusson's cheerful presence, embodied in his whistling. No wonder Mansfield feels she can rest in the midst of what Fergusson called living paint.

Just over a week later, Fergusson was a witness, with the painter Dorothy Brett, at Murry and Mansfield's wedding; soon after that, Mansfield went to Cornwall in an attempt to recover her health and to be close to her friend, the American painter Anne Estelle Rice. While she was there, she heard that Leonard and Virginia Woolf disliked the design that Fergusson had done for the Hogarth Press's edition of Prelude: 'To Hell with other people's presses!'[11] She also sat for Rice twice; one of the pictures is lost but the other is 'the great painting – me in that red brick red frock with flowers everywhere'.[12] Her hairstyle in the portrait certainly resembles that in *Poise*: not a bob but with the hair fringed and cut short to frame the face, with long hair piled on top of the head in a chignon. The day after Mansfield wrote the letter about sitting for Rice, she received from Murry a copy of the art magazine *Colour*, which contained an article on Fergusson's work and a reproduction of *Poise*. I give her response to it, in her reply to Murry, in full, as it seems to me extremely unlikely that Fergusson would have completed a portrait of her two years earlier and not shown it to her, and equally unlikely that she would be as objective as she seems to be if it were a portrait of her:

> You know Poise is extraordinarily fine, but having gone so tremendously far as Fergusson *has* gone I don't think the *mouth* is quite in the picture – It is – it is more 'in the picture' than most of his other mouths are – but I think it might be more *sensitive* . . . more 'finely felt.' Of course I can hear his 'to Hell with rosebuds' but I won't be put off by it: its too easy & begs the question anyway. To exaggerate awfully (as I always do) he really seems sometimes to fit women with mouths as a dentist might fit them with teeth – & the same thing happens in both cases: the beautiful *individual* movement (mobility) of the face is gone – Looking at *Poise* again this mouth seems more nearly right than any other – Perhaps that's what sets up the irritation in me. I must say as a picture it properly fascinates me.[13]

Her tone is that of a friendly critic, not invested with the self-consciousness that a portrait would stimulate in someone as protective of her own image as Mansfield was.

Though I can find no evidence that there is a 'missing' portrait of Mansfield by Fergusson, and I am convinced that the blue-eyed woman in *Poise* is not Mansfield, I should be delighted if any reader has information about a missing picture by Fergusson. It appears in the background of a photograph of Mansfield and Murry taken in Chaucer Mansions in October 1913, reproduced here. It is clearly a street scene, probably painted in Paris in about 1907 – where is it now? The reappearance of *Poise* is happy evidence that missing works by Fergusson do resurface, even though I cannot be persuaded that the eyes in the picture are the ones that seemed to Anne Estelle Rice 'to send out a penetrating beam into the crannies and recesses of one's nature and there was no escape from the searching scrutiny, often disconcerting and I'm sure not flattering'.[14]

Notes

1. Colin Gleadell, 'The Mysterious Mansfield', *The Telegraph*, 12 May 2015 <http://www.telegraph.co.uk/luxury/art/70985/market-news-the-mysterious-mansfield.html> (last accessed 20 November 2015).
2. Katherine Mansfield, *The Memories of LM* (New York: Taplinger, 1972), p. 22.
3. Gillian Boddy, *Katherine Mansfield: The Woman and the Writer* (Ringwood, Victoria: Penguin, 1988), p. xiv.
4. Vincent O'Sullivan and Margaret Scott, eds, *The Collected Letters of Katherine Mansfield*, 5 vols (Oxford: Clarendon Press, 1984–2008), Vol. 1, p. 131. Punctuation and spelling are erratic in the letters and journals. I quote them as they appear in the text.
5. Margaret Morris, *The Art of J. D. Fergusson* (Perth: J. D. Fergusson Art Foundation, 2010), p. 98.

6. *Letters*, 2, p. 164.
7. *Letters*, 2, p. 35.
8. John Middleton Murry, ed., *The Journal of Katherine Mansfield 1904–1922: Definitive Edition* (London: Constable, 1954), pp. 123–4.
9. Morris, p. 119.
10. Margaret Scott, ed., *The Katherine Mansfield Notebooks*, 2 vols (Minneapolis: Lincoln University Press and Daphne Brasell Associates, 1997), Vol. 2, p. 133.
11. *Letters*, 2, p. 203.
12. *Letters*, 2, p. 245. The painting is now in the Museum of New Zealand, Te Papa Tongarewa in Wellington.
13. *Letters*, 2, p. 246.
14. Anon., *Katherine Mansfield in Her Letters and Works: Exhibition 25 April–16 May 1958* (London: New Zealand House, 1958), p. 5.

Poise by J. D. Fergusson: A Rediscovered Portrait of Katherine Mansfield?

Rachel Boyd Hall

In the autumn of 2014, a long-lost painting by the Scottish artist John Duncan Fergusson re-appeared on the art market, having been consigned to an attic in Giverny, France, for the best part of a century. Dated 1916, *Poise* was last seen at Fergusson's one-man exhibition at the Connell Gallery, London, in May 1918 and had been reproduced in June that year in *Colour* magazine with an article entitled, 'J. D. Fergusson: His Place in Art'. In remarkable condition, this striking portrait, notable for its clarity of design and colour, expressing both the self-assurance of the model and balance of the composition, justified its description as a rediscovered masterpiece. Upon its purchase by Richard Green, I contacted the Fergusson Gallery in Perth, who suggested that 'the sitter for this extraordinary work may very well be Katherine Mansfield'.[1]

There is, in the manner in which Fergusson constructed his likenesses, emphasising the lines or planes of the sitter's face, their individual hairstyle and characteristic articles of clothing, a striking resemblance to the author. Beyond these elements, the artist did not feel bound to reproduce the model's features slavishly. In fact, Fergusson did not need the model before him in order to recreate 'the feeling' of seeing her. The increasing intimacy of the artist and author at this time, however, provided opportunities to capture Mansfield's likeness and made it more tangible as a female, fellow creative with whom he felt an affinity. This companionable closeness, also felt and shared by Mansfield's husband, John Middleton Murry, led to an open and honest exchange of ideas, the sharing of each other's work and passionate support of it. Knowing the author well, it is possible that Fergusson knew Mansfield was completing 'The Aloe' and, though excited at the prospect of this new direction, felt unable to progress with her writing in 1916.

157

Poised, like Fergusson was, between the production of new, thoroughly modern work and its exposure in 1918, could the painting's title refer to Mansfield's exhilarated state of creative stasis?

Photographs of Mansfield at this time at the National Library of New Zealand document not only her distinctive hairstyle with blunt, angular fringe and jaw-length bob, but also a wide-collared white blouse with lapels reaching almost to the shoulders, as modelled in the painting. The fine facial features and neat, raised coiffure (though grown long and piled high in the years that followed) also correspond with the only known portrait of the author by the American artist, Anne Estelle Drey (née Rice), dated 1918 in the Museum of New Zealand, Te Papa Tongarewa. One of Mansfield's closest female friends, Rice was introduced to John Middleton Murry by Fergusson, who had been her partner in Paris until 1913 and was a fellow contributor to *Rhythm*. Rice and Mansfield became close friends until the latter's death, and in 1918 spent time together in Cornwall, where Rice painted her portrait of Mansfield, recounting tales of 'Johnny'.[2]

During the First World War, Fergusson painted several portraits of female friends and acquaintances with whom he felt a genuine kinship (despite overtures and the prospect of a definite sale, Fergusson declined a commission to paint Lady Ottoline Morrell).[3] They included Mrs Julian Lousada, the wife of his solicitor, in *Complexity*, and on several occasions, the dancer Kathleen Dillon (his partner, Margaret Morris's pupil) in works such as *Rose Rhythm, Simplicity* and *Summer*, all of which were included in the artist's Connell Gallery exhibition. Writing of this period of Fergusson's art, Sheila McGregor concludes:

> One other portrait of the war years is worth mentioning, because the sitter was possibly Katherine Mansfield, who took a flat with John Middleton Murry opposite Fergusson's studio in Redcliffe Road 1917–18. The present location of the portrait 'Poise' is unknown, but Kathleen Dillon has suggested that the model could well have been Katherine Mansfield.[4]

This statement, adding the weight of a contemporary acquaintance's account to the identity of the sitter, was based on the author's conversation with Fergusson's frequent model, and with Angus Morrison, the pianist for Morris's dance classes and club. These first-hand sources also provided 'much of the background information about Fergusson's life during the First World War'.[5]

Mansfield herself wrote about *Poise* to Murry, having received a copy of *Colour* magazine in Cornwall on 18 June 1918. While expressing her fascination for the painting, the representation of the mouth (arguably the least accurate feature of her portrayal) provoked an understandably passionate, and amusing, response:

> Colour came [. . .] The reproductions are very beautiful – I have had a good look at them – You know Poise is extraordinarily fine, but having gone so tremendously far as Fergusson has gone I don't think the mouth is quite in the picture – It is – it is more 'in the picture' than most of his other mouths are – but I think it might be more sensitive . . . more 'finely felt.' Of course I can hear his 'to Hell with rosebuds' but I won't be put off by it: its too easy & begs the question anyway. To exaggerate awfully (as I always do) he really seems sometimes to fit women with mouths as a dentist might fit them with teeth – & the same thing happens in both cases: the beautiful individual movement (mobility) of the face is gone – Looking at Poise again this mouth seems more nearly right than any other – Perhaps that's what sets up the irritation in me. I must say as a picture it properly fascinates me.[6]

The irritation or slight was enough to preoccupy the author and was referred to a third party, Anne Estelle Rice. The following day, Mansfield wrote to Murry: 'I showed her Colour, & on her own she remarked that Fs "mouths" always troubled her – in fact she entirely agreed with me about them. This, from her, was a relief to me.'[7] Though full of the force of an immediate reaction, this was not the first time Mansfield had seen the painting. In a letter to the artist Dorothy Brett on 22 May, she recounts attending the Connell Gallery's private view, and entreats her, 'BE SURE you see J.D.F's show if you can. I popped in at the Private View and I thought it *wonderful*.'[8] Before the exhibition opened, and while still in London on 12 May, Mansfield encouraged Brett to see Fergusson's work at the Burlington Galleries, declaring his most recent to be the best: 'its the late Fergusson who really is IT. There's not much at this show but it *is* worth a visit. Then Fergusson's show is on Thursday. I would love love love to go there with you.'[9] It is even possible that Mansfield and Murry, as well as visiting and promoting the show, helped Fergusson select which pictures to exhibit. Months before, in December 1917, Mansfield wrote to Murry from her Chelsea studio, 'Fergusson wants to show you & me his work all that he has got there. I have a sort of idea he is going to give you summat. If we can manage to get to the studio before I go – we must.'[10]

While clearly supportive of his work, Mansfield was not the only critic of Fergusson's portrait style. Nor was she the only sitter whose features he adapted to complement a painting's overall decorative design. In his review of the 1918 exhibition, the critic for the *Morning Post* reproached the artist for 'subordinating the expression of character to the pursuit of pattern'.[11] For Shelia McGregor, these portraits mark 'the beginning of a certain standardisation in Fergusson's portraiture, the impulse to suppress individuality in accordance with a mannequin-like ideal of beauty'.[12] Raymond Drey, the journalist and art and theatre critic husband of Anne Estelle Rice, also observed:

> Some of his portraits suffered from this tendency to over-emphasise a voluptuous curve, and pigmentation of the lips and to change slender necks into columns of sculptural form. This heightened the femininity of the sitter at the expense of character and individuality.[13]

A comparison of Fergusson's portrait, *Complexity*, of Mrs Julian Lousada with that painted by Ambrose McEvoy around 1920 (Touchstones, Rochdale) further demonstrates this aspect of Fergusson's style, accentuating the lines of the sitter's face (in particular the hairline) and heightening her colouring to fit his chosen palette. In the cool, clear light of *Poise*, the sitter's blue eyes resonate with the blues of her dress or jacket, the painting behind her and the articulation of shadows.

The anonymous author of the article in *Colour* magazine seems to have spoken with the artist of his aims and offers an explanation of Fergusson's portrait style as represented at the Connell Gallery exhibition:

> They are not copies of nature, not *portraits* in the ordinary sense, nor decorations, but the visualisation of an impression on the mind and sense of the painter [. . .] His *portraits*, therefore, may differ not only from the superficial aspect of the persons they represent, but his rendering of one and the same personality must change with the change of environment and with the change in him from day to day – nay, possibly from hour to hour. Yet if there be a strong characteristic in his 'sitter' – and Fergusson never attempts to *portray* anyone who does not interest him – this prevailing characteristic, or at least the effect it has upon the artist, will appear and reappear again, irrespective of the change in time and circumstance.[14]

The definition of portraiture as 'the visualisation of an impression on the mind and sense of the painter' closely corresponds to a comment Fergusson made to Margaret Morris on 20 August 1916 from Edinburgh, regarding the representation of Kathleen Dillon in the carved stone version of *Summer*: 'Tell K I'm putting the feeling of the last time I saw her, into my sculpture – full and round.'[15]

Mansfield certainly had the opportunity to sit for Fergusson in 1916. She notes in her journal in November, at 3 Gower Street, both a significant gift and a revitalising, if frustratingly enigmatic event: 'Johnnie has given me his fountain pen [. . .] I have rather a cold, but I feel absolutely alive after my experience of this afternoon.'[16] We also know that Mansfield visited Fergusson's studio, as she gives a vivid description of her immersion in this artistic haven, two years after *Poise* was painted:

> 'Well sit down Mansfield, and reposez-vous' said Ferguson, 'and I'll get on with my dressing.'
> So he went into his bedroom & shut the door between, and I sat on the end of the sofa. The sun came full through the two windows, dividing the studio into four – two quarters of light and two of shadow. But all those things which the light touched seemed to float in it, to bathe and to sparkle in it as if they belonged not to land but to water; they even seemed, in some strange way, to be moving. When you lean over the edge of the rock and see something lovely and brilliant flashing at the bottom of the sea it is only the clear, trembling water that dances – but – can you be quite sure? . . . No, not quite sure, and that little Chinese group on the writing table may or may not have shaken itself awake for just one hundredth of a second out of hundreds of years of sleep. Very beautiful, oh God is a blue teapot with two white cups attending, a red apple among oranges addeth fire to flame – in the white bookcases the books fly up and down in scales of colour, with pink and lilac notes recurring until nothing remains but them, sounding over and over.
> There are a number of frames, some painted and some plain, leaning against the wall, and the picture of a naked woman with her arms raised, languid, as though her heavy flowering beauty were almost too great to bear. There are two sticks and an umbrella in one corner, and in the fireplace – a kettle, curiously like a bird.
> White net curtains hang over the windows. For all the sun it is raining outside. The gas in the middle of the room has a pale yellow paper shade and as Ferguson dresses he keeps up a constant whistling.
> Reposez-vous.
> Oui, je me repose . . .[17]

Is it possible that this passage is a recollection of Mansfield sitting for the artist? Unlike other portraits at the time, which feature predominantly nondescript decorative, floral backgrounds, it seems fitting that Fergusson set *Poise*, and perhaps Mansfield, in his white, modernist studio, according her the status of a fellow artist within his creative working environment.

Though Mansfield mentioned Fergusson in her correspondence in 1913, from 1916 onwards her references to 'Johnnie', 'Fergusson' and 'JDF' increase as their relationship deepened, the artist becoming second only to Murry in importance in Mansfield's life: 'Ma Parker yesterday went to my heart. She said suddenly "Oh Miss, you do make the work go easy." What could be a sweeter compliment. Its one I could pay to you & to J.D.F. but nobody else alive.'[18] In one of the few known letters she sent to Fergusson from France, on 15 January 1918, Mansfield wrote, 'I thought last night it is a bad thing during this war to be apart from the one or two people who do count in one's life.'[19] In the spring of 1917, Mansfield took a studio at 141a Church Street, Chelsea, and records Fergusson visiting her there on 21 August, declaring, 'This man is in many ways extraordinarily like me. I like him so much; I feel so honest with him.'[20] Around the same time, Murry took rooms at 47 Redcliffe Road across the street from Fergusson's studio and, according to Margaret Morris, the artist dined with the writers once a week. When they married on 3 May 1918 at South Kensington Register Office, Fergusson and Dorothy Brett acted as witnesses and Mansfield gave her husband a painting by Fergusson as a wedding gift. She also remembered the artist in her will. Murry, too, considered Fergusson a kindred, creative spirit and at the artist's request, wrote the catalogue foreword for his exhibition at the Connell Gallery, which he described as 'like clinching our comradeship in art'.[21]

Bearing in mind the closeness of their friendship, Fergusson's gift of the pen and the studio setting, is it possible that *Poise* could refer to the creation of art in general and the author's writing at the time specifically? Mansfield began writing the first version of 'Prelude', originally 'The Aloe', in 1915 and continued in Bandol as the year ended and 1916 began. She writes in her journal, on 22 January:

> Now, really, what is it that I do want to write? I ask myself, Am I less of a writer than I used to be? Is the need to write less urgent? [. . .] But no, at bottom I am not convinced, for at bottom never has my desire been so ardent. Only the form that I would choose has changed utterly. I feel no longer concerned with the same appearance of things.[22]

The following month, on 16 February, she writes in a notebook to her brother, Leslie Beauchamp, killed in France on 7 October 1915:

> The Aloe is right. The Aloe is lovely. It simply fascinates me, and I know that it is what you would wish me to write [. . .] It is good, my treasure! My little brother, it is good, and it is what we really meant.[23]

While aware of the significance of 'The Aloe' and the new direction she wished to follow, Mansfield wrote very little following her return from France 'apart from letters and occasional jottings in her notebooks'.[24] On 8 December, she writes, 'And even in my brain, in my head, I can think and act and write wonders – wonders; but the moment I really try to put them down I fail miserably.'[25]

Both artist and writer were conscious of the significant direction their work was taking in 1916, of the fulfilment of their ideas and of creative breakthroughs, and were supportive of each others' endeavours. They brought their art to the public's attention two years later: Fergusson at the Connell Gallery exhibition in May, introduced by Mansfield's husband Murry, and Mansfield with the publication of Prelude by the Hogarth Press in July, a few copies of which featured illustrations by Fergusson on the blue paper wrapper.[26]

It is certainly possible, probable even, considering the resemblance, Fergusson's style and method of portrayal, the studio setting and the significance of their relationship, that *Poise* is a portrait of Katherine Mansfield. Unfortunately, this is impossible to prove due to the scarcity of her writing at the time and the survival of what the editors of her letters define as 'a good deal less than half of her correspondence'.[27] What is evident is that *Poise* fascinated and affected Mansfield, even after its creation and display. Writing a review of *Kew Gardens* by Virginia Woolf for the *Athenaeum* in 1919, Mansfield includes the following line, as much a description of her own work in 1916 as of her peer's three years later: 'Poise – yes, poise. Anything may happen; her world is on tiptoe.'[28]

Notes

1. Email correspondence, 13 April 2015.
2. Letter to John Middleton Murry, 12 June 1918: 'And then there was Anne's meeting with Johnny and her first visit to his studio – worth hearing that – – – .' Vincent O'Sullivan and Margaret Scott, eds, *The Collected Letters of Katherine Mansfield*, 5 vols (Oxford: Clarendon Press, 1984–2008), Vol. 2, p. 236. Hereafter referred to as *Letters*, followed by volume and page numbers. Letter to Murry, 17 June: 'Anne came early & began the great painting – me in that red brick red frock with flowers everywhere. Its awfully interesting even now. I must tell you the things she has told me about Johnny – They are revealing.' *Letters*, 2, p. 245.
3. Letter to Murry, 13 December 1917: 'Johnny came yesterday. He was so very particularly nice [. . .] H.L. says she'd like a portrait. I told him yesterday. Of course he said *No*. (Burn this letter. Burn it to bits, please).' *Letters*, 1, p. 344.
4. Shelia McGregor, *J. D. Fergusson: The Early Years 1874–1918*, PhD Thesis (Courtauld Institute of Art, University of London, May 1981), p. 118.
5. McGregor, p. 259, footnote 4.
6. *Letters*, 2, p. 246.
7. *Letters*, 2, p. 248.
8. *Letters*, 2, p. 184.
9. *Letters*, 2, p. 169.
10. *Letters*, 1, p. 358.
11. *Morning Post*, 29 September 1918, cited in Sheila McGregor, *John Duncan Fergusson*, unpublished manuscript, p. 4.
12. McGregor, *John Duncan Fergusson*, p. 4.
13. Raymond Drey, 'Some memories of John Duncan Fergusson', *Apollo*, October 1962, p. 623.
14. 'J. D. Fergusson: His Place in Art', *Colour*, June 1918, p. 101.
15. Margaret Morris, *The Art of J. D. Fergusson, A Biased Biography by Margaret Morris* (Glasgow and London: Blackie, 1974), p. 115.

16. John Middleton Murry, ed., *Journal of Katherine Mansfield* (London: Constable & Co., 1954), p. 119.
17. Margaret Scott, ed., *The Katherine Mansfield Notebooks*, Vol. 2 (Minneapolis: Lincoln University Press and Daphne Brasell Associates, 1997), p. 133.
18. Letter to Murry, 13 December 1917, *Letters*, 1, p. 344.
19. *Letters*, 2, p. vii.
20. Murry, p. 123.
21. 17 March 1918; C. A. Hankin, ed., *The Letters of John Middleton Murry to Katherine Mansfield* (London: Constable, 1983), p. 139.
22. Murry, p. 93.
23. Murry, p. 98.
24. *Letters*, 1, p. 259.
25. Murry, p. 119.
26. 'I have heard from Virginia who dislikes the [Fergusson] drawings very much. So does Leonard. Well, they would – wouldn't they?' Letter from Mansfield to Murry, 29 May 1918. *Letters*, 2, p. 203.
27. *Letters*, 1, p. xxii. Vincent O'Sullivan suggests this scarcity of material was the result of Mansfield's intent and Murry fulfilling her instructions, citing a letter from Mansfield to Murry of 7 August 1922: 'Please destroy all letters you do not wish to keep and all papers.' O'Sullivan continues, 'In her formal will she made the same request.' *Letters*, 1, p. xxi.
28. Katherine Mansfield, 'A Short Story: Kew Gardens by Virginia Woolf', *Athenaeum*, 13 June 1919, p. 459.

Patriarchal Pink: Gender Signification in Katherine Mansfield's 'The Little Governess'

Bronwen Fetters

Feminist critic Ruth Parkin-Gounelas has classified feminine features in Katherine Mansfield's writing, including the use of tag questions, which indicate a need for external reinforcement, frequent underlining, capitalisation and italics, which indicate repeated emphases, and 'diminutive vocabulary'.[1] I would add that Mansfield's recurrent use of colour and visual imagery throughout her stories and written correspondence is likewise a stereotypically feminine feature. But Mansfield employs both her gendered writing style and use of colour to subvert normative patriarchal parameters. In a letter to her husband, John Middleton Murry, we see this counterintuitive process of using accepted female gender norms to subvert patriarchy paradoxically, not only in her writing, but in her actions as well. Mansfield is angry at Murry but she employs 'mock-feminine deferral to masculine authority' to prove a point.[2] She writes:

> Not that I think for one minute that you don't treat me au GRAND sérieux or would dare to question my intelligence, of course not. All the same – there you are – Alone, I'm no end a fillaseafer but once you join me in the middle of my seriousness – my deadly seriousness – I see the piece of pink wool I have put on your hair (and that you don't know is there). Queer isn't it? Now explain that for me.[3]

In this short excerpt, Mansfield uses the previously described features of female writing along with the gender-charged trope of pink wool to resist systemic expectations of femininity. Parkin-Gounelas writes of the wool, 'The color is of course part of a system whereby gender polarization is encoded from the cradle. As Mansfield sees it, her collusion in this process is as conspicuous as is the male's oblivion of it'.[4] Thus, the pink wool acts as a symbol of this larger situation. With the piece of pink wool that she places on his head, Mansfield uses something from within the female system to undermine him, and Murry remains unaware.

Mansfield's fiction performs this same process of resisting, while working within, the gender system. In 'The Little Governess' (1915), Mansfield employs a feminine writing style, especially in her repeated use of colour. By aligning the gender-marked colours of pink and blue with varying levels of male and female space and with varying levels of safety and danger, she makes a statement about the victimisation of women. Mansfield writes a text that reads antagonistically toward men – one that understands that the mentality of blaming women for the harm that comes to them 'merely ignores the methods that patriarchal ideology sets in place to condition the dependency of women'.[5] With this honest and dismal portrayal of young female disillusionment, Mansfield challenges gender norms and addresses the problem of sexual violence toward women.

'The Little Governess', a story which 'focuses on vulnerability of women in a world dominated by male power',[6] opens with a warning from the lady at the governess bureau. She tells the little governess to find the train compartment marked 'Ladies Only', always to lock the lavatory door, and to avoid roaming the corridors of the train, saying,

> 'Well, I always tell my girls that it's better to mistrust people at first rather than trust them, and it's safer to suspect people of evil intentions rather than good ones. . . . It sounds rather hard but we've got to be women of the world, haven't we?'[7]

This warning from the woman at the bureau shows the societal expectation for women to close themselves away in order to keep safe. Women are charged with not only reactionary but also preventative duty in the case of danger. Sydney Janet Kaplan notes how '[t]he little governess is not merely an emblem of woman as victim, but a representation of ideology's construction of woman as a *target* for victimization'.[8] Under this framework set forth by the woman at the bureau, blame for any harm done to the little governess will be her own since she must relegate herself to female space lest she get *herself* into any trouble.

The narrative then shifts to the little governess's pleasant memories from the first leg of her trip: a boat ride. During this agreeable moment in the text, she finds herself quite literally in female space. The Ladies' Cabin of the boat is filled with friendly passengers and strong female camaraderie. In contrast to the rest of the short story, the little governess is surrounded solely by women in this scene, and it is here she is happiest. Mansfield writes, 'The stewardess was so kind and changed her money for her and tucked up her feet. She lay on one of the hard pink-sprigged couches and watched the other passengers' (51). In the Ladies' Cabin, the little governess finds comfort. When the stewardess sits down with a piece of knitting, presumably on one of the 'pink-sprigged' couches, the little governess smiles and thinks to herself how much she likes travelling (51). The couches in the room exude femaleness, as they are marked not only by colour but also by the delicate floral pattern of the fabric. Within the cabin, the women perform stereotypically female duties such as pinning their hats, adjusting their dressing-cases and doing their hair. The mood is congenial but this soon changes. When the little governess steps off the boat, she feels a 'cold, strange wind' and looks up to see the 'masts and spars of the ship black against a green glittering sky' (51). Janka Kaščáková calls this cold wind 'a foreboding of the misfortunes [the little governess] will inadvertently bring upon herself'.[9] Exiting the safe, pink, feminine world of the Ladies' Cabin, the little governess enters the grim, dark, phallic world where 'masts and spars' stand erect before her, the world of which she has been forewarned.

Shortly after leaving the boat, the little governess encounters a 'horrible' man who takes her luggage (52). She stands up to him but, in response, he takes the Dames Seules label off her compartment door, which removes its status as female space. An old man enters the compartment. Using free indirect discourse, Mansfield describes the little governess's impressions of his appearance, noting, 'He had a white moustache and big gold-rimmed spectacles with little blue eyes behind them and pink wrinkled cheeks' (54). The two gender-marked colours appear on the man's face: blue eyes and pink cheeks. Shortly after, though, as the little governess decides whether or not to trust the man, she focuses on his pinkness, ignoring the blue eyes. Mansfield writes, 'But not having a beard – that made all the difference – and then his cheeks were so pink and his moustache so very white' (54). No longer in exclusively female space, the little governess looks for familiarity with the old man and finds it in his clean appearance, lack of a beard, and pink face – all feminine traits. When he asks if she speaks German and she responds positively, the two begin to build rapport, and she 'blushed a deep pink colour that spread slowly over her cheeks and made her blue eyes look almost black' (54–5). The two gender-marked colours here appear on her face as well, though the little governess's cheeks turn a darker shade of pink than the man's and her blue eyes turn almost black. Though the man has entered into what used to be female space, the little governess still retains the functional safety of the female compartment due to the trust she feels toward the man. Blueness is minimised and made subject to pink, but both colours darken, indicative of what is to come.

As the odd pair shares the compartment, the little governess becomes more comfortable with the old man. She looks out the window of the train and 'A cold blue light fill[s] the window panes' (56). However, the blueness is not negative for the little governess this time. The cabin increasingly loses its status as feminine space, the longer the man inhabits it. As the little governess conforms to this new reality, previous elements of comfort and security begin to appear peculiar and new ones take their place. Mansfield writes,

> How pretty it was! How pretty and how different! Even those pink clouds in the sky looked foreign. It was cold, but she pretended that it was far colder and rubbed her hands together and shivered, pulling at the collar of her coat because she was so happy. (56)

Earlier, when she exited the cabin on the boat and felt the 'cold, strange wind', she wished to be back in the Ladies' Cabin with the woman 'who had smiled at her in the glass, when they both did their hair' (51). Now the little governess pretends to be even colder than she actually is. A previously negative sensation thrills her and awakens a fascination for things unknown and unexplored.

They pass a town. The little governess observes more sights: 'Look! look what flowers – and by the railway station too! Standard roses like bridesmaids' bouquets, white geraniums, waxy pink ones that you would never see out of a greenhouse at home' (56–7). Here the colour pink is made alien again as the little governess sees pink geraniums that she would never – italicised never – see at home. As she continues to share space with the man, the previously accepted feminine world becomes foreign, and so does the colour pink. Even so, the man gives strawberries to her in an attempt to build trust further. In this sexualised scene, the pink-fleshed berries are large and the juice runs down her fingers. This trope of forbidden fruit represents female sexual maturity.[10] The old man uses the berries in an attempt to awaken the little governess sexually, but as she eats them, she thinks of the man as her grandfather instead of as a lover. Then Mansfield writes, 'The sun came out, the pink clouds in the sky, the strawberry clouds were eaten by the blue' (57–8). Here seems to be a turning point for the little governess. Mansfield equates the strawberries with the pink clouds and, as such, the feminine world. In this scene, then, the pink strawberry clouds are consumed by the blue clouds even as the female space is infiltrated by the male. Though she has not awakened sexually, the old man has still succeeded. The little governess trusts him fully as surrogate grandfather. After she eats the berries, she feels as if 'she [has] known the old man for years' (58), and she tells him all about her future as governess in Germany. He invites her to accompany him for a day of sightseeing in Munich. Despite the warning from the lady at the governess bureau, despite the 'cold, strange wind' she felt on the dock, and despite all better judgement, the little governess agrees, thinking 'he was so old and he had been so very kind – not to mention the strawberries. . . .' (58).

After the train arrives in Munich, the little governess and the old man spend the day together. In this new and exciting world, she finds adventure. The warning from the lady at the governess bureau seems silly to her now and she trusts the old man – her 'grandfather' – as he shows her the culture of the city. He does not appear to have any 'evil intentions,' as described in the advice for young female travellers at the beginning of the story (51). After several generally pleasant excursions together, the old man asks the little governess to accompany him back to his apartment, telling her that his old female housekeeper will be present as well. The little governess agrees, laughing and exclaiming, '"I've never seen a bachelor's flat in my life"' (60). After continued exposure to increasing levels of male space, the little governess feels comfortable entering this new domain. They enter a 'dark' passage, and right as he goes to open the door, the old man remarks, 'Ah, I suppose my old woman has gone out to buy me a chicken. One moment' (60), a comment which leaves readers to wonder whether the housekeeper ever existed or if she was a fabrication of feminine familiarity, created by the old man to abate the little governess's potential uneasiness with the completely male space of his apartment.

As they enter, the old man asks what she thinks of the space and she does not know what to say, as she finds it 'very ugly – but neat and [. . .] comfortable for such an old man' (60). After he asks the question, however, he kneels down and '[takes] from the cupboard a round tray with two pink glasses and a tall pink bottle' (60). He pours the wine into the little pink glasses with quivering hands. These emblematic vessels receiving the liquid represent the old man's carnal desire for the little governess. She becomes uncomfortable and tells him that she wishes to leave. These small, pink glasses are foreign in the male space of the apartment, which becomes evident to the little governess as she herself begins to feel foreign in the space. Kaplan writes that 'by situating this young female protagonist in an alien environment, alone, with-out the traditionally supportive interactions of the female community, Mansfield exposes women's vulnerability in the world of men' (389).[11] Upon seeing this pink symbol of female vulnerability and his attempt at exploitation, she speaks up to the old man, and full discomfort sets in as she begins to realize his true intentions. He takes advantage of her:

> It was a dream! It wasn't true! It wasn't the same old man at all. Ah, how horrible! The little governess stared at him in terror, 'No, no, no!' she stammered, struggling out of his hands. 'One little kiss. A kiss. What is it? Just a kiss, dear little Fräulein. A kiss.' He pushed his face forward, his lips smiling broadly; and how his little blue eyes gleamed behind the spectacles! (61)

Blue eyes are the last thing the little governess sees before the old man kisses her. She no longer notices his lack of beard, neatness or pink cheeks. In this moment of danger and disillusionment, his 'little blue eyes' pierce through the spectacles, betraying her trust, and prove true the warning from the lady at the governess bureau: 'It's better to mistrust people at first rather than trust them' (51).

In a story that heavily utilises colour imagery, the final two paragraphs exclude any mention of colour. The image of the 'little blue eyes' is the last colour-marked image readers see – an image that symbolises danger's association with the male gender. For the inconsolable little governess on the tram, the world is now full of 'old men with twitching knees' (61). Janet Wilson writes that 'The Little Governess' falls into a type of Mansfield story wherein the protagonist becomes awakened in some way by travel. In these stories of adolescent female vulnerability, 'the young subject [. . .] is susceptible to compelling but disillusioning romantic encounters, often occurring when they are in transit'.[12] During this last leg of the little governess's trip, it seems she has reached complete disillusionment, equating all males on the tram – and in the world – with the old man who has taken advantage of her. She arrives back at the Hotel Grünewald, and it is interesting here to note that the male waiter, who was unpleasant to the little governess earlier in the story, polishes a tray of glasses, reminiscent of the pink symbols of the female from the preceding scene. The waiter delivers the final devastating news: Frau Arnholdt is gone and is not to return. He smiles, obviously pleased with this outcome. Yet again, it is a male who gives the final jab. The little governess is left violated, jobless and entirely mistrusting of men.

As the little governess ventures further away from the safety of the Ladies' Cabin, she rejects the innocence and purity of completely female space. Initially, she experiences excitement, even happiness, as she leaves the pink world behind her. Old comforts become alien; the strawberry clouds are eaten by the blue. But then, at the hands of the old man, the little governess experiences ultimate disillusionment. She loses her chance of a job and the possibility to return back to female space as governess to the Arnholdt children. Perhaps, though, Mansfield wishes for it to be this way. Maybe the story makes an additional statement that women should not have to return to the all-female world of pinning hats and changing nappies. Rather than the polarised nature of male and female space, a spectrum exists between blue and pink. Purple space, perhaps? A space where women do not receive blame for their own victimisation. One where they can freely walk the corridors of the train. One where they can trust people before mistrusting them. Until then, Mansfield and her characters work within the system, within female space – one piece of pink wool at a time.

Notes

1. Ruth Parkin-Gounelas, 'Katherine Mansfield's Piece of Pink Wool: Feminine Signification in "The Luftbad"', *Studies in Short Fiction*, 27: 4 (1990), pp. 495–507 (p. 495).
2. Parkin-Gounelas, p. 496.
3. Vincent O'Sullivan and Margaret Scott, eds, *The Collected Letters of Katherine Mansfield*, 5 vols (Oxford: Clarendon Press, 1984–2008), Vol. 4, p. 104.
4. Parkin-Gounelas, p. 496.
5. Sydney Janet Kaplan, *Katherine Mansfield and the Origins of Modernist Fiction* (Ithaca, NY: Cornell University Press, 1991), p. 390.
6. Kaplan, p. 389.
7. Vincent O'Sullivan, ed., 'The Little Governess', *Katherine Mansfield Selected Stories* (New York: W. W. Norton, 2006), pp. 51–62 (p. 51). Hereafter all references to this story will be included parenthetically in the text.
8. Kaplan, p. 390.
9. Janka Kaščáková, '"Blue with Cold": Coldness in the Works of Katherine Mansfield', in Janet Wilson, Gerri Kimber and Susan Reid, eds, *Katherine Mansfield and Literary Modernism* (New York: Bloomsbury, 2011), pp. 188–201 (p. 192).
10. Kathryn Simpson, '"Strange Flower, Half Opened": Katherine Mansfield and the Flowering of "the Self"', in Janka Kaščáková and Gerri Kimber, eds, *Katherine Mansfield and Continental Europe: Connections and Influences* (New York: Palgrave Macmillian, 2015), pp. 185–201 (p. 190).
11. Kaplan, p. 389.
12. Janet Wilson, 'Katherine Mansfield's Stories 1909–1914: The Child and the "Childish"', in Kaščáková and Kimber, pp. 221–35 (p. 221).

Apples and Pears: Symbolism and Influence in Daphne du Maurier's 'The Apple Tree' and Katherine Mansfield's 'Bliss'

Setara Pracha

We discovered the *cimetière* on a hill. The *gardien* told us that she was first buried in the Fosse commune – the common grave for the poor – but her *beau-frère* had her moved and placed where she is now, with just a plain slab stone in memory. Her husband, Middleton Murry, had never been near it. I bought some flowers and put them on her grave. I wish I had the money to pay for it to be kept in order. I can't forget it.[1]

This essay focuses on a comparative analysis of the short stories 'Bliss' (1918) by Katherine Mansfield and 'The Apple Tree' (1952) by Daphne du Maurier,[2] two stories that illustrate key literary parallels: the use of dramatic irony, 'organic unity'[3] and liminal spaces.[4] In recent years, literary criticism has repositioned Mansfield as a vital contributor to the development of literary modernism. Her influence upon other writers is still being explored and the short stories of du Maurier, herself erroneously regarded as merely a popular novelist, indicate both Mansfield and modernism as primary influences. Clare Drewery argues that there are 'few comparative discussions of modernist women's short stories'[5]; this study attempts to redress such an imbalance by showing how a close reading of Mansfield and du Maurier's stories illuminates the current debate on genre and gender within shorter fiction.[6]

Mansfield died in 1923, when du Maurier was only sixteen, but she was a significant influence on du Maurier, who commented that '[s]urely Katherine Mansfield would not have been so easily discouraged?', when trying to overcome the difficulties of living as a writer.[7] In this we see that du Maurier is not only taking literary inspiration from Mansfield, but also using her as a model for living, as well as for the development of her fiction. In a letter from du Maurier to her governess, Maud Waddell (known in the du Maurier family as Tod), the twenty-one-year-old fledgling writer comments:

I met someone who used to know Katherine Mansfield very well, and apparently K.M. used to live at Hampstead at one time and told this friend how terribly interested she was in the du Maurier children and that she longed to talk to us, and used to watch us for hours playing about on the heath. [. . .]

Isn't it wonderful Tod? Probably when Madam and I used to dash about as Red Indians and schoolboys, Katherine Mansfield watched us. If only she'd spoken to us. It's so odd because she honestly is quite my favourite writer, and I've always felt how sympathetic she must have been. I'm sure I should never have started writing stories if I hadn't her example before me.[8]

However, there is more substance to this comparison than mere proximity and timing, as both story content and form indicate a closer relationship between the two authors. Du Maurier's work is currently undergoing a period of critical reassessment, indicated by Virago's recent republication of her novels and short story collections. However, this repositioning has yet to reach her shorter fiction, which reveals a social awareness and moral didacticism worthy of greater critical attention. Mansfield's influence on style and symbolism in du Maurier's writing is crucial in this study, and the stories chosen perfectly illustrate the importance of the liminal in modernist texts, a space in which 'pivotal individual and cultural change' is caused by 'life's significant milestones such as adolescence, mourning, death and old age'.[9] Mansfield's influence is clearly discernible in du Maurier's stories, which, like Mansfield's, range from satirical thrusts at the bourgeois dinner-party set to accounts of lives on the margins, and more generally, to what Drewery calls the modernist focus on the 'inner life, fragmentation, ambiguity, epiphany, and the relationship between the individual and society'.[10]

It was, perhaps, from reading Mansfield's stories that du Maurier learnt her trick of composing a memorable first line. Both Mansfield's 'Bliss' and du Maurier's 'The Apple Tree' begin *in media res*: 'Although Bertha Young was thirty she still had moments like this when she wanted to run instead of walk'[11]; 'It was three months since she died when he first noticed the apple tree.'[12] This mode compels immediate identification with the protagonist and encourages narrative empathy, something that is subverted later for dramatic effect as the stories increasingly become 'narratives of madness, told from within'.[13] 'Bliss' and 'The Apple Tree' centralise marital disharmony against a bourgeois domestic backdrop, using symbols from nature to explore psychological states and epiphanic moments. A modernist focus on time is apparent in the form and structure of the stories: 'The Apple Tree' surveys a twenty-five-year marriage framed within one seasonal year that starts in early spring, whilst 'Bliss' sketches the life of a married couple within a single day. Both stories illustrate self-deception as the greatest danger to health and happiness, and unconscious, not conscious, desires as primary behavioural motivation.

The unconscious is vulnerable when individuals undergo trauma, and both stories set the potential for personal epiphany in a context of the trauma of loss. The threshold state of bereavement, literal and metaphorical in these texts, is a potent catalyst for the transition into the speaking subject, and the 'in-between space of the garden', where much of the action occurs, shows that liminal spaces, and indeed the stories themselves, 'are occupied only on a transitory basis'.[14] This is apt because both stories are preoccupied with the challenge of a personal trauma (infidelity and bereavement respectively), which could serve as a catalyst for growth, or as confirmation that a character cannot develop beyond the patterns of stasis in which they find themselves caught. Both Bertha and Buzz fall into the latter category, and this aspect of their characters is drawn against the persistent and, for them, unsettling vitality of the trees in their gardens. The abiding naïvety of Bertha Young's immature worldview makes the reader question her childlike interpretation of events as she totters on the verge of womanhood without finally making the crossover. Likewise, in 'The Apple Tree', du Maurier offers her male protagonist, Buzz, as a man who is trapped in a pattern of interpreting everything through his guilty fixation with his dead wife. His lack of self-knowledge is illustrated by his determination to destroy the apple tree, which is emblematic of his frustrated anger towards her in death as well as in life.

Du Maurier presents the reader with the character of recently widowed Buzz, a man preparing to enjoy his wife-free retirement in a new pattern of lengthy foreign holidays and visits to the local pub. This bachelor idyll is disturbed, however, when he notices the seasonal changes in two apple trees in his garden, one of which reminds him of his wife, and the other of a Land Girl with whom he shared an illicit wartime kiss. Unable to shake off the memories of either woman, his increasingly erratic behaviour parallels his obsessional malice towards the older tree and his increasing affection for the younger one. His mania escalates in response to a series of minor events, after which Buzz sees the older tree's blossoms as ugly, the fruit rotten, the logs unburnable and their smoke dangerous, and he is finally successful in chopping down the hated tree. Determined to dispose of the evidence, he behaves as if it is the remnants of a body rather than the logs from a tree in his own garden: 'The logs lay there [...] one charred limb above another, black and huddled, like the bones of someone darkened and dead by fire. Nausea rose in him. He thrust his handkerchief into his mouth, choking' (131). Buzz, with even the onomatopoeia of his name dependent on the existence of a 'midge', is found to be unable to live without the tree: unable to provide for himself, unable to entertain himself, and unable to remain sane.

'Bliss' presents Bertha's apparent happiness as being a symptom of hysteria arising from a lack of sexual intimacy with her husband, Harry. This is hinted at in the reader's first encounter with the pear tree, about which Bertha 'couldn't help feeling, even from this distance, that it had not a single bud or a faded petal' (99). Her perception of the tree is governed by how she feels about it, and this feeling arises in a woman who lacks self-knowledge until she is faced with the 'strange and almost terrifying' possibility that '[f]or the first time in her life [she] desired her husband. Oh, she'd loved him – she'd been in love with him, of course, in every other way, but just not in that way' (107–8).

The story takes place on a spring evening during which Bertha's fears and preoccupations are projected on to the tree, which remains in a state of changeless perfection – neither immature ('not a single bud') nor ageing ('not a single [. . .] faded petal'); rather it is in 'fullest, richest bloom' and stands between the stages of fertilisation and fruiting timelessly (99–100). Its immaculate stasis grips Bertha with both its beauty and its implied stagnant, unbearable permanence. The narrative implies that this is the moment that both are caught in, and both are presented as incapable of change because Bertha, and therefore the pear tree that she sees as her proxy, resist, fear and flee from the thought of change – at least as far as provoking it herself. Yet, the sensual and sexually charged verbs used to describe the moonlit pear tree – 'stretch [. . .] point [. . .] quiver [. . .] grow [. . .] touch' – signify that the pear tree will be fertilised, bear fruit and complete its natural cycle, whereas Bertha's life will remain the same (106). At the end of the story, and after witnessing indications of marital infidelity, her plaintive cry of 'Oh, what is going to happen now?' is answered in the last word of the story, which is 'still' (110). This parallels the denouement of 'The Apple Tree', where Buzz's shout of 'let me go' is addressed to the inanimate tree stump and is met with silence and 'darkness' (159).

In these darkly skewed versions of marriage, the trees serve as an objective correlative for clandestine desires, and a reminder of that first taste of forbidden fruit in Genesis. The trees in both stories are a transformational force, crystallising the doubts, fears, hopes and dreams of characters in liminal states (new motherhood, bereavement) and spaces (thresholds, gardens). The seamless dipping into the thoughts of Bertha and Buzz reveal their inner preoccupations and a tendency to project their emotions on to external objects. 'The Apple Tree' reveals Buzz's guilty preoccupation with his dead wife, Midge. At the beginning of the story Buzz immediately notices the tree and identifies it with her: 'It was a trick of the light perhaps. [. . .] the likeness was unmistakable' (114). This builds until at the end of the story when Buzz kills the tree, which is in his mind an attempt to make Midge die a second time, thinking as he approaches it, '[s]he was almost within reach' (158).

Both stories show two women competing for one man's attention, and both men are attracted to women who are unlike their wives. Names have a heavy significance in these sexual triangles of temptation and exclusion, and both of the 'other women' are suitably titled. In 'Bliss' it is the taciturn Pearl whose name suggests beauty and purity, who fascinates Harry with her maturity, sophistication and poise; for Buzz it is May, the Land Girl, who is as young and fresh as the season her name evokes. The name 'Pearl' evokes the image of a precious, desirable object indicating high status for the wearer but the precious jewel is also made by an irritant, a grain of sand, over time. Du Maurier, like Mansfield, puns heavily on names in the text and May is a spring month of burgeoning fecundity in nature, as well as a verb of ability and permission. 'I may' is equivalent to 'I can', a pertinent detail in a plot centralising sexual infidelity. The nineteen-year-old May is 'cheerful and pretty and smiling [. . .] when she smiled it was as though she embraced the world' (122), whereas Midge is described as being 'dejected [. . .] stooping [. . .] worn out' and Buzz sees her as a 'fundamental blight upon good cheer' (114–15). Buzz calls May a child, even though he desires her as a woman, whilst Bertha regards her youth as an advantage, overstating the blessings of her life in a way that undermines the argument even as she makes it:

> Really – really – she had everything. She was young. Harry and she were as much in love as ever, and they got on together splendidly and were really good pals. She had an adorable baby. They didn't have to worry about money. They had this absolutely satisfactory house and garden [. . .] and their new cook made the most superb omelettes . . . (100)

The final superfluous statement trails off into nothingness, rendering the previous statements suspect and the whole passage unconvincing. This listing of superficial details strongly marks Bertha's lack of conviction that she has a happy marriage; conversely, Buzz's constant reiteration of Midge's faults hints at a deep regret over a *not* unhappy marriage.

Significantly, it is spring in both narratives, the season of rising sap, increased energy and sexual activity that produces fruit, and babies. The sensuousness of the adjectives describing the fruit in 'Bliss' is saturated with the language of desire: the apples are '*stained* with strawberry pink', the pears '*smooth* as silk', and the grapes have 'a silver *bloom*' (my italics, 96). Bertha has developed an enthusiasm for a woman she has recently encountered, Pearl Fulton, with whom her husband, Harry Young, is having an affair. Bertha considers Pearl '"a find"' (98), resulting in a personal betrayal on two counts, as she has unwittingly brought another one of the 'beautiful women who have something strange about them' (99) into her home, and into her marriage. 'Why be given a body?' (95) and 'Why have a baby?' (97) are the unanswered and unanswerable questions Bertha asks herself and – implicitly – the reader, unable to articulate answers in a social system in which she is a decorative object rather than a functioning, speaking subject. On a first reading of 'Bliss', Bertha appears to be a woman whose domestic situation positions her as diametrically opposed to Midge in 'The Apple Tree'. Bertha is a happy wife, delighting in her marriage, baby daughter, friends, home and staff, whereas Midge carries the 'impossible burden' of 'dreary routine of unnecessary tasks' through 'interminable changeless years' (114–15). However, when Bertha wonderingly states, 'How idiotic civilisation is!' (95), she is tacitly commenting on her own idiocy in maintaining a complicit silence regarding her lack of status and power. There is the sense that the feelings of this young wife will grow until they become Midge's 'long-term reproach', a resentment deeply felt but unspoken and dangerous. Domestic authority is a recurring theme in twentieth-century women's writing, and Mansfield's and du Maurier's feminism is implicit, not explicit; yet while it is not a political principle, 'its underlying presence is everywhere'.[15] This implicit feminism shows itself in the foregrounding of female desires; the acknowledgement and exploration of the traditionally female domestic sphere; and in the way that these stories, and the works of Mansfield and du Maurier more broadly, scrutinise the roles that woman are given or create for themselves in homes, relationships and power structures. Thirty years before Midge's tale of unending domestic responsibilities, Bertha irresponsibly forgets her keys 'again' and is consequently treated like a child by the staff, including the nurse who does not trust her with her own baby. For Bertha, the pear tree's beauty, stability and fruition are a natural complement to her position as wife and mother: 'And she seemed to see on her eyelids the lovely pear tree with its wide open blossoms as a symbol of her own life' (100). What she cannot yet see is that having successfully married within her class and produced a child, she now has a merely social and decorative function.

Desire – legitimate and illicit – unifies and unites the stories. Midge wants Buzz's attention and she has evidently not had it; he will not even

177

touch the tree that is her avatar. In 'Bliss' it is spring and, startlingly, Bertha desires her husband for the first time. In parallel to du Maurier's fecund apple trees, which are potent symbols of two sexually unfulfilled dead women, the pear tree in Mansfield's story is in full bloom:

> The windows of the drawing room opened onto a balcony overlooking the garden. At the far end, against the wall, there was a tall, slender pear tree in fullest, richest bloom; it stood perfect, as though becalmed against the jade-green sky. Bertha couldn't help feeling, even from this distance, that it had not a single bud or a faded petal. (100)

'[B]ecalmed' is cruelly ambiguous in describing Bertha through the tree which stands as her proxy. She is without purpose as a mother, wife or housekeeper, and is therefore as becalmed as the pear tree she regards as symbolic of her life. In her misreading of its symbolic plurality she mirrors Buzz in 'The Apple Tree', whose delusions conflate his deceased wife with a tree and cause his presumably fatal entrapment by its stump in wintry darkness. Buzz is so determined to pursue his vendetta that he loses sight of all judgement and follows a course of action that leaves him injured and alone in the snowy garden. At the end of the story we see the discrepancy between the real and the perceived as Buzz shouts '"let me go", as though the thing that held him there in its mercy had the power to release him' (159). This is a clear indication that we should doubt both Buzz and Bertha as witnesses because we are clearly shown that their worldviews are inaccurate and partial.

In 'Bliss', Bertha's sartorial choices simulate the image of the tree: in a white dress with green stockings and shoes and jade beads, she is the daytime image of the tree, while Pearl is the nighttime vision dressed in ethereal silver. Significantly, Pearl Fulton is dressed as a goddess, as Artemis–Diana, 'with a silver fillet binding her blonde hair', deities symbolised by the moon. These are apposite and balanced costumes for the two women in this story, one of whom is the figurehead of Harry's household and the other the mistress of his secret desires.

In the climactic scene Harry throws down Pearl's coat, puts his hands on her body, turns her violently towards him and whispers, '[t]omorrow' – the promise of a future assignation (100). In passion, Harry is grotesquely and bestially transformed into an animal with quivering nostrils and a 'hideous grin', while celestial Pearl retains her 'sleepy smile' and 'moonbeam' fingers (109). The fingers are suggestive of Pearl's magically enchanting abilities as a woman who has not only caused girlish Bertha to 'fall in love with her' (99), but also has her husband Harry within her grasp. Bertha plans to tell Harry what the two women have shared when they are in bed together that night: an act of intimate relation planned after non-existent intimate relations, which places the 'new and mysterious' Pearl right in between them in the marital bed.

Both Buzz and Bertha are subject to extreme states of fear charged with sublimated sexual violence:

> At his last words something strange and almost terrifying darted into Bertha's mind. And this something blind and smiling whispered to her: 'Soon these people will go. The house will be quiet – quiet. The lights will be out. And you and he will be alone together in the dark room – the warm bed. . . .' (107)

This Lawrentian passage recalls D. H. Lawrence's own short story, 'The Blind Man' (1922), in its evocation of the mysteries of erotic sensuality but Mansfield, like du Maurier, privileges trust and intimacy over sex.[16] The pathos arises from the fact that both focalisers feel the loss of that which they never had: a fulfilling marriage. The leitmotif of the cats in 'Bliss' echoes the behaviour of mistress and adulterer: the black cat (Harry) follows the grey one (Pearl) while Bertha looks on, stammering, unsure and unable to articulate the implications of what she witnesses. It is notable that in her most adult role, that of hostess, Bertha misses the significant fact that both Harry and the sole unaccompanied female guest are the only ones late for dinner. In 'The Apple Tree', Midge also sees evidence of marital infidelity and stands staring at the couple made by her husband and the nubile Land Girl. She never mentions their intimacy, though years pass, whilst Bertha's childlike and immediate plea of 'What will happen now?' correspondingly positions her as a cipher in a grown-up world; without the power to direct events, both wives are solely reactive.

To Buzz, the apple tree symbolises his wife – dejected, depressed, weary and overburdened – and it is only through the proxy of the tree that he is able to even come close to confronting the awful reality of Midge's life. The 'clamouring brothers and sisters' are the old tree's intemperate overabundance of apples, and a reminder of the fruitlessness of the marriage. Buzz will not even touch the tree that reminds him so strongly of Midge, and earlier in the story he yawns, taking up a book while she anxiously waits, in the hope of amorous advances.[17] This raises the issue of whether the lack of children results from the husband's sexual indifference, and suggests that his impotent fury at the tree is provoked by his fury at his own impotence. Midge is 'eager yet uncertain' and 'desperately anxious to attract' her husband (135) – descriptions that also apply to Bertha Young in 'Bliss'. In spite of his wife's desire for intimacy, Buzz looks elsewhere for flirtation, finding his wife's attempts to please him as pathetic and detestable as the old apple tree which, once she is dead, constantly evokes her memory. Du Maurier specialises in writing weak, middle-aged men of questionable sexuality – James Fenton, Maxim de Winter, Buzz – highlighting the uncomfortable question of whether a marriage minus intimacy and children is actually a marriage. From Mansfield's narrative the reader initially learns that 'bliss' may not include physical passion, as Bertha Young loves her husband Harry but 'just not in that way', as she understands that he is simply 'different' to her (108). She holds herself responsible for her frigidity, and although 'it had worried her dreadfully at first to find that she was so cold', eventually 'it had not seemed to matter' (108). Of course, it *does* matter.

Power – sexual, maternal, domestic, economic – is a major theme in both narratives, as, for example, in 'Bliss', when the nurse transforms Bertha, 'little B's' biological mother, into the pathetic figure of a 'poor little girl in front of the rich girl with the doll' (97). Bertha pleads with the nurse for permission to feed her infant daughter in 'Bliss', whilst in 'The Apple Tree' patriarchal structures are reversed and, with looking-glass polarity, Midge's household routines discomfit Buzz at every turn. The culturally determined defining features of womanhood and femininity are explored in a subtext that places the metaphor of woman-as-nature-symbol against apparently mundane events. An example of this is Bertha's outfit for the dinner-party in 'Bliss': 'A white dress, a string of jade beads, green shoes and stockings. It wasn't intentional. She had thought of this scheme hours before she stood at the drawing-room window. Her *petals* rustled softly into the hall' (my italics, 100). Bertha's metaphorical petals, included in the description as literal, illustrate that she is a woman who will, dryad-like, remain as silent as the tree until the open-ended conclusion of the story. Her naïvety ensures that the reader does not have access to her undeceived self, just as we only have access to Buzz when he is at his most self-deceptive, and thus neither character can deliver authentic clues to the realities of their lives. The swift change of tack between direct speech and free indirect thought is a habitual pattern with du Maurier, who uses the practice in a Mansfieldian manner to focus attention on the discrepancies between a character's inner life and their interactions with others. In common with Midge in 'The Apple Tree', Bertha and Pearl are silenced within the text despite the free indirect style used to convey Bertha's inner life. In Midge, du Maurier enacts a rewriting of Ovid's myth of metamorphosis whereby – according to Greek myth – a victim of abuse can escape sexual violence only by being turned into a tree and forever silenced.[18] In this latter-day version, Midge's silence does not preclude power, or indeed violent revenge if she is read as an actual revenant haunting Buzz instead of an aspect of his psyche. Bertha is betrayed by the myth of domestic bliss promised by marriage and motherhood, and remains helplessly mute, whereas in this reading Midge enacts a startling revenge on her husband through his own belief in the tree as her vengeful avatar. His obsessional mania proves fatal; there is no escape from the inside of your own head. 'Bliss' begins the narrative for which 'The Apple Tree' is a literal closure.

In Dominic Head's thorough examination of the modernist short story, he defines some of the characteristic devices employed by Mansfield and others, devices he cites as particular to the genre. One of these is the 'tension between the narrative voice and its own self doubts'.[19] Du Maurier is an expert in creating narrators who are hesitant, arrogant and self-betraying. As Head goes on to state, in Mansfield's writing the complexity of characterisation develops at the exact point where the narrative authority begins to fragment. At the core of each text there is a struggle for articulation, shown by frequent ellipses and tangents, interruptions and abrupt endings, a struggle that shows us human beings at the extremes of human experience.

Mansfield's repeated use of ellipses in thought serves to highlight the omissions in speech, foregrounding the things characters are unwilling, or unable, to say. This is a technique borrowed by du Maurier, as Buzz continually trails off when conflating the apple tree with his wife, whose trademark sigh of 'Oh well . . .' always starts an unfinished sentence, something Buzz interprets as 'part of her long-term reproach' against him (116). Midge is incapable of articulating her feelings, even when she witnesses her husband's betrayal with the Land Girl, and throughout Mansfield's story Bertha Young cannot clothe her feelings in words, whether she is thinking of cats or collusion. The final ellipsis in 'Bliss' comes after those telling words: 'And she saw . . . '; before the apparently factual description of Harry and Pearl together there is an indication of the gap between Bertha's perception and the reality that she chooses not to recognise (110). What is apparent happiness is expressed by Bertha in her irrepressible ability to laugh, to 'laugh at – nothing – at nothing, simply', and this echoes the hysterical laughter of Linda Burnell in Mansfield's 'Prelude' (1917), another wife with no power over her fertility and, thus, her future. 'No, no, I am getting hysterical,' says Bertha, caught in the grip of uncontrollable emotion (96). For women, excessive laughter, as Elaine Showalter's book on female madness, *The Female Malady*, illustrates, is a behaviour with potentially dramatic consequences.[20]

181

Mansfield and du Maurier's short fiction negotiates the boundaries of patient narratives in which individuals relate their experience of altered mental states and, as Gail A. Hornstein comments, 'We may be frightened as we read such stories. [. . .] Mental patients show us how much terror or suspicion it is possible to feel before collapsing under the weight or committing suicide.'[21] Du Maurier's work persistently features patient narratives, and in 'The Apple Tree' she afflicts both Midge, who is sickly while alive, and Buzz, who loses his comfort, sanity and life. Although Buzz's bereavement elevates him to the status of sovereign master of his household, the garden encircles the house and him; the silent apple tree that embodies Midge, his wife, has more power and significance than she ever did when alive. Buzz imagines the apple tree speaking to him in the bitter tones of Midge's unspoken resentment of twenty-five years of wifehood: 'is this my reward after all I have done for you?' (145). His subconscious supplies the barbs she never spoke in life.

In 'Bliss' Bertha cannot articulate her position as object because she cannot comprehend it. This shift from subject to object status is evident to the reader, however, in the subtle move from 'want[ing] to [. . .] laugh [. . .] at nothing, simply' (95), to 'simply' running at the end of the story, coming close to actualising her desire but instead manifesting the urge to flee from the truth. Pearl Fulton's comment echoes nightmarishly in Bertha's mind: '"Your lovely pear tree – pear tree – pear tree!"' (109), as if the pear tree that Bertha sees as a symbol for her own life now carries the negative attributes of being static, silent and redundant. '"Oh, what is going to happen now?" she cried. But the pear tree was as lovely as ever and as full of flower and as still' (110). This lack of movement emphasises Bertha's lack of capacity to make decisions or be in charge of herself as woman, wife or mother.

Patient narratives centralise the disenfranchised, marginal and weak. Drewery applies Kristevan theory to modernist fiction by women, stating that '[t]he stories imply that to stay silent, to accept a position that is culturally or linguistically "outside" is to be disempowered, to risk marginalisation', before adding Judith Butler's refinement that 'there cannot be an absolute "outside" from which the boundaries of discourse can be exceeded or countered'.[22] The implication that to accept silence is also to accept marginalisation is demonstrated with great force in both of these stories, and this is made more terrifying by the eternal and inescapable boundary that a character's mind presents for them. Unable to exceed or counter such a limit, Bertha and Buzz unknowingly create and accept reduced roles for themselves, subsiding into a passivity that is equivalent to, or even enacts, the end of life.

These works argue for an understanding of modernism that is uniquely feminine – that the concerns of modernism are especially relevant to the lives of women. This can be seen in the impact of the newly industrial and urbanised culture of the twentieth century and in the social changes effected by two world wars, altering the family unit and women's lives beyond recognition. Seen from this perspective, du Maurier is not a writer of escapist fantasies; rather, she is a writer of failed escape attempts. Like Mansfield, du Maurier recognises marriage as a potentially dangerous trap rather than an escape to greater freedoms. In the words of Head: '[m]arriage, far from being the promised state of fulfilment, is presented as destructive of the female'.[23] The female characters in du Maurier's stories seek a man for either financial support or sex, or both – but never for love alone. Mansfield is concerned with concealed hypocrisy, the limits of rebellion and freedom, and both writers present women at all stages of their lives: girlhood, adolescence, courtship, marriage, motherhood and dotage. If, as Nina Auerbach states, '[r]ebellion is dispossession', then du Maurier's heroines are constantly re-adjusting their positions in line with male actions in a world where even 'good women could sap their will'.[24] Both writers are equally convincing in their depictions of male characters whose motivations are authentic to a startling degree. As Auerbach states of du Maurier, in a comment that could easily refer to Mansfield:

> Daphne du Maurier's uncanny fictional ability to become a man without ever revering men or making a case against them is utterly unwomanly – some might even call her self-transformations antiwomanly – but I continue to admire du Maurier's audacity in choosing roles beyond her own, roles she plays with sympathetic penetration.[25]

This subtlety of characterisation is more significant when considering the new role of the individual in modernist thought, and this speaks to a new figuring of the male protagonist: often an alienated, disenfranchised, anxious individual, living in fantasy. Fantasy is as central to the genre of short-story writing as it is to modernism and these are stories which incorporate dreams, visions and delusions to work through the major social, cultural and political changes experienced by their authors.

In du Maurier's stories, 'Mazie', 'Piccadilly' and 'Panic' (1955),[26] there are the grubby, mean locales and pathetic denizens we associate with Mansfield's stories, 'Miss Brill' (1920) and 'The Daughters of the Late Colonel' (1920). Yet, these themes of decay and decline belie narratives which are spiced with the sharp humour characteristic of du Maurier, a humour that tempers her moribund tales with lightness and redeems them from irrepressible gloom, also a notable feature of many of Mansfield's stories. Du Maurier invites us into a conspiracy of mocking laughter which is reminiscent of Mansfield at her ambiguous best, and while a close reading of Mansfield's stories makes it plain that the most painful of her plots are seasoned with her customary biting wit, du Maurier's tales, so redolent with glee at human flaws and foibles, have yet to be critically addressed.

This essay reveals how, through their short fiction, Mansfield and du Maurier are closely engaged in a negotiation of influence that is made more powerful as a text presence by the biographical proximity of the authors. Mansfield's influence on du Maurier's writing is clear from the appreciative comments in du Maurier's letters:

> I've been reading 'Bliss' etc, by Katherine Mansfield. The stories are too wonderful [. . .] and some of them leave one with a kind of hopeless feeling. [A] sort of feeling that life is merely repetition, and love monotony. Oh, it's not really that but a kind of helpless pity for the dreariness of other people's lives. [. . .] There is one story called 'The Dill Pickle'. Oh God! and another – I've forgotten the name – about a poor woman – So dreary, hopeless, pathetic, But wonderful, and wonderfully written.[27]

Du Maurier's comments suggest that what caught and kept her interest in Mansfield's writing was the latter's urge to fictionalise lives not customarily depicted, and more importantly, to depict the transgressive and illicit aspects of those lives. The rich seam of textual correlations between du Maurier and Mansfield's writing remains unexamined, yet each writer provides us with a valuable means of accessing the work of the other. This essay begins this examination, but is also intended to be an invitation to wider, deeper and greater parallel readings of Mansfield and du Maurier. The symbolism of fruit runs through both the stories discussed above, symbolising generation and degeneration, temptation and revulsion, in stories which offer myth in a modernist style.

Notes

1. Daphne du Maurier, *Myself When Young* (London: Virago, 2004), p. 164. Here du Maurier describes visiting Katherine Mansfield's grave at Fontainebleau as the 'highlight' of a trip to France in 1927.
2. Mansfield also wrote a story called 'Autumns: I', published in *Signature*, 1 (4 October 1915), pp. 15–18, signed 'Matilda Berry' and later retitled 'The Apple Tree' by John Middleton Murry.
3. Sydney Janet Kaplan, *Katherine Mansfield and the Origins of Modernist Fiction* (Ithaca, NY: Cornell University Press, 1991), p. 3.
4. Mansfield's 'Bliss' and du Maurier's 'The Apple Tree' were both titular stories in their original short story collections. The Virago republication in 2004 of du Maurier's

The Birds and Other Stories privileges 'The Birds' in the title as the better-known du Maurier story, following Alfred Hitchcock's film adaptation.

5. Clare Drewery, *Modernist Short Fiction by Women: The Liminal in Katherine Mansfield, Dorothy Richardson and Virginia Woolf* (Farnham: Ashgate, 2011), p. 8.

6. See Dominic Head, *The Modernist Short Story: A Study in Theory and Practice* (Cambridge: Cambridge University Press, 2009); and Emma Liggins, Andrew Maunder and Ruth Robbins, eds, *The British Short Story* (Basingstoke: Palgrave Macmillan, 2011).

7. Du Maurier, *Myself When Young*, p. 177.

8. Letter from du Maurier to Maud Waddell, 19 June 1928, pp. 2–4, Special Collections, Exeter Archives, University of Exeter. Packet labelled 'Letters to Tod 1920–1930', EUL MS 206 add.1. Permission to reproduce excerpts from du Maurier's unpublished letters is given by her son and literary executor, Christopher Browning.

> It sounds silly, Tod, but I can't help feeling there's something queer in all this – if K.M. was so terribly interested in us as children and then she died, and then I got mad about her work and longed to write too – it seems as if her influence was knocking about the place somewhere. You'll think me an awful fool, and don't tell anyone.

9. Drewery, p. 2.

10. Drewery, p. 8.

11. Katherine Mansfield, 'Bliss', in *Bliss and Other Stories* (London: Penguin, 1962), p. 95. All further references will be to this edition and placed parenthetically in the text.

12. Daphne du Maurier, 'The Apple Tree', in *The Birds and Other Stories* (London: Gollancz, 1952), p. 114. All further references will be to this edition and placed parenthetically in the text.

13. Gail A. Hornstein, 'Narratives of Madness, as Told From Within', *Chronicle of Higher Education*, 25 January 2002 <http://www.gailhornstein.com/files/Narratives_of_m.pdf> (last accessed 16 July 2015).

14. Drewery, p. 3.

15. Kate Fullbrook, quoted in Kaplan, p. 11. 'Katherine Mansfield's feminism came about as a matter of course, so much so that overt discussion of it as a political principle is absent from her writing while its underlying presence is everywhere.'

16. D. H. Lawrence, 'The Blind Man', in *England My England and Other Stories* (New York: Seltzer, 1922), pp. 71–97.

17. This scene is evocative of Ernest Hemingway's short story 'The Cat in the Rain', from the collection entitled *In Our Time* (New York: Boni & Liveright, 1925). Here the American husband stolidly reads on while his wife continually, and vainly, attempts to focus his attention on her.

18. Ovid, *Metamorphosis*. The beautiful naiad, Daphne, is chased by lustful Apollo and, as she pleads to be spared, her father, the river god Pineios of Thessaly, turns her into a laurel tree. There are also correlations with the character of Ariel in *The Tempest*.

19. Dominic Head, *The Modernist Short Story: A Study in Theory and Practice* (Cambridge: Cambridge University Press, 2009), p. 117.

20. Elaine Showalter, *The Female Malady: Women, Madness and English Culture* (London: Virago, 1987), p. 130.

21. Hornstein, p. 6.

22. Drewery, p. 121.

23. Head, p. 123.

24. Nina Auerbach, *Daphne du Maurier – Haunted Heiress* (Pennsylvania: University of Pennsylvania Press, 2000), p. 7.
25. Auerbach, pp. 8–9.
26. Du Maurier, *Early Stories* (London: Todd, 1955). The introductory note states that the stories were written between 1927 and 1930, and first published in journals and magazines.
27. Du Maurier, letter to Maud Waddell, 4 February 1924, pp. 4–6.

REVIEW ESSAY

'The Thing Needed': Katherine Mansfield, Psychology and Relationships

Todd Martin

Sarah Ailwood and Melinda Harvey, eds, *Katherine Mansfield and Literary Influence* (Edinburgh: Edinburgh University Press, 2015), 227 pp., £70, ISBN 9780748694419

Meghan Marie Hammond, *Empathy and the Psychology of Literary Modernism* (Edinburgh: Edinburgh University Press, 2014), 216 pp., £70, ISBN 9780748690985

Janka Kaščáková and Gerri Kimber, eds, *Katherine Mansfield and Continental Europe: Connections and Influences* (Basingstoke: Palgrave Macmillan, 2015), 282 pp., £55, ISBN 9781137429964

Gerri Kimber, *Katherine Mansfield and the Art of the Short Story* (Basingstoke: Palgrave Macmillan, 2015), 114 pp., £45, ISBN 9781137483874

Anna Plumridge, ed., *The Urewera Notebook*, by Katherine Mansfield (Edinburgh: Edinburgh University Press, 2015), 128 pp., £30, ISBN 9781474400152

Facing the dehumanisation caused by growing industrialisation and the existential crisis of the First World War, some authors began to question all but the most superficial human interactions. Others, like Sherwood Anderson, proffered relationships as the only means of not only staving off isolation but also restoring our humanity. In 'Sophistication', the penultimate story of *Winesburg, Ohio*, Anderson's protagonist, George Willard, momentarily connects emotionally with Helen White. The story concludes: 'For some reason they could not have explained they had both got from their silent evening together *the thing needed.* Man or boy, woman or girl, they had for a moment taken hold of the thing that makes the mature life of men and women in the modern world possible.'[1] The coming together of individuals, distinct as they may be physically and emotionally, provides 'the thing needed' to exist more fully in the modern world.

While psychology has tended to emphasise one's relation to the self, it also explores the extent to which we are relational beings. But while some contend that we are mere physical beings who interact in a material world, others maintain that we have limited human agency which enables us to interpret our external realities. To us literary critics and theorists, these attempts to find patterns in the universe in order to understand how we fit into the world at large – whether we consider that meaning-seeking as spiritual or not – seem tantamount to what we value in literature and what it reveals about ourselves and the state of our world. And if we are more than mere material beings, the implications are profound for our understanding of relationships. Social and physical contact becomes our means of knowing others, and in knowing others we more effectively begin to see our own place in the world around us.

The ability to connect with the 'other' is the focus of Meghan Marie Hammond's book, *Empathy and the Psychology of Literary Modernism,* in which she focuses on the 'inner turn' evident in some modernist writers, a response stemming from some of the same concerns expressed by Anderson, and, like Anderson, the authors she discusses explore the potential of empathising with another. Hammond considers Henry James, Dorothy Richardson, Katherine Mansfield, Ford Madox Ford and Virginia Woolf alongside prominent contemporary thinkers and theorists of empathy (or 'feeling with'), which she distinguishes from sympathy (or 'feeling for'). She emphasises techniques authors use to draw others into the minds and experiences of their protagonists, arguing that modernists' use of 'internal monologue, stream of consciousness narration, narrative marked by anachrony and fragmentation, and rapidly shifting character focalization' are used to 'provide an immediate sense of another's thoughts and feelings' and thus establish 'fellow feeling' (4).

Of Mansfield, however, Hammond suggests that her 'character minds always leave our readerly desire to empathise frustrated' (91), privileging instead Mansfield's communal focus and shifting perspectives in stories like 'Prelude' and 'At the Bay'. She contends that Mansfield's narrative process, while approaching the empathic, falls short in that readers' experiences are mediated by a narrator whose presence precludes a full immersion into her protagonists' experience. In this, she comes into contention with Gerri Kimber's assessment of Mansfield, as expressed in *Katherine Mansfield and the Art of the Short Story*, in which Kimber notes that one of the reasons Mansfield is appreciated by scholars and general readers alike is that she brings us so completely into the minds of her characters. One way that Mansfield accomplishes this, according to Kimber, is through granting access to the interiority of her characters, particularly via her 'impressionistic evocations of epiphanic moments' (5). Noting Mansfield's rejection of the conventional plot structure and dramatic action and her move toward a more character-driven story, Kimber reveals Mansfield's interest in the inner life of her characters and how they respond to their circumstances. By revealing the working of her characters' minds, Mansfield allows the reader to identify with the character through shared experience. But it is the degree of that shared experience that Hammond calls into question.

In *Empathy and the Psychology of Literary Modernism*, Hammond sets out to explore the influence of psychology on the development of modernism. Her intent is to explore the significance of theorists such as Vernon Lee and E. B. Tichener (he coined the term 'empathy' in 1909), who have been generally overlooked in literary studies. Hammond provides an overview of the development of ideas concerning the ability to know another's mind. She is interested in the way various psychological discourses address a concern with the 'psychological distance between individuals' and the attempt to move toward a more subjective understanding of the 'other' (3). What is particularly valuable about Hammond's study is that she provides a new context for understanding the aesthetic shift in the early twentieth century, showing how contemporary trends in psychology helped lay the foundation for the technical innovations of literary modernism.

To demonstrate these influences, Hammond pairs specific authors with specific theorists of empathy and explores how the literary authors' narrative techniques demonstrate attempts to break down psychological distance, developing a means of thinking and feeling with others. But while Hammond provides valuable context in revealing the ideas of these psychologists and their views concerning the ability to empathise, there are some inconsistencies in whether the kind of empathy being explored in the text is between the author and her characters, the reader and the protagonist, or the protagonist and the other characters. Each is discussed with varying degrees of importance in each chapter, seeming to privilege whichever most effectively conveys the perspective of the given theorists.

Further, the shifting perspectives on empathy make her connection with particular authors somewhat arbitrary. In her introduction, for example, she draws on Edith Stein's definition of empathy as "'the experience of foreign consciousness'" (9) and suggests that to experience empathy is to lose oneself in the new identity. However, as she reveals the various thinkers' views of empathy, there are obvious variations in the degree to which the theorists believe this can occur. That there are differing perspectives on empathy simply shows the variations of the individual psychologists' understanding and exploration of the subject; however, this undermines the continuity of Hammond's application. For example, in her discussion of Ford Madox Ford, Hammond looks at the theories of Vernon Lee and, in particular, her theory of aesthetic empathy, which is 'similar to the process in which "we 'put ourselves [. . .] in the skin' of a fellow creature . . . attributing to him the feelings we should have in similar circumstances"' (122). However, something similar is dismissed in the previous chapter, in which Hammond discusses Mansfield alongside Max Scheler. Scheler rejects Theodor Lipps's notion that 'what the in-feeler brings to the object is key to shaping his experience in the object' (71), because Scheler 'disregards the long-prevailing theory that sympathy works by analogy' and 'fixates on the idea that Lipps's empathy works primarily through projection. For Scheler, the fundamental danger of empathy as projection is that it leads us to "impute our own experience to others"' (93).

The problem is not, of course, that the theorists have conflicting views of empathy and how it works but that Hammond pairs each theorist alongside an author whom she suggests is best understood by that particular perspective. Doing so, however, seems a little disingenuous, especially as there is no direct influence or connection between the theorists discussed and the individual authors. The result limits an understanding of some of the authors' perspectives on empathy. For example, Hammond considers how Mansfield approaches the inner territory of some of her characters' minds but, privileging the narrative structures of her later stories like 'Prelude' and 'At the Bay', Hammond focuses her discussion on Mansfield's portrayal of community. In so doing, she offers a valuable reading and insight into some of Mansfield's stories but she overlooks Mansfield's own explanation of her experience of writing, one that more fully reflects Hammond's discussion of Henry James and the author's relation to his subject. In an oft-quoted passage from a letter to Dorothy Brett written on 11 October 1917, Mansfield reflects on 'becoming' the duck she writes about: 'There follows the moment when you are more duck, more apple or more Natasha than any of these objects could ever possibly be, and so you create them anew.'[2]

Whatever these oversights suggest about the overall structure of the book, however, they affect Hammond's individual readings of the authors only inasmuch as they limit further speculation on their use of empathic techniques. She offers, for example, an insightful discussion of Virginia Woolf's notion of androgyny and its relation to Woolf's resistance to the notion of 'pure' empathy. And although Hammond emphasises interactions between Mansfield's characters over the author/character or reader/protagonist connections developed in earlier chapters, she does provide valuable readings of some of Mansfield's more famous stories.

In opposition to Hammond's conclusions about Mansfield's employment of empathy, Gerri Kimber's discussion of her impressionism and the abstract in *Katherine Mansfield and the Art of the Short Story* suggests that Mansfield brings the reader into the experience of the character. Drawing on Mansfield's statement that 'If one remained oneself all of the time like some writers can it would be less exhausting' (10), Kimber notes that 'One of Mansfield's greatest strengths is her ability to "become" her fictional characters and to depict with acute psychological insight the workings of their minds, as well as delineating their physical attributes' (11). This emphasis on the physical attributes is taken up later by Kimber in her chapter on symbolism, in which she discusses how Mansfield uses concrete images to convey feeling.

As Hammond points out, and Kimber reiterates in her book, Mansfield explores the individual mind and the isolation of many of her characters, a common plight of the modernist protagonist. There was a growing trend at the turn of the twentieth century, according to Hammond, about how to combat this isolation and to attempt to connect with other individuals, something she reveals in the way Mansfield emphasises the loneliness of her individuals. Both accounts, then, tie Mansfield back to modernist aesthetics and themes.

Having established the essence of Mansfield's narrative technique, the remaining chapters in *Katherine Mansfield and the Art of the Short Story* unpack various elements of her techniques, such as the development of her use of indirect discourse. Kimber notes that even when Mansfield presents us with an omniscient narrator, the narrator is unobtrusive and very often merges, via the use of free indirect discourse, with the character on the page, thus blurring the line between the reader and the characters' feelings and thoughts. The result, Kimber argues, is an 'intimate method of storytelling' in which, for certain moments, 'we become the character on the page' (16). Kimber's discussion is not exhaustive but she gives a solid overview of the way Mansfield creates 'subjective perception' (27).

Kimber's updated and expanded book, previously published by Kakapo in 2008, remains valuable for its brief yet thorough overview of Mansfield the writer, particularly when exploring her aesthetic and most common themes. In this regard, it is particularly relevant to readers just entering Mansfield studies. This new edition includes expanded discussions and revised readings of some of the stories that more fully demonstrate the techniques that Kimber identifies as characteristic of Mansfield. Kimber's goal is to debunk the misperception that Mansfield's writing is superficial and to reveal to the uninitiated how her form, particularly her use of free indirect discourse, ties her to literary impressionism. Toward this end, Kimber has extended her discussion of Mansfield's literary impressionism. She has also tightened up her discussion of humour in Mansfield, iterating that her comedy is inflected with pathos, providing not only entertainment but also a sociological message, using Stanley Burnell as an example as well as the affected idiolects of children and especially Nurse Andrews in 'The Daughters of the Late Colonel'. Mansfield, Kimber argues, thus enables seeming trifles to become revelations, hiding the darker aspects of the events she portrays. Kimber also elaborates on the influence of M. B. Oxon's *Cosmic Anatomy*, developing her discussion of 'Sun and Moon' more fully as an example. Kimber's attention to detail in the story and its explication is meticulous. Likewise, she offers a tight, thoughtful discussion of the ending of 'The Daughters of the Late Colonel', an esoteric ending whose meaning can be elusive. Kimber also sheds light on the equally elusive ending of 'The Garden Party'.

Finally, Kimber provides an additional chapter, 'Mansfield in Detail', in which she identifies several themes and images that bear greater attention, and the information that she offers will serve as tools for future work in Mansfield studies. She offers a compendium of references on the topic of fairies, and traces the image of lamps as they appear in some of Mansfield's early vignettes and build to 'The Doll's House'. Likewise, she compiles references to the Maori and related themes. This volume is thus an invaluable introduction and valuable tool for the study of Katherine Mansfield.

To the extent that empathy can be achieved through analogy or association of similar experiences, memory can play a significant role in developing degrees of empathy, and some psychologists view memory as a key means of connecting oneself with another. We rely on our remembrance of experiences to define ourselves, and shared experiences provide a means for one to find common ground with someone else. But as Hammond reveals in her discussion of empathy, associations often entail one projecting one's own experience on to the other. This is evident in how early readers of Mansfield, especially the expurgated early editions of the journals edited by John Middleton Murry, attempted to draw on their identification with Mansfield, causing misinterpretations of her life and stories. As Kimber establishes in her book, *Katherine Mansfield: The View from France*, Murry's editions of Mansfield's letters and notebooks created a view of Mansfield as he wanted her portrayed, a view that obscured the reality and complexity of her life. Such mythologising led to misappropriations of her life, prompting French critics, translators and readers to impose on her their own ideals. The first few chapters of Janka Kaščáková and Gerri Kimber's edited collection of essays, *Katherine Mansfield and Continental Europe*, carry this notion into Mansfield's reception on the Continent. Maurizio Ascari, Nóra Séllei and Janka Kaščáková, in their respective essays on Mansfield's reception in Italy, Hungary, and Czechoslovakia and Slovakia, suggest that the quiet suffering of Mansfield found some associative connections for these audiences. In some instances, critics and translators took these associations and built a view of Mansfield that fit their agenda, finding commonality and imposing on her life a character that was not truly her own. Ascari, for example, demonstrates the influence of the Catholic Church and its inclusion of her work in some of its publications, attributing to her a religiosity that was not her own. And both Séllei and Kaščáková point out the impact of translating Mansfield into their respective languages, revealing often purposeful mistranslations or edits towards a deliberate communist context.

Beyond this misappropriation of her personal writings, the relationship one builds with other writers and how one appropriates those into one's own work represents another type of relationship built on the premise of association and memory. While one's ability to feel with someone is tied to the ability to associate one's past experiences with what another experiences, the role of influence requires, on the one hand, a sense of memory of one's encounter with another writer but, on the other, a sense of how that memory is shaped and how it evolves and becomes manifest on one's own writing. To the extent that a writer struggles to understand the role influence plays in her writing, the attempt of the critic to piece that influence together becomes doubly complex, as Sarah Ailwood and Melinda Harvey point out in the introduction to their collection, *Katherine Mansfield and Literary Influence*. This is where their text and that of Kaščáková and Kimber provide a complement to one another, for while their geographical emphases are different, for the most part, there is a strong emphasis on those who influenced Mansfield, as well as those she has influenced. *Katherine Mansfield and Continental Europe*, though, more particularly provides a glimpse of Mansfield through the eyes of her Continental admirers, introducing English speakers to perspectives otherwise limited by language. In this way it enriches an appreciation of the impact Mansfield had, as well as drawing attention to some of the linguistic and cultural challenges faced in a growing cosmopolitan, global literary world.

While the essays by Ascari, Séllei and Kaščáková look particularly at the reception of Mansfield on the Continent, essays by Gerri Kimber, Mirosława Kubasiewicz, Delia da Sousa Correa and Claire Davison each explore the impact of Mansfield's contact with the Continent. Both Kimber and Kubasiewicz explore the connection between Mansfield and Stanislaw Wyspiański. Kimber, drawing on the letters of Floryan Sobieniowski and the newly discovered story, 'A Little Episode', attempts to piece together a period of Mansfield's life that is not fully known. She sheds light on both the possible influence of Wyspiański on Mansfield and particularly the possibility that she travelled to Poland with Floryan Sobieniowski, where she would have encountered Wyspiański's stained-glass window, 'God the Father – Let it Be', which Kimber argues is inspiration for Mansfield's poem, 'To God the Father'. Kubasiewicz, on the other hand, discusses the influence of Wyspiański on his generation, then provides an explication of Mansfield's poem, 'To Stanislaw Wyspianski', arguing that it reveals Mansfield's feelings of social inferiority and the more general feeling of inferiority of women of the day.

In her essay, Delia da Sousa Correa brings the discussion westward to Germany, revisiting Mansfield's stay in Bavaria, a period in her life about which little is known; like Kimber, she attempts to fill in some of the gaps. Rather than looking at Mansfield's personal relationships at this time, however, da Sousa Correa explores the influence of musical Romanticism on Mansfield. In particular, she demonstrates Mansfield's indebtedness and resistance to Wagner, revealing the complexity of influence that permeates the other collection, *Katherine Mansfield and Literary Influence.* Claire Davison then returns to Mansfield's ties to Eastern Europe through her collaborative translations with S. S. Koteliansky, emphasising the 'power of words in the art of code-switching and mistranslating' (117). Providing a pleasing complement to *Katherine Mansfield and Translation,* of which she is the co-editor, Davison points out that 'high Anglophone modernism was galvanized by translation' and believes that Koteliansky's and Mansfield's translations call for further exploration of the impact of their thinking across the Continent, rather than focusing on the 'inward-looking, nationalist, centripetal tendencies that had been so cynically fostered during the war' (136). Such is the value of considering the issue of translation in general but also the value of this book as a whole.

C. K. Stead, whose essay concludes the collection, provides an insightful assessment of Mansfield's stories that take place on the Continent, assessing them in the context of her New Zealand stories, asking whether they ultimately contend for equal prominence in Mansfield's œuvre. He finally rules in favour of the New Zealand stories because they demonstrate the fuller implementation of the technical developments that she had only begun exploring in the European stories. Stead's article provides a well-rounded conclusion to the collection in making a final declarative statement about the role of the Continent in shaping her work.

The remaining essays in the collection are only cursorily tied to the Continent, often exploring thematic notions of foreignness. Kathryn Simpson and Patricia Moran each consider this from a more psychological perspective. Simpson, for example, considers the subjectivity of Mansfield's characters, particularly their repressed unconsciousness, as a way of talking about the 'foreign within', which results in a state of exile in a male-dominated culture. Moran, likewise, takes up the notion of exile but suggests that Mansfield's feeling of isolation caused her to choose language as her 'home', a psychological replacement of 'personal, cultural, and national identity' (202). As a result, Moran connects Mansfield's exilic perspective to her modernist experimentation. Other essays focus on the stories that take place on the Continent. Angela Smith compares Mansfield's and Jean Rhys's ties to colonial modernism and how each subversively addresses an empiric audience by creating characters who experience foreignness but who are not colonial, while Erika Baldt considers the issue of national identity and how it can be manipulated both by the individual and by the observer to create a sense of 'other'. Janet Wilson rounds off the collection in her study of some of Mansfield's early stories, exploring Mansfield's use of the liminal state of childhood to expose the infantilisation of the metropolitan subject. While these last essays may not consider Mansfield's more direct ties to the Continent, they do provide valuable insights into Mansfield's work and her sense of foreignness.

Sarah Ailwood's and Melinda Harvey's *Katherine Mansfield and Literary Influence* overlaps with *Katherine Mansfield and Continental Europe*, not only in that influence is the concern of some of the essays in the latter, but also in that the reach of influences explored in their book includes some of Mansfield's Continental connections. Deborah Pike, for example, considers connections between Mansfield and the French author, Colette. Unfortunately, she tends to aggrandise Mansfield, discussing her alongside Colette in light of the notion of 'vagabondage', suggesting that Mansfield embraces this notion of solitude but overlooking the fact that Mansfield's isolation was not always voluntary. Juliane Römhild explores the influence of Mansfield's cousin, Elizabeth von Arnim, in particular how Mansfield was inspired by her personal story and her writing. She attempts to show the influence of her cousin on Mansfield's portrayal of Germans in her early stories. But of those essays that tie Mansfield to the Continent, Melinda Harvey's essay on Mansfield and Chekhov stands out. Revisiting the influence of Chekhov on Mansfield, especially since the fervour over the issue of her plagiarism has subsided with the influence of translation studies and changes in how one conceives of appropriation of a text, Harvey traces Mansfield's own manuscript practice along with her translation of Chekhov to show how Mansfield's own writing process and developing notions of translation demonstrate the influence of Chekhov.

As a whole, the essays in *Katherine Mansfield and Literary Influence* distance themselves from Harold Bloom's 'anxiety of influence'. Instead, they explore another type of anxiety – that of negotiating between originality and borrowing, clearly demonstrated in Harvey's essay on Mansfield and Chekhov. What makes this collection valuable is that, like *Katherine Mansfield and Continental Europe*, it explores Mansfield beyond her own circle. The collection looks both forwards and backwards, addressing influences on Mansfield as well as her influence on others. Special attention is given to the ambiguity of her influence on New Zealand and Australian literature in the wake of her death, expanding our understanding of her significance beyond the confines of England.

A few of the essays address influences on Mansfield that seem obvious but which have not always received much critical attention. Michael Hollington, for example, explains how Dickensian motifs are evident at an early age in Mansfield's writings and how they continue throughout her writing life, in particular her means of characterisation. While Mark Houlahan explores how Mansfield's characters use Shakespeare, he is more interested in exploring how Shakespeare helped to rekindle the relationship between Mansfield and Murry, providing them with a common ground for discussion. Both of these essays are useful, and although neither is as fully developed as it could be, each begins a conversation about Mansfield's literary forebears that demands further discussion. Susan Reid takes a different tack, tracing influence through the genre of the manifesto, arguing that Mansfield's stories act as an implied manifesto. She showed how these, alongside her editorials, letters and reviews, begin to serve as a platform to influence others in their writing practice, in particular offering a 'how to' aesthetic as well as a push to urge a subtle style of influence with a moralistic bent, contrasted with Lawrence's violence.

Of course, Virginia Woolf figures significantly in any discussion of influence, as she and Mansfield are often seen as competitors as well as associates, a relationship whose complexity Kathryn Simpson explains through a theory of gift-giving. Simpson explains that the relationship between Mansfield and Woof was one of reciprocation, but that in sharing their ideas and other favours (such as publication), they exerted a degree of power over one another by the giving and withholding of 'gifts'. Katie Macnamara, on the other hand, works to undermine traditional readings of Woolf's relationship with Mansfield, focusing on Woolf's use of the term 'underworld'. Although many critics associate Woolf's use of the term in relation to Mansfield as negative, Macnamara makes a compelling case that Woolf's use of the term in relation to Mansfield evolved as she developed a growing sense of empathy for Mansfield's plight, stemming from her own sense of isolation during her own psychological difficulties. In one of the more memorable essays of the collection, she explains that Mansfield's overcoming a social 'underworld' to remain trapped in an 'internal one' becomes an influence on the later topics of Woolf's fiction.

Most of the remaining essays address Mansfield's influence on others, demonstrating that Mansfield studies have come into their own. Naomi Milthorpe draws on an essay that Evelyn Waugh wrote on Mansfield when he was seventeen to establish a sense of influence, even if it is a rejection of Mansfield's modernist aesthetics. While it focuses more on Waugh's relation to literary modernism, Milthorpe provides a connection to Mansfield that has been overlooked until now. Jessica Gildersleeve explores the possible influence of Mansfield on Elizabeth Bowen, despite the fact that Bowen seems to resist it. She uses the trope of the absent foremother and suggests that Bowen's characters' longing in stories are indicative of the desire for a predecessor, an 'anxiety about and longing for literary influence' (43).

The most welcome essays, though, are those that trace Mansfield's influence back to New Zealand and Australia, back to authors who often grew up in the shadow of Mansfield's success and had to contend with her popularity even as they felt obligated to find their own voice. Janet Wilson, for example, shows Mansfield as a rival of Frank Sargeson, who reacts against her aesthetic, preferring realism and an emphasis on the local – a cultural naturalism. As in Milthorpe's discussion of Waugh, though, rejecting Mansfield requires that Sargeson contend with her influence. Bonny Cassidy, on the other hand, connects Mansfield to Eve Langley through Oscar Wilde, suggesting that Langley may have come to Wilde through Mansfield. The parallels that she draws between Mansfield and Langley are interesting but they appear too superficial to amount to any clear indication of influence. Interestingly, Sarah Ailwood traces Mansfield's influence on Australian literature more generally, specifically through the work of Nettie Palmer. Tracing Palmer's interactions with Mansfield's personal writings to establish a 'dialogic energy' that developed between the two, Ailwood suggests that Palmer used Mansfield as a catalyst to draw attention to Australian literary culture, noting the lack of opportunities at home to push for more local outlets for writers.

As a whole, the collection provides a broad perspective on the influences both on and of Mansfield, though some of the essays tend to rely too heavily on circumstantial ties. More generally, it provides a strong case for a return to the exploration of influence as a valuable means of exploring an author's literary inheritance as well as her own literary legacy.

Our interpretations of our experiences and our influences – if one allows for human agency – help us to make sense of our past and reveal ourselves in relation to them. In this way, memory plays a significant role in the way that Mansfield reflects on her childhood in her fiction. And while there is little doubt about the autobiographical nature of her New Zealand stories, most critics are careful to recognise that these are filtered through memory which must necessarily be selective due to the very nature of memory. The result is that whatever biographical significances these later stories have, they have been filtered through Mansfield's own remembrances of her past, which are coloured by her nostalgic feelings for home. One of the values of Anna Plumridge's new edition of *The Urewera Notebook* is that, as she points out, it is one of the few glimpses of Mansfield's perspective on New Zealand not filtered through memory. It provides the perspective of a young colonial woman who, while she cannot fully escape her Eurocentric background, explores the country of her birth up close and directly. For this reason, Plumridge sets out to bring the full value of the notebook to light, and in order to do so she provides an overview of the critical attention the notebook has received and traces the strategies and reception of the various editions of the notebook even as she justifies her own editorial choices. The result is a validation of the need for this new edition that follows the precise order of the notebook without attempting to force it into a coherent narrative, but one that also provides a scholarly apparatus that allows readers to appreciate the notebook more fully in its full context. This small but beautiful volume offers both general readers and scholars access not only to the notebook, but also to contextual information about the journey and the places that Mansfield visited along the way, bringing the notebook to life and allowing it to speak more fully to the experience of Mansfield. But it also offers valuable scholarly apparati, including historical contexts, an overview of previous editions of the notebook, and helpful textual notes which include explanations of various plants and Maori phrases.

The beauty of the volume lies in part in the collection of previously unpublished photographs of the areas that the camping party visited. One photo shows the campers sitting around their tents at Eskdale with the horses and wagon in the foreground and another shows the group stopping for lunch, possibly in the Urewera. Of particular interest is a photo taken at Runanga, of a paddock where the group camped. Plumridge suggests that this was probably the paddock that inspired 'The Woman at the Store', arguing that this is the more likely location, as opposed to Ian Gordon's account that it was the couple at the Rangitaiki Hotel.

What makes Plumridge's book a particularly valuable addition to Mansfield scholarship, though, is the detailed itinerary that she has developed through great effort. She provides a new, more accurate timeline and detailed account of the day-to-day journal, not only as drawn from Mansfield's notebook, but also supplemented by the materials and letters of the other members of the camping expeditions, as well as contemporary historical documents. The notebook itself provides an often impressionistic description of what Mansfield experienced, offering more of a personal shorthand of the events, which at their best evoke the immediacy of the memory. Plumridge's itinerary helps to put things into context. However, while Plumridge provides valid reasons for retaining the precise order of the original notebook as recorded, her version of the notebook would have benefited from some cross-references to her detailed itinerary, allowing the reader to see more clearly where some of the descriptions from the notebook would most likely fall along the journey.

Overall, the book provides valuable insights into the notebook and includes contexts that illuminate Mansfield's own European influences and suggest a possible corrective to her attitude toward colonial society. It offers a balanced view of Mansfield's experience, neither trying to romanticise it nor overlooking her complex feelings toward her home country and her appreciation of two conflicting cultures, showing her as 'a complex mixture of conventional and insightful thinking' (19).

Psychological approaches to literature get to the heart of why we study literature to begin with: to enable us to appreciate others' experience of the world more fully. As Hammond points out, we may not be able to access these experiences fully in a direct way through empathy, but our imaginations provide us with the ability at least to approach these experiences. The possibility of empathy, even if it must be filtered through our imaginations, signals the value of literature as a window into understanding our own and others' humanity, for, by some accounts, the thing that makes us human is our ability to establish relationships, relationships which rely on a deep feeling for another.

As each of the studies under consideration demonstrates, the life and work of Katherine Mansfield enrich our understanding of the self and our relationship with others. Mansfield certainly knew, better than most, the debilitating effects of exile and isolation as well as the deep-seated desire for human companionship. Yet, even as she often explores the causes and effects of such isolation on the individual in her stories, she likewise offers the potential means of breaking down those barriers so that something akin to Anderson's 'the thing needed', if not fully realised, is approached.

Notes

1. Sherwood Anderson, *Winesburg, Ohio* (New York: Bantam Books, 1995 [1919]), p. 228. Emphasis added.
2. Vincent O'Sullivan and Margaret Scott, eds, *The Collected Letters of Katherine Mansfield*, 5 vols (Oxford: Clarendon Press, 1984–2008), Vol. 1, p. 330.

Notes on Contributors

Maurizio Ascari teaches English Literature at the University of Bologna, Italy. His publications include books and essays on crime fiction, transcultural literature and inter-art exchanges (*Cinema and the Imagination in Katherine Mansfield's Writing*, 2014). He has edited and translated works by Henry James, Katherine Mansfield, William Faulkner and Jack London, among others.

Polly Dickson is a doctoral candidate with the departments of German and French at the University of Cambridge, UK. Her thesis focuses on mimesis and mimicry in the works of E. T. A. Hoffmann and Honoré de Balzac. Her current position is visiting research scholar at New York University, USA.

Louise Edensor is a doctoral candidate at the University of Northampton, UK, and a lecturer in Children's Literature, Media and Foundation studies at Middlesex University in Dubai. Her thesis explores Katherine Mansfield's construction of the self. She has recently contributed a chapter to the forthcoming *Katherine Mansfield's French Lives*, edited by Clare Davison and Gerri Kimber.

Bronwen Fetters is a student at Huntington University, Indiana, USA. She served as an assistant editor for *American Myths, Legends, and Tall Tales: An Encyclopedia of American Folklore* (forthcoming 2016). Her research interests include modern American literature, women's literature and feminist literary criticism.

Rachel Boyd Hall completed her Master's at the Courtauld Institute of Art before becoming a Researcher at the Richard Green Gallery, London, UK, specialising in nineteenth- and twentieth-century works of art.

Meghan Marie Hammond is a postdoctoral fellow at the University of Illinois in Chicago, Illinois, USA. She holds a PhD in English from New York University, USA. Her first monograph, *Empathy and the Psychology of Literary Modernism*, was published in 2014. She is also the co-editor of *Rethinking Empathy Through Literature* (2014).

Clare Hanson is Professor of Twentieth-Century Literature at the University of Southampton, UK. She has published widely on twentieth-century women writers and has written books on Mansfield and Woolf, in addition to editing Mansfield's critical writings. Her current research focuses on literature and science, and she is working on a study of genetics and the literary imagination.

Gerri Kimber, Visiting Professor at the University of Northampton, is co-editor of Katherine Mansfield Studies and Chair of the Katherine Mansfield Society. She is the deviser and Series Editor of the four-volume *Edinburgh Edition of the Collected Works of Katherine Mansfield* (2012–16). She is the author of *Katherine Mansfield: The View from France* (2008) and *Katherine Mansfield and the Art of the Short Story* (2015).

Eve Lacey is a writer and trainee librarian. 'Katherine Mansfield, in the Archives and the Hereafter' won the inaugural Persephone Essay prize in 2015. Eve is the editor of *Furies* (2014) and *The Emma Press Anthology of Sea* (forthcoming 2016).

Todd Martin is Professor of English at Huntington University, USA, where he teaches twentieth-century British and American literature. He has published on such various authors as John Barth, E. E. Cummings, Clyde Edgerton, Sherwood Anderson, Julia Alvarez, Edwidge Danticat and Katherine Mansfield. He is co-editor of Katherine Mansfield Studies and serves as Membership Secretary of the Katherine Mansfield Society.

Paula Morris (Ngati Wai) is author of the story collection *Forbidden Cities* (2008), the essay 'On Coming Home' (2015) and seven novels, including *Rangatira* (2011); she was fiction winner at both the 2012 New Zealand Post Book Awards and Nga Kupu Ora Maori Book Awards.

Avishek Parui is an Assistant Professor in English in the Department of Humanities and Social Sciences at the Indian Institute of Technology Guwahati, India, and an Associate Fellow of the UK Higher Education Academy. He has a PhD in English from Durham University, UK, and his research interests include modernism, masculinity studies, memory studies and posthumanism.

Allan Pero is Associate Professor of English at the University of Western Ontario, Canada. He is currently working on a book-length study of camp and modernism, a volume of essays on Edith Sitwell with Gyllian

Phillips (now under consideration), and *The Encyclopedia of Cultural Theory* with co-editor Kel Pero.

Nina Powles is a writer from Wellington, New Zealand. She has an MA in Creative Writing from the International Institute of Modern Letters at Victoria University, Australia. She is the author of the poetry chapbook *Girls of the Drift* (2014) as well as several poetry zines. She is currently writing a series of poetic biographies of New Zealand women, Katherine Mansfield among them.

Setara Pracha is a writer, researcher and lecturer based at the University of Buckingham, UK, developing material on Daphne du Maurier. She is a former postgraduate Ondaatje Scholar at Massey College, University of Toronto, Canada, where she specialised in postcolonial studies, and her research interests lie in areas of difference, the writing of gender, diasporic literature, and twentieth-century literature reflecting the complexity, comedy and cross-cultural fertilisation of hybridity.

Angela Smith is an Emeritus Professor in English Studies at the University of Stirling in Scotland. Her books and articles focus mainly on modernist writers, including Katherine Mansfield, Virginia Woolf and Jean Rhys, and on Scottish and colonial artists, particularly the Scottish Colourist J. D. Fergusson and the Canadian Emily Carr.

Rebecca Thorndike-Breeze is a Lecturer in the Massachusetts Institute of Technology's Comparative Media-Studies/Writing division in the USA, where she teaches writing and communication. She earned her PhD in literature from Northeastern University, Boston, USA. Her work explores how realist, modernist and graphic works of fiction confront fraught problems of affect, recognition and community.

Index

206

The Montana Stories (Mansfield, K.),
  141–3, 146, 147n
Moran, Patricia, 2, 8n, 16, 19, 22n, 25–6,
  37n, 59, 66n, 102, 111n, 197
Morrell, Ottoline, 2, 142, 158
Morris, Margaret, 7, 152–3, 155n–6n, 158,
  160, 162, 163n
Morris, Paula, 6, 127, 158, 204
Moses, Omri, 24, 33, 37n
Murry, John Middleton, 2, 7, 16, 23–4,
  29, 36n, 39–40, 44, 48, 52, 54n–5n,
  72, 79, 86, 100–1, 108, 111n, 113,
  144, 150, 153–5, 156n, 157–9, 161–3,
  163n–4n, 165–6, 172, 184n, 195, 198
  'The Meaning of Rhythm', 24, 36n
Myers, Frederick, 41, 54n
  *Human Personality and Its Survival of
    Bodily Death*, 41, 54n

narrative memory, 118–19
New, W. H., 104, 112n
The New Age, 4, 8n, 24, 39, 41–4, 54n–5n
New Zealand, 6, 41, 49, 128, 138–9, 150,
  158, 197–200
Nicoll, Maurice, 43
notebooks *see The Katherine Mansfield
  Notebooks*

occult, 39, 43
Oedipus complex, 14, 16, 18, 20, 41, 52
Orage, A. R., 4, 39–44, 53n–5n
O'Sullivan, Vincent, 4, 8n, 21n–2n, 36n,
  40, 53n–4n, 66n, 79n, 98n, 155n,
  163n–4n, 171n, 202n
Ouspensky, P. D., 39, 44, 53
Oxon, M. B., 4, 38, 40–2, 54n–5n, 194
  Cosmic Anatomy, 4, 38–41, 44–6, 49–51,
  53, 55n, 194

Palmer, Nettie, 200
'Panic' (du Maurier, D.), 183
Paris (place), 24, 44–5, 48, 113–14, 152–3,
  155, 158
Parkin-Gounelas, Ruth, 80n, 165, 171n
Parui, Avishek, 6, 113, 204
Pater, Walter, 1–2, 30
  'The Child in the House', 2
Pero, Allan, 6, 100, 204
'Piccadilly' (du Maurier, D.), 183
The Picture of Dorian Gray (Wilde, O.), 114,
  120
Pike, Deborah, 197

Plumridge, Anna, 7, 189, 200–1
  The Urewera Notebook, 7, 189, 200
plurisignification, 4, 51
The Poetics of Space (Bachelard, G.), 13,
  21n
Poise (Fergusson, J. D.), 7, 151–2, 154–5,
  157–63
Pound, Ezra, 39
Powles, Nina, 6, 205
Pracha, Setara, 7, 172, 205
'Practical Religion' (Wallace, L.), 44
'Prelude' (Mansfield, K.), 37n, 56, 154,
  162–3, 181, 190, 192
Principles of Psychology (James, W.), 24, 28,
  37n, 66n, 82, 97n–8n
La Psicosintesi (Assagioli, R.), 43
'Psycho-Egyptology' (Wallace, L.), 44
'Psycho-Egyptology-II' (Wallace, L.), 44
Psychoanalysis and the Unconscious
  (Lawrence, D. H.), 8n, 52, 55n
'Psychology' (Mansfield, K.), 23, 27, 100,
  106, 110
'The Psychology of Dreams' (Young, J.),
  43, 55n
The Psychology of the Emotions (Ribot, T.),
  56, 58, 60–1, 66, 66n

Queer Phenomenology (Ahmed, S.), 3, 13,
  20, 21n

Randall, A. E., 4, 41–2, 54n
  'The Heart of Hamlet's Mystery', 41,
  54n
Reid, Susan, 52, 55n, 171n, 198
Rhys, Jean, 197, 205
Rhythm, 24, 36n, 153, 158
Ribot, Théodule, 4, 57–61, 64, 66, 66n–7n
  The Psychology of the Emotions, 56, 58,
  60–1, 66, 66n
Rice, Anne Estelle, 137, 152, 154–5,
  158–60
Richardson, Dorothy, 36n, 56, 66n, 190
Richmond, Kenneth, 54n
Römhild, Juliane, 198
Rose Rhythm (Fergusson, J. D.), 7, 152–3,
  158
Ryan, Judith, 2, 8n

sadomasochistic, 114, 121–2
Saint Teresa of Avila (Bernini), 104
Sargeson, Frank, 199
savoir, 6, 101–2, 106

Join the Katherine Mansfield Society

Patron: Dame Jacqueline Wilson

Annual membership starts from date of joining and includes the following benefits:

- Free copy of Katherine Mansfield Studies, the Society's prestigious peer-reviewed book series published by Edinburgh University Press
- Three e-newsletters per year, packed with information, news, reviews and much more
- Regular email bulletins with the latest news on anything related to KM and/or the Society
- Reduced price fees for all KMS conferences and events
- 25% discount on all books published by Edinburgh University Press
- Special member offers

Further details of how to join are available on our website:
http://www.katherinemansfieldsociety.org/join-the-kms/
or email us: kms@katherinemansfieldsociety.org

The Katherine Mansfield Society is a Registered Charitable Trust (NZ) (CC46669)